OUTSOURCING THE BOARD

In this groundbreaking work, Stephen M. Bainbridge and M. Todd Henderson change the conversation about corporate governance by examining the origins, roles, and performance of boards with a simple question in mind: Why does the law require governance to be delivered through individual board members? While tracing the development of boards from quasi-political bodies through the current "monitoring" role, the authors find the reasons for this requirement to be wanting. Instead, they propose that corporations be permitted to hire other business associations – known as "Board Service Providers" or BSPs – to provide governance services. Just as corporations hire law *firms*, accounting *firms*, and consulting *firms*, so too should they be permitted to hire governance *firms*, a small change that will dramatically increase board accountability and enable governance to be delivered more efficiently. *Outsourcing the Board* should be read by academics, policymakers, and those within the corporations that will benefit from this change.

Stephen M. Bainbridge is the William D. Warren Distinguished Professor of Law at UCLA School of Law, where he teaches courses in corporate law and governance. Bainbridge has written over a dozen books and a hundred law review articles. He is best known as the originator of the director primacy theory of corporate governance. In 2008, 2011, and 2012, he was named by the National Association of Corporate Directors as one of the hundred most influential people in the field of corporate governance. His blog, ProfessorBainbridge.com, has been named five times by the ABA Journal as one of the Top 100 Law Blogs.

M. Todd Henderson is the Michael J. Marks Professor of Law and Mark Claster Mamolen Research Scholar at the University of Chicago Law School. Henderson researches and teaches in a wide range of fields from corporate law to American Indian law. His work has appeared in leading law reviews and has been covered in publications including *The Wall Street Journal* and *The Economist*. Henderson is a frequent commentator in the media and at conferences around the world on topics of corporate governance. He serves as a strategic advisor to several start-up companies.

Outsourcing the Board

HOW BOARD SERVICE PROVIDERS CAN IMPROVE CORPORATE GOVERNANCE

STEPHEN M. BAINBRIDGE
UCLA School of Law

M. TODD HENDERSON
University of Chicago School of Law

CAMBRIDGE
UNIVERSITY PRESS

CAMBRIDGE
UNIVERSITY PRESS

University Printing House, Cambridge CB2 8BS, United Kingdom

One Liberty Plaza, 20th Floor, New York, NY 10006, USA

477 Williamstown Road, Port Melbourne, VIC 3207, Australia

314–321, 3rd Floor, Plot 3, Splendor Forum, Jasola District Centre, New Delhi – 110025, India

79 Anson Road, #06–04/06, Singapore 079906

Cambridge University Press is part of the University of Cambridge.

It furthers the University's mission by disseminating knowledge in the pursuit of education, learning, and research at the highest international levels of excellence.

www.cambridge.org
Information on this title: www.cambridge.org/9781107193697
DOI: 10.1017/9781108149792

First published 2018

Printed in the United States of America by Sheridan Books, Inc.

A catalogue record for this publication is available from the British Library.

Library of Congress Cataloging-in-Publication Data
NAMES: Bainbridge, Stephen M., author. | Henderson, M. Todd, author.
TITLE: Outsourcing the board : how board service providers can improve corporate governance / Stephen M. Bainbridge, M. Todd Henderson.
DESCRIPTION: Cambridge [UK] ; New York, NY : Cambridge University Press, 2018. | Includes bibliographical references and index.
IDENTIFIERS: LCCN 2017058381 | ISBN 9781107193697 (hardback)
SUBJECTS: LCSH: Directors of corporations – Legal status, laws, etc. | Corporate governance – Law and legislation.
CLASSIFICATION: LCC KF1328 .B35 2018 | DDC 346/.06642–dc23
LC record available at https://lccn.loc.gov/2017058381

ISBN 978-1-107-19369-7 Hardback
ISBN 978-1-316-64512-3 Paperback

In memory of my friend and mentor, Mike Dooley.
Stephen M. Bainbridge, Los Angeles

For Mom & Dad, who gave me everything, and
for Saul Levmore, my intellectual hero.
M. Todd Henderson, Chicago, Illinois

Contents

Preface

Corporations are central to our modern society, and the board of directors is the central node of control of corporate power. In the popular imagination, boards are sinecures for friends of the CEO, and this is certainly true in some cases. But it is also certainly the case that corporate boards perform much better today than when either of us was in law school. Nevertheless, boards are still underperforming. Don't take our word for it: Directors themselves routinely report that most directors are not up to the task of managing ever-increasingly complex and risky global businesses. Failures abound, both big and small. This should not surprise us. The board is a group of part-timers of loose affiliation who do not work at the company they are hired to manage. And yet the board is the way that shareholders, creditors, employees, and governments regulate the behavior of corporate activity.

We are law professors who study this odd phenomenon – the law leaning so heavily on boards despite their obvious shortcomings. Over the past several decades, we have read countless articles and judicial opinions that criticize boards and propose fixes to improve them. We've written a few too. But, while there have been improvements on the margin, large and persistent gaps remain. The world is only getting more complex for corporations, as markets expand and share ownership transitions increasingly to passive investing, and the need to rethink corporate governance is acute.

Undeterred by the failures of reformers of all kinds, including ourselves, we decided to rethink boards at a fundamental level. Instead of proposing a tweak – More independence! Less independence! More diversity! More elections! – we went back to first principles, asking why boards exist at all, why they have persisted for so long despite the shortcomings, and why the law prescribes the way in which corporate governance services are delivered. We were surprised with the answers we came to when we dug into the first two questions, but it is really the last question – why the law mandates boards look the way they do – that hints at our proposal to remake the corporate board. Unlike other services provided to corporations, like legal, accounting, or strategic consulting, governance or board services must be provided by a group of unaffiliated, sole proprietors. Corporations hire law firms and accounting firms but legally must not hire board service firms. Board members must be individuals.

This book explores those questions and the answers we came up with. It explains why we find the current state of corporate governance woefully lacking in many respects. More importantly, however, it offers both a solution and a roadmap for making the legal and cultural changes necessary to effect that solution. We hope you will come to agree that one major advantage of our proposal vis-à-vis most corporate governance reform proposals is that we do not rely on complicated fixes. Our mantra is simple: Let markets work.

Although this book is intended for corporate governance scholars and policy makers, we hope it is accessible to board members, corporate executives, legislators, judges, and the interested public. It is a book by two academics, but it is not written in high academic style. So, if you've got this far, don't be turned off thinking this is going to be a dry casebook filled with citations and equivocations. We hope this ride through the history, practice, and (hopefully) future of corporate boards is as entertaining as it is informative and thought provoking.[1]

---

[1]   We originally proposed the BSP idea in a law review article aimed at an academic audience, Stephen M. Bainbridge & M. Todd Henderson, Boards-R-Us: Reconceptualizing Corporate Boards, 66 *Stan. L. Rev.* 1051 (2014). This book vastly expands, as well as updates, revises, and repurposes that article so as to reach a general audience.

Acknowledgments

There are too many people to thank, so we won't try to thank everyone who contributed ideas to this book. The idea originated at a conference hosted by Stephen M. Bainbridge at the Milken Center at the UCLA Law School several years ago, and has been road-tested in various forms with countless colleagues at universities, law firms, business schools, and other venues across the world. We have received valuable contributions from scholars, board members, executives, pundits, and our friends. You know who you are, as do we. We are grateful for your help.

Introduction

In the spring of 2001, Enron was riding high. Its stock was trading north of $80 per share, and according to *Fortune* magazine, it was America's most innovative company for the sixth year running. Chairman Kenneth Lay had built Enron from an old-school pipeline company into the seventh largest business in the United States, with more than $100 billion in revenues and over 20,000 employees around the world. Six months later, Enron was bankrupt. The empire Lay built turned out to be as fleeting as that of Ozymandias, king of kings.[1] Within a few years, Lay was dead, and his chief deputies Jeff Skilling and Andy Fastow were in prison. (Skilling will be incarcerated until 2019.) The 20,000 employees were out of work, many with their retirement accounts (put in Enron stock) worthless. Enron's collapse also rippled through the larger economy, helping to lead America into its worst recession in decades. What happened?

Congress held hearings. The Senate subcommittee investigating Enron's collapse put the blame on Enron's board of directors:

> [T]he Enron Board of Directors failed to safeguard Enron shareholders and contributed to the collapse of the seventh largest public company in the United States, by allowing Enron to engage in high risk accounting, inappropriate conflict of interest transactions, extensive undisclosed off-the-books activities, and excessive executive compensation.[2]

The short answer from Congress: the board of directors failed.

The legislation that came out of these hearings – the Sarbanes-Oxley Act (SOX) of 2002 – flowed directly from these findings. It made the biggest changes to corporate governance in the United States since the Great Depression. Under SOX, boards are required, among other things, to be more independent and to change the composition of key committees. Directors are now personally liable for the accuracy of financial statements.

The focus on the board as the source of Enron's failure and as the place to reduce corporate fraud was reasonable. State law provides that businesses are to be run by a board of directors, acting as agents of shareholders and other corporate stakeholders. If the board runs the company as the law requires, then when the company is run badly, the board is to blame. *Quod erat demonstrandum.*

But in the Enron case, there was something strange about blaming the board. Just before the collapse, *Chief Executive* magazine declared the Enron board one of the five best in corporate America.[3] This was a widely shared view, and rightly so. Enron's board was stacked with luminaries from business, academia, and government. The board had seven CEOs or former CEOs across a variety of industries, as well as the former dean of the Stanford Business School and the former chair of the Commodities Trading Futures Commission. These were not yes-men or cronies of the CEO. The board was independent of management and had all the committees a good board is supposed to have. Board members showed up, by all accounts took their work seriously, and engaged the best consultants, accountants, and lawyers money could buy. It was in many ways a model of modern corporate governance wisdom and best practices. In fact, an article in the Harvard Business Review, written after Enron's collapse, cheered the composition of Enron's board, concluding "no corporation could have had more appropriate financial competencies and experience on its board."[4]

Maybe the Enron board just blew it. Perhaps. But the legal response in SOX (and elsewhere) presumed that boards were generally underperforming, and that new legal rules could help them.

After all, the Enron example is not an outlier. Corporate governance failures are a familiar part of modern capitalism in the United States and abroad today. The names are familiar: WorldCom, Adelphia Communications, HealthSouth, Parmalat, Bear Stearns, Lehman Brothers, and on and on. Many of these boards were more or less doing what boards everywhere were doing and according to the best practices of the time. And yet, each failure begat a new solution, usually focused on the board. There are hundreds of academic books, thousands of articles in the academic literature and popular press, and countless proposals to make boards better. More independence! More diversity! More meetings! More shareholder power! More managerial power!

But, like the TSA requirement that everyone take off their shoes after Richard Reid put a bomb in his shoe on a Christmas day flight to Detroit, one gets the sense that the solutions are fighting the last battle or just slogans to make everyone feel like something is being done. The people demand action, this is action, therefore this must be good.

Complaints about boards are hardly new, of course. In the 1970s, Ralph Nader complained that directors resemble "cuckolds" who are "often the last to know when [their] dominant partner – management – has done something illicit."[5] In the 1930s, the late US Supreme Court Justice William O. Douglas dismissed directors as "business colonels of the honorary type – honorary colonels who are ornamental in parade but fairly useless in battle."[6] Indeed, as far back as the 1770s, Adam Smith observed that one could not expect that the directors of a joint stock company, "being the managers rather of other people's money than of their own, ... should watch over it with the same anxious vigilance with which the partners in a private copartnery frequently watch over their own."[7] Corporate governance failures were as much a part of Adam Smith's day as our own.

To be sure, there have been significant improvements in recent years. Modern boards of directors typically are smaller than their antecedents, meet more often, are more independent from management, own more stock, and have better access to information. These are probably good developments. (Although we can't be sure, since there is no way to measure good governance empirically. Governance is impossible to separate from operational performance, although the two may be independent. We return to this in the chapters that follow.)

It'd be surprising if some such improvements hadn't occurred, given that corporate governance reform has been a front burner agenda item for the last several decades and almost every reform proposal put forward focused on the board of directors. Reformers have debated whether boards have too much control over corporate affairs, too little, or just the right amount. Subsidiary debates have raged over such issues as whether board members should be independent, who should appoint them, how they should be elected, how they should be compensated, how long their terms should be, what the standards for their conduct and liability should be, what the optimal board size is, and so forth. At bottom, however, all of these debates come back to the problem of optimizing the board's governance role.[8]

While these debates have generated numerous reforms, too many boards are still broken. Consider the following assessment from a 2014 survey of nearly 800 board members by the consultancy McKinsey & Company:

> Boards aren't working. It's been more than a decade since the first wave of post-Enron regulatory reforms ... [but] most boards aren't delivering on their core mission: providing strong oversight and strategic support for management's efforts to create long-term value.[9]

Unbelievably, just 34 percent of the directors in the survey agreed that their boards understood their companies' strategies! Read that sentence again. One third *of directors* think the people responsible for managing the firm understand the firm. Is it any wonder there are countless proposals to reform the board?

Board failures are leaving a lot of money on the table that ought to be going to corporations and their shareholders. In emerging markets, for example, it is estimated that investors would pay a premium of 20 to 40 percent for companies with stronger boards.[10] The potential for significant gains is confirmed by a study of South Korean and Indonesian corporations whose board effectiveness ratings rose from the median to the top quartile. Those firms' market value rose 13 to 15 percent.[11]

How can this be? How can corporate boards continue to "fall short," to use the language from the McKinsey report, despite the countless best practice documents, corporate gurus offering advice, and legal reforms offered up over the last fifty-plus years?

We think an answer can be found by asking a seemingly simple question: what do all US corporations – and those in almost all other countries – have in common? They are composed exclusively of human beings.[i] We believe most board dysfunction could be substantially cured if that changed.

We don't have in mind a board consisting of chimps sitting around a table hand signing or Hal 9000-like supercomputers blinking at one another.

Instead, we have in mind outsourcing the board of directors' functions to a separate entity. We call the separate entities that would offer other firms board services "board service providers" (BSPs). To be clear, we do not have in mind individual board members forming professional corporations to get the protection of limited liability, but rather all director services for a given corporation being provided by a single business specializing in providing board services. We want to enable companies to outsource the board. After all, many other services businesses need to succeed are provided by other businesses, not by groups of individuals. For example, companies like General Motors and Google hire accounting *firms* to provide their external audit, not a group of individual accountants. BSPs would work the same way.

Thus instead of Boeing hiring thirteen unaffiliated individuals – Robert Bradway, CEO of Amgen; David Calhoun, Managing Partner, Blackstone Group; Arthur Collins, former CEO, Medtronic; Kenneth Duberstein, former White House Chief of Staff; Admiral Edmund Giambastani, former Vice

---

[i] In a number of countries, perhaps most notably the UK, the law permits the use of BSP-like entities. Yet, by all reports, few companies avail themselves of this option. We evaluate why that is the case and propose ways in which those countries could tweak their rules and norms to facilitate greater use of BSPs.

Chairman of the US Joint Chiefs of Staff; Lynn Good, CEO, Duke Energy; Lawrence Kellner, former CEO, Continental Airlines; Edward Libby, former CEO, Allstate; Dennis Muilenburg, CEO, Boeing; Susan Schwab, former US Trade Representative; Randall Stephenson, CEO, AT&T; Ronald Williams, former CEO, Aetna; and Mike Zafirovski, former CEO, Nortel – to provide board services in their individual capacity, Boeing would contract with another business to provide these services. The board-of-directors function would be outsourced to a professional services company, a BSP. Call it Boards-R-Us, Inc. Boards-R-Us would still act through individual agents, of course, and perhaps even hire these thirteen individuals to do the job, but the legal responsibility for managing Boeing would be that of Boards-R-Us the entity.

This may seem like a preposterous idea. In the pages that follow, we hope to convince you that it is not. In fact, we think that when you close the back cover, you'll wonder why we haven't already let companies experiment with this idea.

Consider how many corporate functions are already outsourced. As noted earlier, all public corporations outsource their external audit function to independent accounting firms. Most corporations outsource the vast majority of their legal work to law firms. Many outsource human relations, bookkeeping, payroll, and other functions as well.

The reasons for this are straightforward. Outsourcing happens when other business entities can do the work at lower total cost for a given quality. Consider Apple. If you have an Apple device, turn it over. On the back it says, "Designed by Apple in California. Assembled in China." It doesn't say that it is assembled by Foxconn, a separate entity that has a contract with Apple to build the devices. Why does Foxconn build the devices instead of Apple? Simple: it can do it at lower cost while producing an equivalent quality product. The same rationale can lead businesses to hire other businesses to provide board services, whatever those might be.

But the outsourcing we have in mind is not just hiring someone else to do a given task, but also allowing the task to be done by a formal and legally recognized association of individuals, rather than a group of unaffiliated individuals. Individuals form businesses to share risks, to achieve efficiencies that come from collaboration within a hierarchy, and to increase their individual reputations. We will look at this more closely, but the point is obvious. The reason Boeing hires a law firm for a particular deal or law suit instead of hiring a bunch of individual lawyers working as sole proprietors is because it can get the work done at lower cost for a given quality by hiring a *firm*. Cravath, Swain & Moore or Kirkland & Ellis, legal entities, can do the work better and more efficiently than if the very same lawyers were doing the work on their own. After all, there would be no Cravath and no Kirkland if this weren't the case.

Our proposal to allow businesses to outsource the board is also already used in some places. Outsourcing managerial functions is well established in other types of business associations, excluding corporations. Many limited partnerships, for example, have corporations serving as their general partner. Joint ventures between two or more corporations are common. Some manager-managed limited liability companies have incorporated managers. So why not allow an outsourced board for the business corporation?[i]

In this book, we consider various details of what an outsourced board might look like, and examine the costs and benefits of the BSP approach as compared with the current model. To help you grasp the basics of the BSP model, we propose no other significant changes to corporate governance. In other words, except for the minor changes needed to make the BSP system lawful and function, we hold the current election, role, and liability regimes of boards constant. (We will, however, offer views on how these might be tweaked or implicated if there is widespread adoption of our proposal.) Almost all of the current rules of federal and state law, as well as stock exchange listing standards, governing the nomination and election of directors would apply in a BSP-friendly world, just as they do now. Essentially, all that would change is that instead of multiple individuals, only a single entity would be selected to be the board.

Unlike many current corporate governance reform proposals, our BSP proposal has no ideological bent. To be sure, we think corporations are generally engines for social good. Indeed, it has been well said that the corporation is "the basis of the prosperity of the West and the best hope for the future of the rest of the world."[2] In turn, we believe that corporate boards of directors are one of the most important institutions in our capitalist system. Understanding, explaining, justifying, and improving them has been a key focus of our professional lives.

The critical ideological divide in corporate governance today, however, is not the importance of the corporation or the board – on which all agree – but the relative allocation of corporate power between the board, the top

---

[i]   Our idea is consistent with management guru Peter Drucker's view of outsourcing. Drucker argued that business activities that did not provide "a career ladder up to senior management" should be outsourced. Drucker Institute, Farming Out the Directors (Aug. 26, 2013).

"To get productivity, you have to outsource activities that have their own senior management," Drucker said in an interview that appears in Managing in a Time of Great Change. "Believe me, the trend toward outsourcing has very little to do with economizing and a great deal to do with quality."

Ibid. In our view, however, outsourcing the board function should provide higher quality decision-making and economize on decision-making costs.

management team, and the shareholders. The rise of activist investors, especially since the emergence of hedge funds as activists, has generated great controversy and much spilled ink. We have been players in that debate in the past and doubtless will be again in the future.

Here and now, however, we are neutrals in the Corporate Wars. We believe that BSPs make sense whether you favor board-centric governance, in which the board has most power and shareholder power is limited, or shareholder-centric governance, in which shareholders hold ultimate sway.

Accordingly, if shareholder access to the corporate voting proxy with the goal of more competition for board seats is desired, our proposal can achieve this more directly, at lower cost, and with less downside than the current model. On the other hand, if what would maximize shareholder value is greater managerial control and a longer-term view for board decision making, our proposal could be adapted to this goal as well. In short, corporate governance experts like both Lucian Bebchuk (shareholder power) and Martin Lipton (managerial power) should see the value in our proposed board model. We are trying to reconceptualize the board, not move it in a particular ideological direction.

We emphatically do not suggest that all firms should adopt the BSP approach, any more than we would require all businesses to hire law firms or accounting firms. Sometimes hiring a business to do a job makes sense, and sometimes an individual can do the outsourced work better. Instead, we simply urge that the law and capital markets permit those firms for whom the BSP seems appropriate to adopt it. At present, state corporate law and federal securities law, as well as various stock exchange listing standards, require directors to be "natural persons." Boards must be composed of multiple, unaffiliated human beings. As far as we can discern, there is no jurisdiction in the United States in which a BSP would presently be lawful.

This restriction strikes us as both foolish on its own merits and as inconsistent with the general thrust of both state and federal law governing business associations. Corporate law is generally permissive about how companies structure their governance, providing merely a set of default rules that can be altered by contract. Mandatory rules are very rare, and the case for them is weakened when there are significant benefits, as here, that can flow from freedom of choice. In addition, there are many cases in which entities, like our imagined BSPs, are already serving as boards or in board-like capacities. As already noted, unincorporated entities – such as partnerships, limited liability companies (LLCs), and the like – are typically permitted to have business associations serve in the management role played by a corporate board of directors for corporate entities. In addition, several federal statutes, including the Investment Company Act of 1940, permit directors to be incorporated entities, and the Supreme Court has construed portions of the securities laws broadly to include corporations acting as directors when the policy justifications for that result are strong.

Instead of proposing a new one-size-fits-all BSP regime, our goal is simply to replace the current regime, in which various laws and regulations effectively forbid firms from hiring BSPs, with one that removes this categorical bar. We think it is hard to come up with persuasive objections to such an enabling approach. Imagine, for example, there were a state law requiring legal services to be provided by individual sole proprietorships. Such a law might be motivated by a belief that lawyers would be more careful acting alone or that conflicts of interest arising from pooling legal resources outweigh the gains. But whatever the reason, such a rule would generate widespread opposition from lawyers arguing that by pooling their resources they could offer better services to their clients. Clients would object too. While some clients might prefer to hire lawyers unaffiliated with a large firm, others might prefer the costs and benefits of hiring a firm instead of a group of individual lawyers. The same is true for corporate governance. It is unlikely that one size fits all, suggesting that a ban on plausible options must be based on an overwhelming case. This case has not been made with respect to BSPs. On the contrary, we think the case for BSPs is quite strong.

WHY A BSP?

Boards of directors of public corporations face a daunting array of tasks, including hiring and firing the chief executive officer (CEO), setting the CEO's compensation, monitoring the CEO's decisions, ensuring compliance with laws, and, above all, representing the interests of shareholders. Yet, the evidence seems clear that they often fail at most or all of these jobs. Why?

There are many reasons boards fail to police managers adequately or make good decisions. Directors are part-timers with weak incentives and limited information. They also are generalists, meaning the average board is unlikely to have all the experts it needs at any given time. CEOs pick directors based on an unknown set of factors, and shareholders have no information about how decisions are made or how individual directors perform.

Hiring a BSP to provide board services instead of a loose group of sole proprietorships will increase board accountability, both from markets and judicial supervision. For instance, BSPs traded in public markets will be disciplined to provide quality services at competitive prices, and courts may be more willing to enforce fiduciary duties against companies than against individuals. We will show why, but the point is simple: Courts may balk at bankrupting a professor serving on a board but not at bankrupting a BSP.

There currently is no market for directors. They find their way onto boards largely through personal connections, often with the CEO, or the opaque head-hunter process, and because votes are private and decisions are made collectively, the accountability to shareholders is greatly diminished. Although it is possible for any individual to run for a board seat on any company, the publicity and voting costs are prohibitive. A BSP with a national reputation and the ability to provide all director functions would be able to reduce the cost of winning board seats. For instance, BSPs can use their brand and economies of scale to lower the costs of communicating with and persuading shareholders to hire them.

In addition, BSPs will allow boards to deploy experts as needed to address particular problems as they arise. When board members currently need outside expertise, it all too often comes from outsiders hired by or influenced by the CEO, which creates serious conflict-of-interest problems. In the BSP model, by contrast, we assume that the board-service company would have an internal expert staff backing up the individuals who provide the board functions. Allowing these experts to be under the same roof would reduce this conflict-of-interest problem, as well as transaction costs. BSPs will be able to produce and deploy expertise at lower overall costs. Finally, service firms have reputations that exceed those of individual members, meaning the potential for slack or opportunism is reduced. When an individual acts alone, only one reputation is at stake, but when a firm acts, it is effectively betting the reputation of the firm each time.[i]

* * *

Academics and other corporate observers often imagine that they have the silver bullet that will fix corporate governance, once and for all. These people propose things like eliminating staggered boards or giving shareholders access to the corporate voting machinery or requiring shareholder votes about executive pay. They believe all companies should be required to do what they think is best. We are skeptical that academics have any silver bullets in their guns, and have yet to see a one-size-fits-all approach to governance that we would support as a requirement. Given this, how can we subject you to a book-length corporate governance proposal?

We think our idea to outsource the board is different from the typical proposal in an important way. That is why we call the idea "revolutionary." We believe in markets and that, to quote business-law academics Frank Easterbrook and Daniel Fischel, "[t]he best structure cannot be derived from theory; it must be developed by experience."[3] As such, our proposal is

---

[i] Conflict problems arising from BSPs could be handled through rules limiting cross selling of services, just as Sarbanes-Oxley did for accounting and consultancy services.

just that – an idea that law should allow corporations to try. We may be wrong. If so, no businesses will use a BSP, or those that do will find it doesn't deliver the supposed benefits. Those that persist in using it despite this will be ground under by the competition.

But we may be right. And, if we are, then firms that use a BSP may achieve new efficiencies in corporate management, resulting in lower costs of producing economic activity. Corporate transparency about governance will be increased, and there will finally be a market for governance, as distinct from the market for corporate control. We may be able to finally isolate a measure of governance that is distinct from operational performance, thus bringing a market test to the question of optimal corporate governance. After all, the answer as to optimal governance in general or for a particular company is not in the mind of a corporate law scholar or gadfly, but in the thousands of minds that will experiment with new governance arrangements. There may be entrepreneurs with ideas about how to run firms using boards better, but are unwilling or unable to take over those firms or to take on the economic risk. We propose to let those entrepreneurs try.

PLAN OF THE WORK

To make our argument, the book proceeds as follows.

Chapter 1 traces the history of the board of directors. Our goal is to uncover the origin story in the hope of explaining why boards look the way they do, centuries later. As it turns out, the modern board owes much to its ancient ancestors; this is not a good thing. Board are, despite recent improvements, stuck in the past, and it is a past that does not fit with modernity.

In Chapter 2, we turn to the question of what do boards do today? Corporation statutes tell us that the corporation's business and affairs "shall be managed by or under the direction of a board of directors,"[i] but if this statutory command ever reflected real-world practice, it has long since ceased to do so. In order to assess the merits of the BSP model, we therefore need to identify the real-world functions performed by modern boards of directors.

A modern board's job has three components: management, oversight, and service. The balance between them has varied over time and from firm to firm, as we shall briefly demonstrate with a review of the historical development and evolution of the board. As we shall see, however, the long-term trend has been

---

[i] This language is from Delaware General Corporation Law § 141(a), the most important source of corporate governance law in the United States. Delaware is home to more public corporations than any other state. Other states have similar statutory commands.

to emphasize the board's role as monitors of the top management team. This trend has been given even more power in recent years, with increasing compliance obligations being imposed on boards of directors by both federal securities laws and state corporate law. Boards are more removed from the day-to-day job of running the firm than ever in the history of corporate affairs, and yet law leans on board members more and more.

In Chapter 3, we observe that boards of directors have long had a bad press and explain why that has been the case. From Adam Smith in the 1770s, to William O. Douglas in the 1930s, to the Securities and Exchange Commission (SEC) in 2009, critics have complained about boards. While there is some evidence that many modern boards outperform their predecessors, it would be Pollyannaish to deny that there is still much room for improvement in board performance. The aftermath of the financial crisis of 2007–2008, for example, revealed widespread board failures in areas such as enterprise risk management. Still another widely asserted criticism is that boards have failed to rein in allegedly runaway executive compensation.

Accordingly, Chapter 3 will briefly review the leading criticisms that have been launched at the board of directors as an institution over the years, with special emphasis on recent critiques. We will examine complaints about board performance during the financial crisis, for example, as well as such current arguments as the lack of board diversity.

Chapter 4 asks why boards fail. We argue that boards fail because they devote inadequate time to their jobs, because they misspend the time they do devote to their jobs, and because they have inadequate information, improper skill sets, and insufficient incentives. Many of these problems are longstanding, of course, but we believe that they have been significantly compounded by the increased emphasis in recent decades on director independence. As a result of stock exchange listing standards mandating director independence and pressure from corporate governance reformers, the percentage of board members who are independent has risen dramatically. As a result, boards today are dominated by part-timers, the vast majority of whom have full-time employment elsewhere, which commands the bulk of their attention and provides the bulk of their pecuniary and psychic income.

In Chapter 5, we come (the reader may well say, at last!) to our description of board service providers. Instead of a corporate board composed of a group of individuals acting as independent contractors, we have in mind a business entity, be it a partnership, LLC, corporation, or other association, acting as the board of another company. In our model, the board would be an "it," not a group of "hes" and "shes." Instead of nominating and electing a slate of unrelated individual independent contractors to serve as board members, a BSP would be chosen to provide director services.

We propose that the BSP be selected by the shareholders, but leave it to the market to develop solutions to the problems presented by corporate elections. We also hint here and there about alternatives to standard, annual elections.

Chapter 6 argues that BSPs could deliver, at least in some instances, better corporate governance at lower costs. We demonstrate that claim by mapping the BSP model to the functions played by the modern board: management, service, and monitoring management. In each of these areas, the BSP has the potential to make improvements or at least do no harm.

In doing so, Chapter 6 identifies a number of ways in which BSPs could help reduce the pathologies of the current board model of corporate governance. A significant advantage of the BSP model is the potential to ameliorate the problems identified in Chapter 5 by taking advantage of the potential economies of scale and scope inherently created when economic activity is brought within an organization rather than conducted by individuals. In addition, BSPs would be more accountable than the group of individuals currently providing board services; indeed, we believe that the accountability of the whole would be greater than the sum of the liabilities of the parts.

Chapter 7 will address issues such as the role of the BSP in the overall team that includes outside legal counsel, independent financial advisors, independent accountants, and other service professionals. It will also consider issues such as how the BSP is compensated by the company and the internal incentives within the BSP.

Chapter 8 explores the legality of BSPs under current law, which admittedly creates numerous obstacles to affecting our proposal, all of which therefore require rethinking. The most obvious hurdle is the requirement – embedded in a surprisingly large number of provisions of state corporation law, stock exchange listing standards, and various federal laws – that directors be "natural persons." Chapter 8 identifies the legal barriers to creating BSPs and argues that they should be eliminated so as to allow BSPs to become an option for corporations hiring board services.

In addition to reviewing US law, Chapter 8 will examine the law of other countries to determine the extent to which they permit the use of BSPs. Particular emphasis will be placed on the UK example, where BSPs are permitted but rarely used.

The final chapters of the text explore where BSPs fit into various current corporate governance topics. Chapter 9, for example, reviews how BSPs can be adapted to the emerging federal corporate governance scheme effected by SOX and the Dodd-Frank Act of 2010. Chapter 10 explores how BSPs could be reconciled with the increasing demand by investors for proxy access. Chapter 11 offers BSPs as an alternative to quinquennial board elections, an idea promoted by two lawyers with long experience in the trenches of the Corporate Wars.

Chapter 12 examines the emergent school of thought contending that shareholder activism is a response to alleged shortcomings of the monitoring model. As the argument goes, businesses have grown exponentially in size and complexity in recent decades, while traditional boards have been unable to adapt to these changes. The problem is compounded by legal changes – such as Sarbanes-Oxley § 404 – that have heaped a series of new duties on boards that distract directors from monitoring aspects of the firm not governed by the various new compliance regimes. Proponents of this line of argument contend that boards need to evolve to a "thickly informed" director model, in which the board would develop deep knowledge about the company and its industry, which would require significant changes in what directors do and how board structure might evolve to support this broader role. In our view, the BSP model is an ideal vehicle for implementing such a post-monitoring board.

Finally, Chapter 13 anticipates and responds to likely objections to our proposal.

A NOTE ON TAKING THE BSP MODEL GLOBAL

Our focus admittedly is focused on the United States. It is the system we know best, after all. At least for the time being, it also remains the largest economy in the world with the vast majority of large corporations. Improved corporate governance, however, increasingly is a matter of global concern. The last several decades have seen numerous official and quasi-official studies of corporate governance offering recommendations for change in many countries, such as the United Kingdom's famous Cadbury Report. In addition, numerous transnational organizations have issued similar surveys and recommendations, such as the Organization for Economic Cooperation and Development's regularly updated Principles of Corporate Governance. Throughout the book, we therefore devote attention to the relevant legal rules and economic situations of both developed countries and emerging markets. The chapter on why boards fail, for example, includes discussion of the reasons boards do so in emerging markets, which turn out to duplicate the problems of US companies while adding unique additional factors into the mix. The chapter on BSPs and the law likewise includes an analysis of the laws in the United Kingdom and a number of other major economies.

Having said that, however, our emphasis is on the unitary board system predominant in common law countries. Although there are many similarities between that system and the dual board system found in many civil law countries – most famously in the German system of codetermination – there are also many critical differences in the duties and roles of boards in the two systems. Even more differences emerge when one broadens one's perspective to include extra-legal considerations such as best practices, social norms, and cultural expectations. In our view, some of those differences – especially with respect to employee representation – loom sufficiently large to justify our focus on countries with a unitary board system (or, at least, a unitary board option).

Notes

1. "Ozymandias" by Percy Bysshe Shelley.
2. S. Rep. No. 107–70, at 3 (2002).
3. Marleen A. O'Connor, The Enron Board: The Perils of Groupthink, 71 *U. Cin. L. Rev.* 1233, 1273 (2003).
4. Jeffrey A. Sonnenfeld, What Makes Great Boards Great, *Harv. Bus. Rev.* (Sept. 2002), https://hbr.org/2002/09/what-makes-great-boards-great.
5. Ralph Nader et al., *Taming the Giant Corporation* 64 (1976).
6. William O. Douglas, Chairman, Sec. & Exch. Comm'n, Address at a Luncheon of the Fort Worth Clearing House Association (Jan. 8, 1939), in *Democracy and Finance: The Addresses and Public Statements of William O. Douglas* 46 (James Allen ed., 1940).
7. Adam Smith, *An Inquiry into the Nature and Causes of the Wealth of Nations* 700 (Edwin Cannan ed., Random House, Inc. 1937) (1776).
8. See, e.g. Melvin A. Eisenberg, *The Structure of the Corporation: A Legal Analysis* 170–185 (1976) (arguing that board reforms focused on director independence would improve monitoring of management); Lisa M. Fairfax, Sarbanes-Oxley, Corporate Federalism, and the Declining Significance of Federal Reforms on State Director Independence Standards, 31 *Ohio N.U. L. Rev.* 381, 387 (2005) (noting that SOX, for example, "focus[ed] on director independence" and sought to "eliminate those ties that hindered directors [sic] ability to objectively monitor corporate officers.").
9. Dominic Barton and Mark Wiseman, Where Boards Fall Short, *Harv. Bus. Rev.*, Jan–Feb 2015.
10. Simon C. Y. Wong & Dominic Barton, Improving Board Performance in Emerging Markets, *McKinsey Q.* 35 (2006), https://ssrn.com/abstract=899920.
11. Ibid.
12. John Micklethwait & Adrian Wooldridge, *The Company: A Short History of a Revolutionary Idea* xv (2003).
13. Frank H. Easterbrook & Daniel R. Fischel, The Corporate Contract, 89 *Colum. L. Rev.* 1416, 1420 (1989).

PART I

CORPORATE BOARDS

In this Part, we set out the basic facts about boards – why we use them, what they do, how they are doing, and why they aren't measuring up – in order to set the table for our proposal to permit corporations to serve as the board for other corporations.

1

A Brief History of the Board

Before we can rethink the board, we have to understand it. In this chapter, our goal is to trace the origins of the board looking for insight into current practice. After all, using a board of individuals to oversee other decision-makers is not a natural state of affairs nor obviously the most efficient governance model. So why do we use corporate boards? Where did the practice originate and what can the genesis story of boards tell us about how they should be used today?

THE POLITICAL ORIGINS OF CORPORATE BOARDS

In the summer of 1791, Alexander Hamilton (cue the music!) petitioned the New Jersey legislature for a charter for a corporation to promote industrial development of the Passaic River near the town of Patterson, NJ, about fifteen miles west of Manhattan. Hamilton, then Secretary of the Treasury, teamed up with financier William Duer and four others to create "The Society for Establishing Useful Manufactures" (SUM), as a means of expanding the young nation's industrial base. Initially, Hamilton wanted Congress to fund the project, but he couldn't get the votes. He decided to raise private capital to build the manufacturing facilities. The promoters of SUM raised $600,000 (about $10 million in today's dollars) from investors to "produce paper, sail linens, women's shoes, brass and ironware, carpets, and print cloth."[1]

To manage the company, Hamilton appointed a "governor" and "deputy governor" to manage the day-to-day operations, but required they be overseen by a board of thirteen directors chosen by the shareholders. SUM was governed as a representative democracy, just as it would have been had it been created and funded directly by Congress. It was, like most companies at the time, a hybrid of public and private. Two-thirds of the thirty corporations chartered up to this point in America were for infrastructure or other projects that fit easily within the ambit of government services.[2] In a very real sense, early corporations were government by other means. This is one reason they needed the imprimatur of the government, in the form of a bespoke, legislature-issued charter.

In the case of SUM, the outsourcing of government in its hands was apparent from its charter. For example, the board of directors was delegated with legislative and executive powers of the state, including being able to take land for its own use by process of condemnation. It was thus natural for the founders of these companies to design their governance structure to mimic that of government.

The governance structure did not work as intended. Duer was appointed governor, then promptly squandered the fortunes and opportunities of the venture. By early 1792, Duer was in jail and the money he'd "borrowed" from SUM to engage in financial speculation was gone for good. Indeed, Duer spent the rest of his life in debtor's prison.[3] The board, which had the job of monitoring the governor, thus had failed too, making SUM arguably America's first corporate governance scandal.

Hamilton was not content to see his dream die, so he took over SUM, acting as perhaps the first private equity workout specialist. But even he couldn't turn around SUM's fortunes and, by 1796, the factories lay idle and Patterson was "a ghost town."[4] The dream of an industrial center was eventually realized when the War of 1812 provided a need for the United States to build up its manufacturing base. Cotton mills came first thanks to the plentiful water power that drove the millwheels. Steel production and locomotive manufacture came by the mid-nineteenth century. Silk revitalized the area's textile industry after the Civil War. Ultimately, Patterson and SUM thrived well into the early twentieth Century.

But the lasting legacy of SUM was its corporate governance structure – the board of directors – that became the norm for American corporations. SUM's charter became a template for corporate governance, and by 1811, when New York passed the first antecedent to modern corporate legislation, the idea of a board of directors was baked into corporate law. That statute provided that "the ... concerns of such company shall be managed and conducted by [directors], who ... shall be elected ... as shall be directed by the bylaws of the said company."[5] This requirement persists today. The Delaware General Corporation Law (DGCL), the most influential corporate law for modern American companies, for example, provides that, "[t]he business and affairs of every corporation ... shall be managed by ... a board of directors."[6]

The idea of using a board to oversee SUM did not originate in the summer of 1791. In fact, Hamilton had used the same governance approach six months earlier when, in the winter of that year, he helped establish the first Bank of the United States. The Bank was proposed to serve a public purpose – to create financial infrastructure for the nation[i] – just as SUM was designed to provide a manufacturing base. The Bank as a governmental venture was not popular among prominent political leaders. Secretary of State Thomas Jefferson and Representative James Madison argued that establishing the Bank exceeded the federal government's powers under the Constitution. To overcome these objections, Hamilton structured the Bank as a private, nongovernmental entity, the same strategy he would later deploy for creating SUM. This was sufficient to garner enough votes in Congress and President Washington's signature. Befitting its public purpose, the Bank was to be governed by a board of twenty-five directors, elected annually by the shareholders, the biggest of which was the US government.[7] As with SUM, political governance befitted the public purpose of the enterprise.

If SUM provided the template for the first corporate law statutes, and if the Bank of the United States provided the template for SUM, where did Hamilton's idea for governing the Bank come from? According to law professor Franklin Gevurtz, Hamilton borrowed the governance model used by the Bank of England.

The 1694 charter of the Bank of England vested management authority in twenty-four directors, and it is likely that this would have been a ready and powerful example for early American officials.[8] As in America with the Bank of the United States, the Bank of England was originally chartered to bring stability to England's financial situation following a costly war with France. Also like the later Bank of the United States, the Bank of England was a private company cloaked with public purpose.[ii] The two were also alike in that Parliament created the Bank of England (with the Tonnage Act of 1694), just as Congress created the Bank of the United States (with the Bank Act of 1791). It is not surprising, therefore, that both banks borrowed their governance model from politics – the directors were chosen by the shareholders to represent the interests of each bank's stakeholders, just as representatives to the House of Commons or Congress represented citizens.

In stark and revealing contrast, most businesses at this time or at any point in human history up to this date did not use boards or any other type of collective governance approach. Given the nature of economic production at the time,

---

[i] The Bank was the agent of the government in collecting taxes, making payments, and issuing loans, among other things.
[ii] The Bank of England was nationalized in 1946, and is now the central bank of the United Kingdom.

most businesses were akin to modern sole proprietorships or partnerships. These were most often family-run affairs, under the control of a single individual, usually the pater familias. Economic activity was not collectively managed, but governed and directed by individuals. As Professor Gevurtz notes, this was true even for some big business of the era. He cites the examples of the Peruzzi (1275–1343) and Medici (1397–1494) companies, which were "partnerships operated under the domination of a family leader or trusted manager."[9] These were purely private affairs, and they were governed as such.

The connection between the board of directors and politics is plain from these examples, but it can be made even clearer by looking back to antecedents to the Bank of England. Gevurtz locates the origins of modern corporate boards in medieval Europe, on both the continent and in England. The reason for using a group to oversee a single authority arose from the explicitly political origins of corporations. Early corporations were not private entities seeking private ends, but rather government entities in disguise. Outsourced government was governed like government. This should not be a surprise. The examples of the banks and of SUM are illustrative. But the political nature of early boards can be more clearly seen several hundred years earlier in the proto-corporations of Europe.

In England, two early companies that pioneered the modern board of directors approach were the Company of Merchants of the Staple (royal charter in 1319) and the Company of Merchant Adventurers (royal charter in 1505). These "companies" were established to consolidate the various exporters of wool and cloth (respectively) from England to the Continent. The idea was to achieve economies of scale and to increase regulatory control over English tradesmen operating on the Continent. (Traders were based initially in Antwerp, far beyond the reach of the English monarch.) The function of these companies was governmental – the policing of merchants through a sort of proto self-regulatory apparatus. For instance, the twenty-four directors of the Company of Merchant Adventurers did not direct the strategy of the various English tradesmen operating in the export business, but rather promulgated rules and sat in judgment of their alleged misbehavior.[10] After all, if one English merchant defrauded a wool buyer in Belgium, this would potentially harm all English wool merchants, since they might get a reputation for shady dealing as a group. If the English merchants were less able to be regulated by the local authorities and beyond the reach of their sovereign, this presented a problem for the noncheating traders. If you think you might be cheated and you can't sort the good traders from the bad ones before the fact, then you will lower the amount you are willing to pay for a certain quantity and quality of wool. A "corporation" of all traders internalizes these potential negative effects and raises overall quality.

These early corporations were not business corporations as we think of them, but rather government-sponsored trade associations. The Financial Industry Regulatory Authority, the private regulator of stock brokers, is a better analogy to these early firms than Google or General Motors.[11] And their use of a board was overtly political and regulatory.

This approach to early corporate governance happened in parallel in continental Europe. In the sixteenth century, several of the provinces of the Netherlands were engaged in trade with the East Indies. In 1602, these provincial trading companies were consolidated under the single umbrella of the Dutch East India Company (Verenigde Oostindische Compagnie or VOC). The VOC was a cartel. Like all cartels, it was established to limit competition and set prices, as well as to better police misbehaving traders. After all, if one province treated its partners in the East badly, it might impact all Dutch traders, even the ones that had not done anything wrong. Economists call these "negative spillovers," and reducing them is a core function of government.

To effectively govern this cartel, the Dutch chose a political model, just as the English did with their wool and cloth cartels. Initially, the board of directors of the VOC, known as the "Council of Governors," had sixty members: twenty from Amsterdam, fourteen from Rotterdam and Delft, fourteen from Hoorn and Enkhuizen, and twelve from Zealand.[12] One way to think about the corporate governance of the VOC, which set the standard for corporate governance in the Netherlands and beyond, is as a representative political body. In return for giving up sovereign control over the provincial trading companies, Rotterdam, Zealand and the other provinces received voting rights in the combined entity. This ensured that provincial interests were represented in the group decision making, and that Amsterdam did not consolidate power.[i] The board of the VOC was akin to the US Senate – the various states vested some of their sovereignty in the federal government, receiving in return two seats each in the Senate.[13]

But it didn't start there. Tracing the history back even further, the governmental nature of early corporate boards can be seen in the first widespread "corporate" enterprise in Europe – the group of German trading posts

---

[i] A sixty-member board eventually proved to be inefficient, so the VOC created a separate board, known as the Collegium, with seventeen members. It wielded the real power over the VOC, and was referred to as the Herren seventeen, or the seventeen gentlemen. It too had proportional representation based on geography.

collectively known as the Hansa. Beginning in the twelfth century, the Hansa, also called the Hanseatic League, was a group of loosely affiliated German city-states that established the first trading network spanning all of Northern Europe.

Consider the example of the Hansa outpost established in Bergen, Norway. The Hansa went there to provide a way of bringing cod fish from the fishing grounds of the far north (near the Arctic Circle) to the rest of Europe. Without modern communications and international business transaction law, there was no easy way to get the fish thousands of miles to its customers. The Norwegian fishermen in the Lofoten Islands did not have any knowledge of how to dry fish for shipment, how to ship them, or how to build relationships with customers in dozens of countries and city-states in lower Europe. The Hansa had all of these things. To ensure a steady supply, the Hansa built their own network of agents to obtain the fish, dry it, and ship it to the heart of Europe. Hansa agents operated in the north to ensure supply, in Bergen to collect, dry, and ship the fish, and in the south to facilitate delivery throughout Europe.

The Hansa in Bergen were far from their masters in Lübeck in what is now Germany. Accordingly, they were governed by a council or board of directors, who oversaw the merchants in all aspects of their lives and business transactions. The governance model was similar to that used by the boards of English analogs discussed earlier. As Professor Gevurtz describes them, "these governing institutions of the Hanseatic merchants acted to preserve the group's trade privileges, to enforce rules of trade, and to adjudicate disputes among the merchants."[4] The governance design was premised on the political nature of the role of the supervising authority. The Hansa board wasn't about giving strategic advice or managing the day-to-day activities, it was about providing a political check on the activities of outposts remote from central, governmental authority.

Interestingly, quasi-governmental entities, like the Hansa, the Merchant Adventurers, the VOC, the Bank of England, and SUM, were needed because of the inability of governmental power to reach the particular activities. In medieval Europe, the kings and princes were relatively powerless over tradesmen operating hundreds or thousands of miles away because of the costs of information transmission and of deploying force across distance. To regulate behavior, the government needed to replicate itself in a different form, and one that was acceptable to the regulated actors and to the more proximate government. Thus, the creation of the cartel of British wool exporters operating in Antwerp. Later, the Bank of the United States and SUM were created as quasi-government entities for a different reason – the political resistance to the government engaging in this particular type of activity. But in all cases, the governance model that begat our modern board of directors was determined by the overtly political nature of the enterprise. Here is how Professor Gevurtz summarizes the history:

> Overall, the development of corporate boards in Continental Europe is consistent with the English experience: corporate boards developed as a governance mechanism for merchant societies (like the hanse) or merchant cartels (like the Dutch East India Company), and only later evolved into the governance mechanism for large business ventures with passive investors.[15]

Boards and parliaments thus arose in medieval Europe contemporaneously, in part because they were serving similar functions. While causation is impossible to determine – were boards copying parliaments, were parliaments copying boards, or were larger forces driving both to happen? – the simple fact that early corporations were not corporations as we know them, but were more like shadow governments, is clear.

THE PRIVATIZATION OF THE CORPORATION AND THE CHANGING ROLE OF THE BOARD

Over time, this role changed as the nature of corporations changed. After the age of exploration ended and the industrial revolution came to England, America, and the Continent, the vast majority of businesses were small, family-run affairs. Sole proprietorships or partnerships were the legal arrangements for nearly all economic activity. At the time the US Constitution was ratified, there were fewer than thirty companies chartered in the Colonies, and most of these were created with government approval to do government work – that is, to build bridges, canals, ports, and so on.[16] It wasn't until the early nineteenth century, when New York liberalized the rules about corporate law – letting anyone incorporate without the government's imprimatur – that corporations became a serious feature of American business.[17]

In a world in which corporations were doing work that required less political oversight by outsiders, such as making cloth, tools, and such, the board evolved. It might have withered away, resulting in a unitary executive model of corporate governance. In that case, the CEO would not have been unaccountable; oversight would have been done by government. But bodies in motion tend to stay in motion, and the board as institution, once established, had strong incentives to stick around. After all, the change in roles did not happen overnight, and at the very least, incumbent and prospective board members had strong reasons to preserve the status quo. Boards had to evolve to survive.

As it turned out, there were many other things boards could provide to shareholders. Accordingly, when their original purpose became less important, boards were deployed for other work. For the tens of thousands of corporations created during the first half of the nineteenth century, the board provided advice, contacts with sources of funding, political connections, credibility with regulators of various kinds, and wisdom about management, production, and markets.

Then, after the Civil War, the growth of large industrial corporations necessitated that the board serve another role – interconnected ownership. During the latter half of the nineteenth century, most state corporate laws forbad companies from owning other companies in other states.[18] Concerns about "foreign" corporations, a race to the bottom, and provincial interests of banks, politicians, and other stakeholders likely drove this policy. Whatever the reasons, however, the improved technology of the post-Civil War era – railroads, canals, pipelines, telegraphy, and so on – made the policy increasingly obsolete. But until law could catch up with business, entrepreneurs needed to find a work-around. Boards were key. Putting individuals on multiple boards allowed investors to control multiple corporations, thus achieving economies of scale. Boards became a mechanism of legal arbitrage or evasion when the law no longer served the social welfare.

An interconnected board was a device that permitted a company in Ohio to own assets in New York, while complying with state law in both states. Some of the directors of the Ohio company could sit on the board of the separate New York company, thus providing continuity of control. These interlocking directors were a key mechanism through which control could be exerted without ownership and without running afoul of state law.

John D. Rockefeller famously exploited this technique to expand his refinery operations from Cleveland to Pittsburgh to New York.[19] He built a network of businesses using clever ownership structures, several of which relied in large part on placing "Standard men" on the boards of pipelines, railroads, gas companies, and countless other businesses.[20] For instance, Rockefeller's brother served as the chair of the board of the Brooklyn Union Gas Company (BUG), which was an entity that rolled up all of the independent gas providers in Brooklyn during the late nineteenth century. BUG entered into long-term contracts with Standard on very favorable terms for Standard, thus locking in a demand for its production of naphtha. Standard didn't have to own BUG because it ran its board.

While modern state law has obviated the need for this work-around, the use of interlocking directors is still common today. According to work by William Domhoff, approximately 20 percent of directors sit on two or more boards,[21] and CEOs are commonly encouraged to "expand their network" by sitting on another board.[22] Just as with the purpose of boards generally, the purpose of interconnected directorships has evolved over time. In the past, it was about control; today it is about the value of information and experience, or what we call the "service" purpose.

Modern corporations evolved away from the trust-like function played by boards during the growth of American industry in the run up to the two World Wars. During the 1950s, American corporations expanded their national and international scope, and boards again changed to play new roles. In an era when American corporations had unrivaled market power and were dramatically expanding operations at home and abroad, boards became advisors to CEOs, offering strategic advice based on experience inside and outside of the company in question. Strategic questions were paramount, so boards evolved into this role, again to survive.

During the early part of the twentieth century, boards of American companies were staffed almost entirely by white men, most of whom had worked at the company for decades. (This was, to some extent, the natural [but lamentable] consequence of labor market restrictions [both legal and cultural] that existed up to this point.) Putting aside the discrimination and focusing on the choice between inside and outside directors, there were pros and cons. On the plus side, these insiders had valuable knowledge about the company and likely worked together as a team better than if the board were a mix of insiders and outsiders. On the negative side, however, their status within the hierarchy meant that they were under the dominion of the more informed, more incentivized, and more powerful CEO. Accordingly, these boards provided some strategic input but little monitoring of the CEO or other management, beholden as they were to company and social hierarchies.

In the 1930s, Yale law professor (and then SEC Chair and Supreme Court justice) William O. Douglas wrote a piece in the Harvard Law Review – "Directors Who Do Not Direct" – arguing that boards were too subservient to management.[23] It issued a call to arms to transfer the board from a tool of management into a monitor of management:

> It is timely to consider the corrective measures necessary if the board is to be employed as a medium for the protection and enhancement of the interests of the corporation and the stockholders, rather than as a convenient devise for the exercise of economic and political power for the selfish interests of those who happen to be in a position of dominance.[24]

Douglas's plea fell on mostly deaf ears for decades. There was some change on the margins, but for the most part, boards at the start of the 1970s looked much like they had for decades. In part, this is because there was little pressure from competitive markets demanding change. (Turns out, law professors agitating for change isn't very effective!)

Toward the end of the 1970s, several influential organizations reinvigorated Douglas's idea of a board playing a more assertive oversight or monitoring role. The American Bar Association, the American Law Institute, and, perhaps most importantly, the Business Roundtable, called for making the board more independent and powerful.[25] The Business Roundtable's initiative – "The Role and Composition of the Board of Directors of the Large Publicly Owned Corporation" – called on boards to add enough independent or outside directors "to have a substantial impact on the board's decision process."[26] Shortly thereafter, the New York Stock Exchange required that all boards of listed companies have audit companies with a majority of independent directors.[27] More women and minorities were seen in the boardroom, although several decades later they make up just about 30 percent of directors.[28]

The next two decades saw the rise of shareholder activism—first in the form of leveraged buyouts (LBOs) and then in the growing power of institutional investors – and accordingly the board evolved more toward an outsider-dominated monitoring board. Shareholders pushed for their representatives on the board and often succeeded. These board members were there to push a particular agenda and to give particular shareholders access to receive and convey information. Some court decisions in Delaware aided the change, focusing as they did on the monitoring role played by the board when making decisions regarding executive pay, mergers, and other significant corporate events.[29] By the 1980s, a majority of directors were formally independent of management.

THE BOARD'S EVOLVING MODERN ROLE

In response to these various forces, the last several decades have seen slow (but steadily accelerating) changes in board practice. Writing in 2004, law professors Lucian Bebchuk and Jesse Fried characterized boards as dominated by management, thus coining the managerial power school of thought.[30] Boards in their telling were mostly failures, being under the thumb of the managers they were supposed to be supervising.

In Bebchuk and Fried's view, managers dominated board members for several reasons: (1) the power of CEOs to appoint directors; (2) the ability of the CEO to reward cooperative directors; (3) the social and psychological influences the CEO has over directors, such as "the power of friendship, loyalty, collegiality, and authority"; (4) the cognitive biases of directors that come from being CEOs or former CEOs themselves; and (5) the time and informational barriers most directors face to making informed and reasoned decisions. In short, Bebchuk and Fried were merely renewing Douglas's call to arms from seven decades previously.

Although some criticized how accurate an account the managerial power view offered in the early 2000s,[31] most commentators believed that by the late 2010s, the strong form of the Bebchuk and Fried account no longer described most cases. Boards were increasingly independent and effective.[32] This was aided somewhat by regulatory changes, both in statutes and in rules. The Sarbanes-Oxley Act (SOX) required new independence for audit committees, and empowered boards to hire their own advisors, independent of the CEO.[33] Dodd-Frank mandated a similar independence obligation for compensation committees.[34] The tenor of both laws was an emphasis on the board as a monitor of the corporation, and not just as a means of reducing agency costs within the firm, but also as a means of ensuring compliance with external law and regulation. The board is in a sense the agent of not just the shareholders but also society writ large.

SUMMARY

The antecedents to the modern corporate board were "a reflection of political practices and ideas widespread in Western Europe in the late Middle Ages," which were developed in order to give "political legitimacy" to corporate activity.[35] As we will argue in the chapters that follow, the need for political legitimacy is no longer as powerful as it once was. Corporations today are not quasi-governments, but rather purely private entities pursuing purely private ends. The principal historical rationale for the board of directors model thus no longer obtains.[i]

While the proposal we set out in this book upsets the formal notion of a board of separate individuals acting as a potential check on corporate activity, as we will explore, there is nothing about our idea that would upset the idea of "consent through elected representatives" continuing as part of the corporate tradition.[36] In fact, our proposal is likely to *increase* the political legitimacy of

---

[i] One of us has elsewhere argued that corporate law favors multimember boards because groups are better than individuals at the sort of critical evaluative judgment that characterizes most board decisions. See Stephen M. Bainbridge, Why a Board? Group Decisionmaking in Corporate Governance, 55 *Vand. L. Rev.* 1, 12–41 (2002) (discussing theory and empirical evidence about group decision making). As we describe later, however, our proposal retains the advantages of group decision-making while simultaneously solving the problems that make the modern board model so frequently dysfunctional.

corporate boards by opening up possibilities for more transparent and active participation of shareholders in deciding who will represent their interests in supervising corporate management.

Notes

1. Franklin A. Gevurtz, The Historical and Political Origins of the Corporate Board of Directors, 33 *Hofstra L. Rev.* 89, 109 (2004).
2. Stephen M. Bainbridge & M. Todd Henderson, *Limited Liability: A Legal and Economic Analysis*, (2016).
3. David J. Cowan, William Duer and America's First Financial Scandal, 97 *Financial History* 20–35 (2009).
4. Russell Roberts, The Society for Establishing Useful Manufacturers, 64 *Financial History* 20 (1998).
5. 1811 N.Y. Laws LXVII.
6. Del. Code. Ann., tit. 8, § 141(a) [hereinafter cited as DGCL].
7. Bank Act, ch. 10, § 4 (1791).
8. Gevurtz, Historical and Political Origins, at 110 (citing Cyril O'Donnell, Origins of the Corporate Executive, 26 *Bull. Bus. Hist. Soc'y* 55, 61 [1952]).
9. Gevurtz, Historical and Political Origins, at 128.
10. Ibid. at 125.
11. For a brief history of FINRA, see William A. Birdthistle & M. Todd Henderson, Becoming a Fifth Branch, 99 *Corn. L. Rev.* 1 (2013).
12. Gevurtz, Historical and Political Origins, at 127.
13. Ibid.
14. Ibid.
15. Ibid. at 129.
16. See Robert E. Wright, The Rise of the Corporation Nation, table 7.1, in Douglas Irwin & Richard Sylla (eds.), *Founding Choices: American Economic Policy in the 1790s* (2010); see also Joseph S. Davis, Essays in Earlier History of American Corporations, in *Eighteenth Century Business Corporations in the United States*, Volume II, table I, 24 (1917).
17. See Herbert Hovenkamp, The Classical Corporation in American Legal Thought, 76 *Geo. L.J.* 1593, 1634–1640 (1988).
18. See, e.g. Joseph H. Beale, Jr., Corporations of Two States, 4 *Colum. L. Rev.* 391, 391–392 (1904) (noting the puzzle of how to think about a corporation operating in two states, since by their nature, corporations are an "act of sovereignty" that can only have power within one state). See also Glenn Porter, *The Rise of Big Business: 1860–1920*, 73 (1973).
19. For good overviews of Rockefeller's career, see Ron Chernow, *Titan: The Life of John D. Rockefeller, Sr.* (2007); Grant Segal, *John D. Rockefeller: Anointed with Oil* (2001).

20. For a discussion of the "Standard Men," see Stewart Holbrook, *The Age of Moguls* (2017).
21. William G. Domhoff, *Who Rules America?: Power, Politics, and Social Change* 30–31 (2006).
22. Brad Feld, "All CEOs should sit on another company's board," *Fortune*, Aug 16, 2012, available at http://fortune.com/2012/08/16/all-ceos-should-sit-on-another-companys-board/.
23. See William O. Douglas, Directors Who Do Not Direct, 47 *Harv. L. Rev.* 1305, 1314 (1934) (arguing for taking "the control or dominance of the board away from the executive management").
24. Ibid. at 1322.
25. See Ronald J. Gilson & Reinier Kraakman, Reinventing the Outside Director: An Agenda for Institutional Investors, 43 *Stan. L. Rev.* 863, 873 (1991) ("Whether one asks the Business Roundtable, the Conference Board, the American Bar Association, or the American Law Institute, the answer to the question of who should monitor management is the same: independent outside directors elected by the shareholders.").
26. The Business Roundtable, The Role and Composition of the Board of Directors of the Large Publicly Owned Corporation, 33 *Bus. Law.* 2083, 2108 (1978).
27. See Stephen M. Bainbridge, *Corporate Governance after the Financial Crisis*, 81–83 (2012) (discussing stock exchange listing standards on director independence).
28. Deloitte, "Missing Pieces Report: The 2016 Board Diversity Census of Women and Minorities on *Fortune* 500 Boards" (2016), available at www2.deloitte.com/us/en/pages/center-for-board-effectiveness/articles/board-diversity-census-missing-pieces.html?id=us:2el:3dp:adbcenpr16:awa:ccg:020617.
29. See Bainbridge, *Corporate Governance after the Financial Crisis*, at 79 (discussing Delaware case law).
30. See Lucian Bebchuk & Jesse Fried, *Pay without Performance: The Unfulfilled Promise of Executive Compensation* (2004).
31. See, e.g. M. Todd Henderson, Paying CEOs in Bankruptcy: Executive Compensation When Agency Costs Are Low, 101 *Nw. U. L. Rev.* 1543 (2007).
32. See generally, Stephen M. Bainbridge, Executive Compensation: Who Decides? 83 *Tex. L. Rev.* 1615, 1638–1642 (2005) (discussing reasons to doubt the continued power of the managerial power model).
33. See Bainbridge, *Corporate Governance after the Financial Crisis*, at 83 (discussing SOX requirements).
34. See ibid. at 128–129 (discussing Dodd-Frank compensation committee rules).
35. Gevurtz, Historical and Political Origins, at 129, 170–173.
36. Ibid. at 173.

2

What Do Boards Do?

In Chapter 1, we answered the question of why we have boards and why they look like they do. Boards were used for political or regulatory oversight of early corporate conduct, which was effectively outsourced government. Boards were thus elected or appointed in ways that resembled representative government. We also saw how boards evolved to serve different roles as social circumstances changed, deemphasizing the need for political oversight and serving instead as sources of information, regulatory arbitrage, or other functions. We situate our proposal for additional innovation in this vein – a further evolution of the board instead of a rejection of it.

In this chapter, we fast forward to today, looking at what boards do now. While we have seen boards serve various functions already, the modern board of directors plays a role that blends a variety of these historical functions in unique ways.

THE ROLES PLAYED BY THE MODERN CORPORATE BOARD

Boards have a great deal of freedom to define their role within the company, subject to two major sets of constraints. One is provided by the legal system of the country – or, in federal systems such as the United States, the laws at both the state and federal levels – in which the corporation was organized. Until relatively recently, the legal constraints on the board's role were surprisingly vague. In most states, the corporation statute simply stated something to the effect that the company was to be managed by the board of directors or employees supervised by the board. To be sure, that barebones statement is constantly being fleshed out in cases claiming that specific board activities are either required by or prohibited by the directors' fiduciary duties to the company and its shareholders. Yet, the law emerging from these cases typically speaks to the process by which the board acts rather than requiring specific actions.[1]

As we shall see, however, legal constraints have become increasingly important in recent decades, especially in the United States since the adoption of SOX and Dodd-Frank.[i] Yet, despite their importance – and the considerable amount of time and effort boards must devote to satisfying these new federal requirements – they cherry picked specific areas for emphasis, while leaving most of what boards do largely unregulated by federal law.

The other set of constraints on boards is provided by the expectations and demands of key constituents or stakeholders. In the United States, for example, proxy advisory services, such as Institutional Shareholder Services (ISS), increasingly influence how boards function and the roles they serve. Large institutional shareholders, like CalPERS (the pension fund for employees of the State of California), typically vote in corporate elections in ways recommended by ISS or its equivalent. More globally, both national and transnational best practice guidelines have proliferated, further influencing board structure and function. In the UK, for instance, the Cadbury Report recommends a variety of corporate governance policies, further commanding corporations to comply with these or explain to shareholders why this has not been done.

Nevertheless, within those constraints, there is a lot of variance in how boards operate. This can be seen to some degree in the way that companies describe the scope for their work and the way in which they do their job.

Apple's Corporate Governance Guidelines, for example, succinctly state that:

> The Board oversees the Chief Executive Officer (the "CEO") and other senior management in the competent and ethical operation of the Corporation on a day-to-day basis and assures that the long-term interests of the shareholders are being served. To satisfy its duties, directors are expected to take a proactive, focused approach to their position, and set standards to ensure that the Corporation is committed to business success through the maintenance of high standards of responsibility and ethics.[2]

In contrast to the almost breathtaking generality of Apple's statement, The Walt Disney Company's statement of board responsibilities delves much more deeply:

> The responsibility of the Board of Directors is to supervise and direct the management of the Company in the interest and for the benefit of the

---

[i] Note that we define legal constraints broadly to include stock exchange listing standards.

Company's shareholders. To that end, the Board of Directors shall, acting directly or through Committees, have the following duties:

1. Overseeing the conduct of the Company's business to evaluate whether the business is being properly managed;
2. Reviewing and, where appropriate, approving the Company's major financial objectives, plans and actions;
3. Reviewing and, where appropriate, approving major changes in, and determinations of other major issues respecting, the appropriate auditing and accounting principles and practices to be used in the preparation of the Company's financial statements;
4. Assessing major risk factors relating to the Company and its performance, and reviewing measures to address and mitigate such risks;
5. Regularly evaluating the performance and approving the compensation of the Chief Executive Officer and, with the advice of the Chief Executive Officer, regularly evaluating the performance of principal senior executives; and
6. Planning for succession with respect to the position of Chief Executive Officer and monitoring management's succession planning for other key executives.
7. The Board of Directors has delegated to the Chief Executive Officer, working with the other executive officers of the Company and its affiliates, the authority and responsibility for managing the business of the Company in a manner consistent with the standards of the Company, and in accordance with any specific plans, instructions or directions of the Board.

The Chief Executive Officer shall seek the advice and, in appropriate situations, the approval of the Board with respect to extraordinary actions to be undertaken by the Company, including those that would make a significant change in the financial structure or control of the Company, the acquisition or disposition of any significant business or the entry of the Company into a major new line of business.[3]

As one parses such statements, three basic board functions keep recurring: management, oversight, and service. Admittedly, this typology suggests that board functions can be situated in distinct silos. In the real world, however, there is a lot of overlap between the various functions. For example, in the 1980s, RJR Nabisco's management spent hundreds of millions of dollars in an ultimately fruitless effort to develop a smokeless cigarette. When the board was finally informed, many directors were reportedly angered by management's failure to consult with them beforehand. The board pulled the plug on the project and the responsible CEO resigned to avoid dismissal.[4]

One could characterize the RJR Nabisco board's role in that instance as managerial, because the board eventually began making decisions about new product development. On the other hand, one could also describe the board's role as supervisory, because most of what the board did consisted of uncovering and undoing poor product line decisions by top management. Yet again, one could describe the board's role here as an oversight failure because the project dragged on at great expense for an extended period before the board even became aware of it.

So, we want to be careful throughout to ensure that we think of the board's role in a nuanced, organic way that describes a spectrum of functions rather than trying to pigeonhole those functions. Having said that, however, having a basic typography of functional roles provides a useful shorthand and means of organizing an analysis of what boards do, what they ought to do, and what they all too often fail to do.

How boards allocate effort between those functions varies widely, depending in considerable part on factors such as the life stage, size, and ambitions of the company. Boards of mom-and-pop corporations often actually manage the company, just as most boards did two hundred years ago. Start-up and growth company boards often have a strong emphasis on service, especially providing access to key resources and constituencies. Big public company boards tend to leave management and service to the top management team, emphasizing oversight of that team as their main job.

In addition, across all companies trends are observable across time, with the importance of different roles increasing and decreasing to meet the needs of the market given external constraints and conditions. We will consider the changing nature of board roles later in the chapter. For now, we turn to describing these various board functions.

MANAGEMENT

New York's 1811 Act Relative to Incorporations for Manufacturing Purposes, which is regarded as the prototypical modern corporation statute, provided that corporations formed thereunder were to be "managed and conducted" not by shareholders but by directors elected by the shareholders. More than a century and a half later, the corporation statute of Delaware – by then well established as the leading corporate law jurisdiction – still mandated that "the business and affairs of every corporation organized under this chapter shall be managed by a board of directors." For a long time, the law took this obligation seriously. As recently as 1956, the Delaware Supreme Court, interpreting that statute, held that "[t]he general rule forbidding the directors to delegate managerial duties applies as well to a delegation of a single duty as to the delegation of several or of all duties."[5]

In the real world, of course, management of a corporation's day-to-day operations had long since ceased to be the primary function of the boards of directors of all but the smallest corporations. At least since the emergence of the first vast industrial enterprises of the nineteenth century, public corporations had simply become too big and complex for boards to manage in any meaningful sense of the word. In addition, board composition had changed in ways that compounded the problem. Directors were increasingly outsiders who had full-time jobs elsewhere and therefore could devote relatively little time to the running of the business on whose board they served. A ban on delegation makes little sense in a world in which directors show up four times a year for a series of meetings.

Although case law had implicitly recognized this trend as early as the 1920s,[6] it was not until 1974 that the DGCL was finally amended to explicitly authorize boards to delegate managerial responsibility to the corporation's employees. Law lagged reality but it did not impede innovation in board practice because of the ambiguity in the term "delegation."[i]

As amended, DGCL § 141(a) stated – as it still does – that "the business and affairs of every corporation . . . shall be managed by or under the direction of a board of directors."[7] The new formulation clarified that supervision of the employees who conducted the corporation's day-to-day operations – rather than conducting those operations themselves – was now legitimately a primary board function.

Accordingly, although it remains a "fundamental precept of Delaware corporation law" that the board "has ultimate responsibility for the management of the enterprise," that law also recognizes that "modern multi-function business corporations" are "large, complex organizations" and that modern boards are composed mainly "of persons dedicating less than all of their attention to that role."[8] Thus, boards are not obliged to run the corporation on a day-to-day basis. Instead, directors "satisfy their obligations by thoughtfully appointing officers, establishing or approving goals and plans and monitoring performance."[9]

Nonetheless, the boards of even the largest corporations typically retain some functions that are best described as managerial in nature. The provision

---

[i]   This stands in contrast to the clear meaning of "natural person," which is the core of the legal rule getting in the way of the innovation we propose in this book.

for board approval of extraordinary transactions in Disney's corporate govern-ance guidelines, for example, reflects key statutory restrictions on such trans-actions mandating such approval. Indeed, modern corporation statutes include many specific mandates that only the board can fulfill. Approval by the board of directors is a statutory prerequisite, for example, to mergers and related transactions, such as sales of all or substantially all corporate assets. The same is true of a slew of other transactions such as the issuance of stock, distribution of dividends, and amendments to the articles of incorporation. Approval by the board of directors of related party transactions involving top managers or board members is a statutory option for substantially insulating such transactions from judicial review for fairness. The board typically has nonexclusive power to amend bylaws. In addition to these and other duties explicitly assigned by statute to the board, courts have held that various other decisions are so important that the board of directors must make them.[10]

Best practice also assigns important managerial roles to the board, as illu-strated by several provisions of Disney's corporate governance guidelines. The requirement that the board review and, in appropriate cases, approve major polices is a common board function. Even more common, and particularly important, is the board's power to hire and fire the top management team, especially the CEO, and set their compensation.

The board's hiring and firing power has taken on special emphasis in recent years, as boards are increasingly under pressure from investors to undertake succession planning well before the incumbent CEO is expected to step down. As the Conference Board observes, succession planning has become "a key element in achievement of the larger goal of 'sustainability' – in the sense of enabling the business enterprise to adapt, thrive and grow in response to changing market conditions and other challenges."[11] In 2009, the SEC responded to investor demand in this area by changing its policy stance on shareholder proposals to "recognize that CEO succession planning raises a significant policy issue regarding the governance of the corporation that transcends the day-to-day business matter of managing the workforce."[12] Instead of allowing companies to routinely exclude proposals by shareholders relating to CEO succession planning, the SEC now routinely requires com-panies to include such proposals in their proxy statements.[i] Coupled with increased media attention on CEO succession planning, which began when

---

[i] SEC Rule 14a-8 permits shareholders to submit nonbinding proposals for a vote at the company's annual meeting using the company's proxy materials. These "precatory" proposals are a source of great controversy, as managers view them as inappropriately hijacking the company's microphone, and shareholders view them as an essential tool for communicating with management and among shareholders.

concerns were raised over Apple's alleged failure to prepare for a successor to Steve Jobs during his final illness, boards now increasingly engage in detailed succession planning. Indeed, as the Disney corporate governance guidelines illustrate, a growing number of companies are formalizing the board's role in this area.

Nevertheless, it's important not to overstate the board's managerial function. In public corporations, management is primarily the responsibility of the CEO and the other C-suite executives. Although the formal principles of both law and best practice state that boards still must make key decisions of the sort just discussed, in practice the board's role even in those areas is often more advisory or supervisory than managerial.

Consider, for example, succession planning. Traditionally, the incumbent CEO took the lead on succession planning – to the extent it was done at all – by identifying potential successors, evaluating them, and presenting a chosen heir apparent to the board. Although some boards now take the initiative by putting succession planning on the corporation's agenda, it remains true that the CEO's informational advantages – especially as to potential inside successors – give the CEO considerable leverage to drive succession planning.

Much the same could be said about merger negotiations. Although board approval is a legal prerequisite for a merger to become effective, the process is generally delegated to the top management team. The CEO and his advisors identify potential targets (or acquirers, as the case may be), set the major terms, determine valuation, and so on. Accordingly, the board's role prior to the final formal approval is at most advisory. It would be a mistake to sign a deal during intermission at the Lyric Opera of Chicago without informing the board (as happened in the famous case *Smith* v. *Van Gorkom*), but as long as the board is informed in advance and kept in the loop, managers take the lead.

Up to this point, we've been considering the role and function of a board in ordinary times. In some extraordinary situations, the board is expected – both by law and best practice – to step forward and take on more active managerial functions. If the corporation becomes the target of an unsolicited takeover bid, for example, the "board of directors has an active role to play" in evaluating and responding to the offer.[13] If the top management team proposes to buyout the public shareholders, the board – or, more precisely, its independent members – must take the lead in evaluating and negotiating the offer. Likewise, to cite but one more example, boards of financially troubled companies are expected to be especially proactive.

Our discussion so far has focused on the role of boards in domestic US corporations, which is reasonably well documented. In contrast, board functions outside the United States, especially in developing countries, are understudied. A recent survey of nonexecutive directors in emerging market companies in twenty-seven Eurasian countries ranging from Poland to Mongolia found that boards commonly perform managerial functions – at least defined as "as active participation in decisions of a strategic nature" – in those countries.[14] Specifically, the survey found that boards make the final decision on strategic issues in over half the studied cases.[15] That figure is more impressive than it seems since over 40 percent of the surveyed companies had a majority shareholder, whom one would expect to be the de facto – if not de jure – final decision-maker.

UK corporate governance puts an interesting spin on the board's managerial role, by holding that that role is not to formulate strategy but to "set the context of strategy."[16] The board sets the broad scope of the company's business but does not set policy. Instead, the board reviews, approves, and sometimes changes management's strategic plans. The board also seeks to provide moral support to good managers and send signals to management about the standards to which they will be held.

SERVICE

The second primary role played by boards is what we call "service." Board members can provide a variety of services to the corporation, but the most common and important are networking and advising management. Indeed, especially insofar as outside directors are concerned, these were generally regarded as the board's primary functions for much of the last century. As famed Delaware Chancellor William Allen observed in 1990, for example, "businessmen or women will view their roles as directors in the same way that they probably wish outside directors on the board of their own companies to view their role – as a source of expert advice and judgment, on call to the CEO but not to be officiously interjected."[17]

We turn now to a brief look at each of these elements of the board's service role – networking and advising management.

Networking

Outsiders can provide access to networks to which insiders do not belong, thereby assisting the firm in gathering resources and obtaining business. Outside directors affiliated with financial institutions, for example, facilitate the firm's access to capital. In addition to simply providing a contact between the firm and the lender, the financial institution's representative can use his board membership to protect the lender's interests by more closely monitoring the firm than would be possible for an outsider. In turn, that reduction of risk should result in the lender accepting a lower return on its loans, thereby reducing the firm's cost of capital. Another example of service is the part played by the politically connected board member. These board members, be they former politicians or their family members, have access to legislators and regulators, and this may aid the firm in dealing with the government, predicting regulatory potholes, or forecasting the likely policies of a particular government. Such board members may also assist with obtaining government contracts, and with clearing red tape and providing the firm with political cover in times of trouble.

The networking function is especially important at startups and other young companies. As leading commentator Ralph Ward observes, at such companies "the board's role is very hands-on and results oriented. Directors are expected to tap their networks heavily to help raise funding, lure talent, and make connections, as well as to actively mentor the often overwhelmed founders."[18] It is for this reason that startup companies routinely seek out venture capital investments despite their relatively steep terms. Venture capitalists invested in a firm take board seats, and they bring their network to bear to help fledgling companies. As the venture investors on the hit ABC show "Shark Tank" always tell entrepreneurs when raking them over the coals on deal terms, sharks are far more valuable than the money they invest, since they connect startups with their network of portfolio companies, suppliers, customers, and financiers.

The same networking role is importunate for financially distressed firms. As Ward noted, albeit with a now somewhat dated metaphor, "bankruptcy is the moment when you as a director must put your Rolodex to work for the company ... This can mean getting on the phone with banks, creditors, suppliers – anyone who can make a difference."[19] The role here is played by workout or turnaround specialists, often referred to as vulture investors. These are the analog to venture investors, just at the death stage instead of the birth stage of companies.

Boards also increasingly play an important role as intermediaries between the top management team and key stakeholders, especially shareholders. Indeed, the Business Roundtable recommends that companies bring the investor relations function into the boardroom:

> When appropriate and in consultation with the CEO, directors should be equipped to play a part from time to time in the dialogue with shareholders on topics involving the company's pursuit of long-term value creation and the company's governance ... Direct communication between directors and shareholders should be coordinated through – and with the knowledge of – the board

chair, the lead independent director, and/or the nominating/corporate governance committee or its chair . . .

Companies should engage with long-term shareholders in a manner consistent with the respective roles of the board, management and shareholders.
Companies should maintain effective protocols for shareholder communications with directors and for directors to respond in a timely manner to issues
and concerns that are of widespread interest to long-term shareholders.[20]

This function became especially important during the last decade because
several of Dodd-Frank's corporate governance provisions encouraged investors
to demand opportunities to meet with the board. The executive compensation
provisions of Dodd-Frank, especially the say on pay rule that requires periodic
shareholder votes on executive compensation, for example, encouraged investors and boards to communicate directly about the amount and rationale of
the CEO's pay and benefits package. Investors preferred to talk directly to
those who set the CEO's pay rather than the CEO who received it.
Conversely, when investors were unhappy with CEO pay, sending the CEO
to meet with them was less productive than sending board members.

Of course, sometimes the message boards must communicate to shareholders is "no." As Chancellor Allen famously observed, so long as the board
considers a matter "deliberately and in good faith," the fact that "some shareholders, even a majority of shareholders, may disagree with the wisdom of
their choice" does not oblige the directors to submit to shareholder wishes.[21]
Assisting the corporation in making its case to investors in such cases is an
especially important board function. This is especially true when the board's
role is defined as being the neutral go-between in the conflict between
management and shareholders. As we consider later in this chapter, there is
nothing sacrosanct about this role for boards. But, if boards are going to play
this role, their network and skills in this regard are important elements of
success.

We observe similar board functions outside the United States. In the UK,
for example, outside directors reported to researchers that they drew considerably on the networks of personal, business, and political contacts.[22]
Conversely, top managers of UK firms stated that having directors with wide
networks gave their firm a competitive edge. In addition, they reported that
boards were helpful in maintaining relations with shareholders and other
stakeholders.

We can speak from a bit of experience as well. When one of us was
approached about being a board member of a public company listed on one
of the world's biggest stock exchanges, the interview focused to a large extent

on the personal and professional network that we would bring to bear for the benefit of the company.

Advising

The second core service provided by boards of directors, especially their outside members, is providing advice and counsel to the CEO. As outsiders, the board members can offer the CEO alternative points of view. This is critical in today's fast-paced world, in which opportunities and threats constantly emerge in new and unexpected ways. Boards with broad experience add value by seeing "the broader business landscape and helping management recognize major opportunities and discontinuities that will affect the business."[23]

A McKinsey report thus observed that:

> "Boards need to look further out than anyone else in the company," commented the chairman of a leading energy company. "There are times when CEOs are the last ones to see changes coming."
>
> This forward-looking imperative comes in part from the way long-term economic, technological, and demographic trends are radically reshaping the global economy, making it more complex to oversee a successful multinational business. As executive teams grapple with the immediate challenge of volatile and unpredictable markets, it's more vital than ever for directors to remain abreast of what's on (or coming over) the horizon.
>
> Second, and compounding the short-term executive mind-set, the length of CEO tenures remains relatively low – just five to six years now. That inevitably encourages incumbents to focus unduly on the here and now in order to meet performance expectations. Many rational management groups will be tempted to adopt a short-term view; in a lot of cases, only the board can consistently take the longer-term perspective.[24]

In short, a critical board function is helping the CEO think outside the proverbial box.

The importance of this role arises in part by the nature of the CEO's dual role of managing the firm and setting its course. As a manager of the company, the CEO may believe that the other employees must have complete faith and confidence in the CEO, thus discouraging the CEO from openly admitting any doubt or shortcomings when it comes to the business. In addition, the CEO likely believes that apparent weakness and indecision invites rivals within the company to undermine the CEO or seek their own way to the top. But, as the person responsible for determining the company's future, the CEO likely needs different perspectives and opinions, and would benefit from admitting uncertainty and doubt about various options. The outside directors, being outside of the managerial hierarchy, can resolve this tension by being the confidante to whom the CEO can have a frank conversation about the business without having that conversation cause negative effects in the management of the business.

The board can also serve as a reservoir of outside expertise. Complex business decisions require knowledge in such areas as accounting, finance, management, and law. Members who possess expertise themselves or have access to credible external experts play an important role in the board's service function. Board consultant Ram Charan, for example, offers the example of General Motors board member John Smale when describing the value of outsider expertise. Smale was a former chairman of the board at Proctor & Gamble, a company that is routinely among the leaders in advertising spending. As a General Motors board member, Smale prompted General Motors to make significant changes in its marketing programs that led to substantial new sales.[25]

The importance of this function is reflected in many widely observed traits of successful boards. Law professor Donald Langevoort observes that:

> Invitations to the board are based heavily on matters like compatibility and "fit." The work of the board prizes consensus, not conflict. Absent some sort of crisis, outside members see their value largely in terms of constructive advice, giving insiders the benefit of an expert external perspective on the company's uncertain world.[26]

Langevoort notes that assigning this role to the board is "somewhat curious," because managers can always get expert advice – or, for that matter, obtain access to outside networks – by hiring consultants and other outside advisors.[27] He uses psychology and behavioral economics to explain the board's advisory role as being a way "to compensate for the cognitive *biases* – as opposed to the deliberate self-interest – of the managers and their organizational culture":[28]

> A sizable body of research in cognitive psychology indicates that, left to their own, managers tend to develop biased constructions of the firm's strategic position. Moreover, they will be overconfident and heavily invested in those beliefs, and hence disinclined to seek out information that would suggest that they might be wrong. Only by giving formal power to a more objective group of outsiders (that is, making them directors) can the insiders be forced both to expose their biases and to take dissonant viewpoints seriously.[29]

* * *

If we think of the board's networking function as being a way of gathering resources for the corporation, it becomes apparent that there is a substantial amount of overlap between the board's networking and advising roles. Complex business decisions require knowledge in such areas as accounting, finance, management, and law. Providing access to such knowledge is a critical part of the board's resource-gathering function. Board members may either possess such knowledge themselves, in which case their advisory function becomes especially pertinent, or have access to credible external sources who do.

This is a classic example of the choice between "building" (that is, having expertise inside a particular firm) and "buying" (that is, hiring the expertise in the market) that firms face in a host of activities. In general, we expect firms to build, or insource, when the costs of doing so for a given level of quality are lower than the costs of buying, or outsourcing. As in many of these decisions, the costs are influenced by subtle factors, such as those described by Professor Langevoort. It appears that boards have an important efficiency advantage when it comes to being able to play Devil's advocate regarding corporate decision making. (We will exploit this same framework and reach a similar conclusion when we consider how the natural person requirement forces board members to buy expertise in the market when it might be more efficient for them to build it instead. In other words, from the perspective of companies, permitting them to outsource the board would permit the board to insource its development of expertise.)

MONITORING

The third and final major role played by boards is a monitor of corporate behavior, with an eye on both risk management and compliance with legal obligations. In the former role, board members are agents of the shareholders, while in the latter role they are agents of citizens or society more broadly as well.

Famed mid-twentieth century corporate lawyer and academic Bayless Manning once observed that the bulk of most of what directors do "does not consist of taking affirmative action on individual matters; it is instead a continuing flow of supervisory process, punctuated only occasionally by a discrete transactional decision."[30] This is even truer today than it was when Manning wrote those words back in 1984. Monitoring management today is not just *a* board function; arguably, it is *the* board's function.

The central role of monitoring is premised on a doctrine that has been a basic principle of US corporation law for at least 100 years; namely, that corporations are to be run for the benefit of the shareholders. As the Supreme Court of Michigan famously explained in *Dodge* v. *Ford Motor Co.*:

A business corporation is organized and carried on primarily for the profit of the stockholders. The powers of the directors are to be employed for that end. The discretion of directors is to be exercised in the choice of means to attain that end, and does not extend to a change in the end itself, to the reduction of profits, or to the nondistribution of profits among stockholders in order to devote them to other purposes.[31]

Much more recently, Delaware Chief Justice Leo Strine confirmed that "a clear-eyed look at the law of corporations in Delaware reveals that, within the limits of their discretion, directors must make stockholder welfare their sole end, and that other interests may be taken into consideration only as a means of promoting stockholder welfare."[32]

Yet, a problem immediately arises thanks to that same law of corporations. Recall that Delaware law assigns responsibility for conducting the business and affairs of the corporation to the board of directors. In turn, the board is authorized to delegate day-to-day running of the firm to top management, and, in the sort of corporations with which we are concerned, always do so. Shareholders have little power either to make corporate decisions or interact with those who do. This creates what economists call a principal-agent problem. The shareholders are the "principal" and the CEO is the "agent," tasked with doing their will. But as when anyone is hired to do anything for someone else, there is a risk of divergence between the will and wish of the principal and the application of them to the task at hand by the agent.

Suppose one morning the CFO reports to the CEO that the corporation was unexpectedly profitable in the last quarter to the tune of an extra $50 million. The CFO suggests paying out the unforeseen earnings to the shareholders as a dividend or via a stock buyback. But the CEO long has had her eye on a new larger and faster corporate jet, whose price tag just happens to be $50 million. Does anybody doubt that many – if not most – CEOs would opt for the jet? Shareholders do not get to ride on the jet, of course, but it can be sold to them as about efficiency of management and as a means of attracting top talent. In any event, unless they are paying close attention, shareholders aren't even likely to know there was a choice.

The problem is pervasive, as explained in an Eleventh Circuit Court of Appeals decision:

All corporations necessarily incur monitoring costs. Because managers generally do not own the corporations they run, their interests may be contrary to the stockholders. Accordingly, management may avoid corporate action because of personal benefit even though the action may be beneficial to the stockholders. The corporation, therefore, necessarily incurs monitoring costs – the expenses that arise from management potentially not acting in the best interests of the company.[33]

The jet example is only the tip of this particular iceberg. Excessive managerial consumption of perks is clearly a problem, although it goes far beyond jets. Bigger offices than necessary, fancy art on the walls, a building designed by Frank Gehry, meetings in Boca Raton; these are all expenses that shareholders might not benefit from but that are routine in corporate America. Federal law tries to inform shareholders, requiring perks more than $50,000 in value to be reported, but nothing on this list other than the jet ride would count, since the others are not technically perks of an individual officer.

But the problem is even bigger still. Shirking by managers (and other employees) is likely a much greater cost to shareholders than the sum of excessive perks. So too are the costs of risk aversion inherent in the divergence between shareholder and manager interests. Simply put, shareholders can (and should) diversify their investments across many companies, thus reducing their exposure to the risks of a particular company. This means shareholders prefer individual companies to take risks that are net-present-value positive, even if they result in bad outcomes more frequently than a risk-neutral CEO would prefer. All else being equal, individual CEOs, who have their employment and a great deal of their wealth tied up in a particular company, are likely to operate a given firm much more conservatively than shareholders would prefer.

The board of directors long has been charged with being one of the primary mechanisms by which corporations monitor managerial behavior for the benefit of stockholders along all these dimensions – perks, shirking, risk aversion, and so on. But how do we make sure that the board does a good job? What keeps the board from sloughing off and letting management run roughshod over shareholder interests? Or, for that matter, what prevents the board itself from doing so?

In a very real sense, those are the critical questions that motivate our proposal. Corporate law and governance has come up with lots of ways to encourage directors to be more effective or to provide alternative means of monitoring management. To date, however, nobody has come up with a better vehicle for doing so than an effective board of directors or a mechanism for ensuring board effectiveness. Hence, the need for BSPs.[i]

---

[i]   Alternatives to board monitoring include shareholder voting, creditor monitoring, the market for corporate control, the market for managerial labor, and regulatory supervision, among others. Boards remain, however, the most promising vehicle for effective monitoring. Boards are more flexible than these other constraints. Boards have better access to information – both

Monitoring Becomes Job One

The relative balance between these functions of corporate boards has shifted over time. Survey data and other forms of fieldwork in the 1970s suggested that boards had a mainly advisory role. Survey data from the 1990s, by contrast, shows an emphasis on managerial functions in the sense of broad policy making and setting strategy. By the end of the 1990s, survey data showed that boards were becoming active and independent monitors of the top management team.[34]

What drove this change in emphasis? Corporate governance reformers in the 1970s recognized, as prominent law professor Melvin Eisenberg observed, that boards were "not fulfilling the policy-making role contemplated by corporate law."[35] Instead, he argued, the task for which the board is "uniquely suited" is that of "selecting and dismissing the members of the chief executive's office and monitoring that office's performance."[36]

This view rapidly became accepted as best practice by leading governance organizations. In 1978, for example, the American Bar Association's Section of Business Law promulgated a *Corporate Director's Guidebook* that advocated separating the managerial and oversight functions with the former assigned to the top management team and the latter being assigned to a board composed mainly of outside directors.[37] A formal statement by the Business Roundtable the same year likewise adopted the monitoring model.[38] The absorption of the monitoring model into generally accepted best practice continued throughout the 1990s.[39] By 1997, Eisenberg was thus able to declare that "key structural elements of the monitoring model – including a board that has at least a majority of independent directors, and audit, nominating, and compensation committees – [were] already well-established."[40]

Much of the impetus behind the rise of the monitoring model came from lawyers and business people concerned about the potential for a drastic expansion of the federal government's role in corporate governance and decision making. If boards could be deployed, or rather redeployed, to monitor CEOs and other managers, this would save the government having to do as much monitoring work. Not only would this mean a smaller government role, but the proponents of the monitoring model believed it would also mean a more efficient regulatory approach.

---

in terms of the speed by which it is acquired and its depth – than do outside constraints. Boards process such information faster than most outsiders, allowing them to act as a corporation's first responder in times of managerial crisis. Lastly, only that board has the power to hire and fire management, which gives it far greater leverage than any outside constraint. See Philip Stiles & Bernard Taylor, *Boards at Work: How Directors View Their Roles and Responsibilities* 4–5 (2001).

The tradeoffs are fairly clear. Board members would have more business expertise than government regulators. They would also have more information at lower cost. Finally, being inside of the firm, investigations and regulation of activities by board members would likely result in less push back and defensive crouch by managers, compared with the same work being done by the government. On the other hand, boards might be expected to be less vigilant than government monitors, given their personal and monetary affiliations with the firm.

This tradeoff might net out in favor of boards as the primary mechanism of social control, especially since government regulators stand ready in the event of board failures. In this sense, monitoring boards are a form of self-regulatory organization, in that they face the same tradeoffs as SROs for entire industries. As in the case of SROs, the situation could be improved if board members could be imbued with public mindedness that would reduce some of the potential risks of incentives and capture or group affiliation that might cause board members to turn a blind eye to unlawfulness or excessive risk-taking. The cases establishing relatively strict fiduciary duties for directors and the push for independent directors can be seen in this light. Directors being tasked with a monitoring/regulatory role cannot be inside directors, since in that case the costs noted earlier would swamp the benefits.

Codifying the Monitoring Model

Best practice is one thing. Legal mandates are quite another. The idea that the board's primary job is monitoring management began moving from the former to the latter in 1977 when the NYSE amended its listing standards to require the board of directors of a domestic listed company to have an audit commit-tee composed solely of directors independent of management. This require-ment grew out of a series of corporate scandals in the first half of that decade, as law professor Jeffrey Gordon notes:

> The 1970s were characterized by a double disillusionment about corporate performance, and the passivity of directors that contributed to it. There were two powerful shocks: first, the unexpected collapse of Penn Central and second, the Watergate-related illegal domestic campaign contributions and "questionable payments," (less politely, probable bribes) to foreign govern-ment officials. The bankruptcy of the Penn Central Railroad, regarded as the bluest of blue chips, resonated in its day like the fall of Enron, and the "questionable payments" scandal revealed at least as much rot as the account-ing abuses in the late 1990s. The reaction was to push the board away from an advisory model to a monitoring model, at least in aspiration. In a sense, much

subsequent corporate governance reform is a working out of the forces put in motion by the 1970s.[41]

As the SEC noted in approving the NYSE rule change, "support for audit committees independent of management" had grown "in the wake of recent revelations of questionable and illegal corporate payments."[42]

It's been aptly noted that declining stock markets and the corporate scandals that often seem to accompany them create fertile ground for corporate governance reforms: "People get religion of sorts about ethics and corporate governance in down markets. When things are going well, they tend to forget about it."[43] Just as the Penn Central scandal gave impetus to the monitoring model of board functions, so did the bursting of the tech bubble and the concurrent Enron scandal at the turn of the millennium.

After the Enron scandal broke, its board of directors appointed a special investigative committee whose report concluded that senior managers "were enriched, in the aggregate, by tens of millions of dollars they should never have received."[44] The report laid much of the blame at the feet of Enron's board of directors, which "failed . . . in its oversight duties" with "serious consequences for Enron, its employees, and its shareholders."[45]

Just as the Penn Central debacle proved to be merely the first in a series of high profile corporate scandals, so did Enron's failure. As a NYSE report opined, the post-dotcom bubble period saw a "'meltdown' of significant companies due to failures of diligence, ethics and controls" on the part of directors and senior managers.[46] Post-Enron congressional investigations found multiple instances in which "directors had extensive social and professional ties with corporate officers and their fellow directors that compromised their ability to be impartial and undermined their ability to provide an adequate check on directors' and officers' conduct."[47]

In response to the Enron meltdown and numerous other high profile corporate scandals, Congress passed SOX.[48] As we'll see in Chapter 9, the Act created new federal rules relating to corporate governance, including director and officer duties, responsibilities of auditors, and obligations for corporate lawyers, many of which were "designed to reduce conflicts of interest or interpersonal pressures in order to make it more likely that the directors will act as judgmental monitors of management rather than as reciprocating colleagues."[49] Still others "require directors to engage in processes that may increase their self-awareness and diligence, or because they increase the ability and incentives to directors to act diligently on behalf of public shareholders."[50]

Unlike Sarbanes-Oxley, the Dodd-Frank back story is not one in which failures by Main Street boards of directors figure prominently. As one of us described elsewhere, however, special interests centered on shareholder activists successfully hijacked the legislative process to pursue goals unrelated to the housing bubble or the credit crisis.[51] Just as was the case with the comparable provisions of SOX, Dodd-Frank's corporate governance provisions were intended to empower shareholders at the expense of both boards and managers.[i]

The UK has similarly emphasized the monitoring role of the board. The Cadbury Report (1992) made the board responsible for oversight of the company's internal controls.[52] The Turnbull Report (1999) emphasized the board's responsibility to oversee the company's risk management strategies.[53] The latest version of the UK Corporate Governance Code provides that the board's independent members "should scrutinise the performance of management in meeting agreed goals and objectives and monitor the reporting of performance."[54] The code also confirms the Cadbury and Turnbull positions on the board's duty to monitor the company's internal control and risk management systems. Like SOX and Dodd-Frank, the code also assigns substantial monitoring obligations to the audit committee in connection with the preparation of the company's financial disclosures.

The extent to which boards function as assertive monitors is debated. In the United States, the evidence suggests that boards today are more effective than they used to be, but still fall far short of what would be ideal.[55] A survey of outside directors of companies in emerging markets found evidence of active board engagement in monitoring management. In particular, the survey found that more than two-thirds of the directors in the study had voted against at least one proposal at some point in their tenure, which the authors took as evidence that the directors were "significantly engaged" with the company.[56] On the other hand, while a small survey of eleven Israeli companies found that their directors spent considerably more time on monitoring than on service, the survey found little evidence of boards vetoing management proposals.[57] The utility of the time spent by Israeli directors on monitoring thus remains, at best, uncertain.

---

[i] Dodd-Frank was an enormous statute covering hundreds of topics, of which only a relatively small handful addressed the governance of public corporations outside the financial sector. For an overview of the statute's governance provisions, see Mirela V. Hristova, Dodd-Frank's Corporate Governance Reform, 30 *Rev. Banking & Fin. L.* 516 (2011). For a review of the major provisions of the Act as a whole, see The Subcommittee on Annual Review, Committee on Federal Regulation of Securities, ABA Section of Business Law, Annual Review of Federal Securities Regulation, 66 *Bus. Law.* 659 (2011).

DIVERSITY

Although our focus in this book will be on the three functions just described, there is another potential purpose for boards that is not frequently mentioned in the academic literature but is an implicit part of conversations about modern boards. The board can be a mechanism for achieving broader social change by providing positions of authority for historically subjugated groups, such as women and racial or ethnic minorities. We consider how BSPs might help on this front later in this chapter. For now, we point out that some progress has been made: in 2015, women comprised approximately 20 percent of directors on boards of the largest five hundred companies.[58] This is a large increase in the past few decades, but it falls far short of the parity that in polls a majority of current directors believe would be the ideal state of affairs.[59]

OVERLAPPING ROLES AND THE CRUDENESS OF CATEGORIES

We've identified three roles for the board: management, service, and oversight. In practice, of course, the lines between them are, at best, fuzzy. If the board terminates the CEO due to lagging corporate performance, for example, we might call that a pure example of the monitoring function. Yet, is not terminating an employee – even one as exalted as the CEO – a managerial task?

If the board terminates the CEO because it believes the lagging performance resulted from bad policy decisions by the CEO, that action could still fairly be called monitoring, but now the managerial component becomes even more obvious. If finding a replacement CEO whose policy preferences are aligned with those of the board drives the subsequent recruitment process, that action takes on an even greater managerial aspect. Providing leadership and guidance to an interim CEO during the interregnum before a new permanent CEO is found is also a common board role, but again is more managerial than oversight in nature.[i]

Not only are the various roles almost impossible to untangle, but it also seems clear that playing each of them has a synergistic effect on overall board performance. For example, performing a management role significantly enhances the board's oversight function. On the one hand, the very presence

---

[i] Not all disciplinary actions rise to the level of termination, of course. In fact, it seems certain that most do not. Yet, lesser punishments are even more difficult for management than are terminations. If the board instructs the CEO to change from one policy to another, for example, that order is just as much a management decision as when the CEO instructs a subordinate to do so.

of independent directors who must give their approval to major corporate decisions should go a long way toward encouraging managers to make better and more faithful decisions.

> The mere fact that the top executives know they have to make formal presentations about key issues on a regular basis to an audience that may probe and criticize, and that has the power to remove them, elicits a great deal of valuable behavior. Executives gather facts more carefully and completely, make ideas and judgments more explicit, anticipate and deal with competing considerations, and find modes of articulation that can withstand scrutiny outside the inner circle. The consequence of all these efforts to better "explain and sell" the executive viewpoint may well be to clarify strategic thinking and improve decision making ... Similarly, the fact the top executives know they have to present a proposed major financing, business acquisition, or compensation plan to a board that will ask questions and has power to say "yes" or "no" will tend to limit the range of proposals that the executives dare propose and push them somewhat closer and more reliably toward plans that benefit shareholders. The impact is valuable, even if clearly imperfect.[60]

On the other hand, exercising their oversight function is one of the key ways in which boards become fully informed.

ROLE CONFLICTS

In addition to being difficult to put into separate buckets, there is an inherent conflict among the board's various roles. Suppose the CEO comes to the board for advice on a proposed project. The board advises the CEO to go forward with the proposal, but the project thereafter fails miserably. The board's role in the original decision inevitably compromises its ability to evaluate and, if necessary, discipline the CEO. The monitoring model seeks to avoid this problem by giving primacy to the board's oversight role.

Yet, in focusing board effort on oversight, the monitoring model raises its own set of problems. One size does not fit all, and some boards may need to play active advisory and service roles, but the emphasis on their monitoring function may deprive them of the time and other resources necessary to effectively accomplish managerial and service functions. Independence heightens the credibility of monitoring on behalf of shareholders and the government, but reduces the efficacy of management, strategy, or valuation advice. This problem has been compounded in recent years, because the net effect of SOX, Dodd-Frank, related regulatory developments, and associated stock exchange listing standards was to significantly increase the emphasis on the board's monitoring function. Independence is the watchword of the day, but it is not an unalloyed good. Independence, like everything, has costs, and these must be constantly measured against its benefits.

These issues have been contested for a long time and yet remain highly controversial. Some commentators think boards should do nothing but monitor management. Some think the law now overemphasizes monitoring at the expense of other legitimate board functions. Our own view is that one size does not fit all, and the law should give boards substantial freedom to set their own priorities to best serve the corporation.

Ultimately, however, what matters for present purposes is understanding what functions boards have historically performed rather than the precise allocation of time between those functions. As we will argue later, BSPs are highly adaptable. They are well suited to perform the monitoring function as required by current law and best practices, but they are equally well suited to performing service and managerial functions. Indeed, as we shall see, because BSPs are less subject to time and expertise constraints than individual directors, they are capable of fully carrying out the monitoring function while also simultaneously providing more effective advisory, networking, and managerial services.

EVOLUTION OVER TIME

The foregoing is a snapshot of board functions in the modern era; approximately since the 1970s. In fact, however, the perceived relative importance of these functions has changed dramatically over time. While early boards were predominately about monitoring or quasi-regulation, as described in Chapter 1, boards during the Industrial Revolution were mostly about management, while boards at the turn of the twentieth century were service boards. As our analysis in this chapter shows, however, today's boards have returned to their lost historical roots, becoming monitoring boards again.

In the thirteenth century, the English king established the board of the Merchants of the Staple to provide quasi-governmental oversight of English merchants that were outside of his power; today, our system of corporate governance, built over the decades by courts, legislatures, and private associations acting in loose concert, delegates enormous regulatory oversight to corporate boards in much the same way. While in the old days it was about the ability of government to extend its reach, this is not the reason for delegation of regulatory authority today – no one doubts the ability of the government to exert control over corporations if they wanted to. Instead, the use of boards to play this role is based on ideas about efficiency – who can provide a given level of regulatory oversight and compliance at the lowest social cost – and perhaps some concerns about the proper extent of government power.

Whatever the reasons, the modern corporate board is unquestionably a monitoring board, even though it also provides other functions. Just as boards did throughout corporate history – boards have always provided a mix of these three core functions, just in different degrees. Every board is a management board, a monitoring board, and a service board. The only question at any point in time and for any board is how much of each is a particular board providing. There are tradeoffs, since devoting board time to monitoring means that it will have less time to assist in management or use its connections to serve the company. It is for this reason that different ages of the corporation have taken on particular board identities.

Change seems again to be on the horizon. Institutional shareholders in charge of passive investment accounts totaling the tens of trillions are now the largest shareholders at nearly all of America's large public companies. These investors do not have the time, expertise, or financial incentive to invest in corporate governance or even corporate strategy. Passive investors are rationally ignorant about governance at individual companies because losses of one company in their portfolio are likely offset by gains by other companies they own. Moreover, improvements in governance inure to all shareholders, thus distorting the cost-benefit calculation for investments in good governance by individual shareholders. It is perhaps for this reason that today's institutional investors are not investing much in governance. Vanguard's governance team employs only 15 to cover about 13,000 companies around the world; BlackRock employs about 20 people for its 14,000 companies; and State Street employs fewer than 10 people for governance issues at 9,000 companies.

Activist investors have stepped into the lacuna of corporate governance created by the rational apathy of the passive investors. These investors have increasingly pressured for their representatives to take board seats, reminiscent of the takeover era of the 1980s. According to PriceWaterhouseCoopers' 2016 board survey, "The board-centric model that took hold in the 1990's due to a number of corporate scandals has continued to transition to an investor-centric model . . . Shareholders are looking for a seat at the board table, putting directors in the spotlight and driving change across the governance landscape."[61]

The recent battle for control of Arconic, part of the aluminum conglomerate formerly known as Alcoa, is illustrative. Hard times came in 2008, and the stock price of Alcoa fell by over 90 percent. The board installed a new CEO, and after a few failed reboots, the company was split in two. Alcoa spun off its aluminum business into a new company also called Alcoa, and renamed the parent company, Arconic. Alcoa took several steps to improve its governance, but Arconic stuck to the old way of doing things. It remained incorporated in

Pennsylvania (Alcoa moved to Delaware), and kept its classified board and unitary executive model (Alcoa ditched them). The board was also plagued by conflicts of interest. The lead independent director, also served as the as the chair of the HP board, on which Arconic's CEO also served. There was also evidence the Arconic board was not as aware as it should be. The board was unaware of a voting agreement that put nearly nine million shares of Arconic stock in the effective voting control of the CEO for two years. To make matters worse, the voting agreement was only revealed to Arconic shareholders after a dead-hand provision had kicked in, causing these shares to be voted for management no matter who owned them. All the while institutional investors sat on the sidelines, rationally apathetic to the underperformance and governance shenanigans.

The situation became so bad that an activist investor, Elliott Management, took a 13 percent stake in Arconic, and began agitating for change. It sought the ouster of the CEO and four independent directors on the Arconic board. Arconic responded by threatening shareholders with a "poison put" – arguing with no obvious legal foundation that a contract with an employee pension trust required a payment of $500 million in the event Elliott were successful in its campaign to remake the board.

Ultimately, the parties settled the case, agreeing to many of Elliott's demands, including the change in directors. The takeaway from this anecdote, however, is the possibility that it portends a change in the role played by modern corporate boards. A role not just of monitoring, but of expressing managerial or strategic views again in a more robust form than in the recent past. What is old is always new again in the board room.

Notes

1. For a useful overview and summary of board duties under state and federal law, see The Corporate Laws Committee, ABA Section of Business Law, Corporate Director's Guidebook—Sixth Edition, 66 Bus. Law. 975 (2011).
2. Apple Corporate Governance Guidelines 1 (2015), http://files.share holder.com/downloads/AAPL/3576932174x0x443011/6A7D49F1-A3AF-4E 69-B279-021B81A93CDF/governance_guidelines.pdf.
3. The Walt Disney Company, Corporate Governance Guidelines 1–2 (2014), https://ditm-twdc-us.storage.googleapis.com/Corporate-Governan ce-Guidelines.pdf.
4. The story is recounted in Bryan Burrough & John Helyar, *Barbarians at the Gate: The Fall of RJR Nabisco* 74–77 (1990).

5. *Adams v. Clearance Corp.*, 121 A.2d 302, 305 (Del. 1956).
6. See *Cahall v. Lofland*, 114 A. 224, 229 (1921), aff'd, 118 A. 1 (1922) (recognizing that the directors' principal role was one of supervision and control, with the detailed conduct of the business being a matter that could properly be delegated to subordinate employees).
7. DGCL § 141(a).
8. *Chapin v. Benwood Foundation*, 402 A.2d 1205, 1211 (Del. Ch. 1979).
9. Ibid.
10. See, e.g. *Lee v. Jenkins Bros.*, 268 F.2d 357, 365–366 (2nd Cir. 1959) (explaining that officers have no apparent authority with respect to extraordinary matters, which are reserved to the board).
11. The Conference Board, CEO Succession Practices 72 (2015).
12. Securities Exchange Commission Division of Corporate Finance, Staff Legal Bulletin No. 14E (CF) (Oct. 27, 2009).
13. *Dynamics Corp. of Am. v. CTS Corp.*, 637 F. Supp. 406, 409 (N.D. Ill.), aff'd, 794 F.2d 250 (7th Cir. 1986), rev'd on other grounds, 481 U.S. 69 (1987).
14. Ralph de Haas et al., The Inner Workings of the Board: Evidence from Emerging Markets 2 (Jan. 23, 2017), https://ssrn.com/abstract=2904663.
15. Ibid.
16. Philip Stiles & Bernard Taylor, *Boards at Work: How Directors View Their Roles and Responsibilities* 31 (2001).
17. William T. Allen, Independent Directors in MBO Transactions: Are They Fact or Fantasy? 45 *Bus. Law.* 2055, 2057 (1990).
18. Ralph D. Ward, *Saving the Corporate Board: Why Boards Fail and How to Fix Them* 99–100 (2003).
19. Ibid. at 120–121.
20. The Business Roundtable, *Principles of Corporate Governance* 25–26 (2016).
21. *Paramount Commc'ns Inc. v. Time Inc.*, 1989 WL 79880, at *2 (Del. Ch. July 14, 1989), aff'd sub nom. *In re Time Inc. S'holder Litig.*, 565 A.2d 281 (Del. 1989).
22. Stiles & Taylor, *Boards at Work*, at 99.
23. Ram Charan, *Boards at Work: How Corporate Boards Create Competitive Advantage* 8 (1998).
24. Christian Casal & Christian Caspar, Building a Forward-Looking Board, *McKinsey Quarterly* (Feb. 2014).
25. Charan, *Boards at Work*, at 11.
26. Donald C. Langevoort, The Human Nature of Corporate Boards: Laws, Norms, and the Unintended Consequences of Independence and Accountability, 89 *Geo. L.J.* 797 (2001).
27. Ibid. at 803.
28. Ibid. (emphasis supplied).

29. Ibid.
30. Bayless Manning, The Business Judgment Rule and the Director's Duty of Attention: Time for Reality, 39 *Bus. Law.* 1477, 1494 (1984).
31. *Dodge v. Ford Motor Co.*, 170 N.W. 668, 684 (Mich. 1919).
32. The Honorable Leo E. Strine, Jr., The Dangers of Denial: The Need for a Clear-Eyed Understanding of the Power and Accountability Structure Established by the Delaware General Corporation Law, 50 *Wake Forest L. Rev.* 761, 768 (2015).
33. *Int'l Ins. Co. v. Johns*, 874 F.2d 1447, 1465–1466 (11th Cir. 1989) (footnotes and citations omitted).
34. For an overview of the relevant surveys, see Renee B. Adams et al., The Role of Boards of Directors in Corporate Governance: A Conceptual Framework and Survey, 48 *J. Econ. Lit.* 58, 64–65 (2010).
35. Melvin Aron Eisenberg, *The Structure of the Corporation: A Legal Analysis* 154 (1976).
36. Ibid. at 162.
37. ABA Section of Corporation, Banking and Business Law, Corporate Director's Guidebook, 33 *Bus. Law.* 1591, 1619–1628 (1978).
38. Statement of the Business Roundtable, The Role and Composition of the Board of Directors of the Large Publicly Owned Corporation, 33 *Bus. Law.* 2083 (1978).
39. See Ira M. Millstein & Paul W. MacAvoy, The Active Board of Directors and Performance of the Large Publicly Traded Corporation, 98 *Colum. L. Rev.* 1283, 1288–1289 (1998) (reviewing best practice guidelines).
40. Melvin A. Eisenberg, The Board of Directors and Internal Control, 19 *Cardozo L. Rev.* 237, 239 (1997).
41. Jeffrey N. Gordon, The Rise of Independent Directors in the United States, 1950–2005: Of Shareholder Value and Stock Market Prices, 59 *Stan. L. Rev.* 1465, 1514–1515 (2007).
42. In re NYSE, Exchange Act Release No. 13,346, 11 SEC Docket 1945 (Mar. 9, 1977).
43. Kathryn Jones, Who Moved My Bonus? Executive Pay Makes a U-Turn, *NY Times*, April 5, 2009 (quoting James A. Allen).
44. William C. Powers, Jr., et al., *Report of Investigation by the Special Investigative Committee of the Board of Directors of Enron Corp.* 3 (Feb. 1, 2002).
45. Ibid.
46. NYSE, *Corporate Governance Rule Proposals Reflecting Recommendations from the NYSE Corporate Accountability and Listing Standards Committee, as Approved by the NYSE Board of Directors* (Aug. 1, 2002).
47. Lisa M. Fairfax, The Uneasy Case for the Inside Director, 96 *Iowa L. Rev.* 127, 149 (2010).

48. Pub. L. 107–204, 116 Stat. 745 (July 30, 2002). For an overview of SOX that emphasizes the new duties it creates for corporate directors and officers, see Brett H. McDonnell, Sox Appeals, 2004 *Mich. St. L. Rev.* 505 (2004).

49. Robert Charles Clark, Corporate Governance Changes in the Wake of the Sarbanes-Oxley Act: A Morality Tale for the Policymakers Too, 22 *Ga. St. U. L. Rev.* 251, 267 (2005). See also Larry E. Ribstein, Market vs. Regulatory Responses to Corporate Fraud: A Critique of the Sarbanes-Oxley Act of 2002, 28 *J. Corp. L.* 1, 26 (2002) (explaining that "corporate reformers have emphasized independent directors as a way to curb insider abuse").

50. Clark, Corporate Governance, at 267.

51. See Stephen M. Bainbridge, Dodd-Frank: Quack Federal Corporate Governance Round II, 95 *Minn. L. Rev.* 1779 (2011) (discussing the corporate governance provisions of the Dodd-Frank Act).

52. Stiles & Taylor, *Boards at Work*, at 62.

53. Ibid.

54. Financial Reporting Council. The UK Corporate Governance Code 9 (Apr. 2016), www.frc.org.uk/Our-Work/Publications/Corporate-Governance/UK-Corporate-Governance-Code-April-2016.pdf.

55. See Stephen M. Bainbridge, *Corporate Governance after the Financial Crisis* (2012).

56. Haas, Inner Workings, at 2.

57. Miriam Schwartz-Ziv & Michael S. Weisbach, What Do Boards Really Do? Evidence from Minutes of Board Meetings, 108 *J. Fin. Econ.* 349 (2013).

58. www.pwc.com/us/en/press-releases/2016/pwc-2016-annual-corporate-directors-survey-press-release.html.

59. Ibid.

60. Clark, Corporate Governance, at 280–281.

61. Paula Loop, Leader of PwC's Governance Insights Center.

3

Grading Boards

In Chapter 2, we set out a typology for considering board performance. Only by knowing what boards are doing and by classifying their activities can we create a framework for evaluating their performance. This evaluation is essential to our project, since our proposed reform is (not to give away the plot of this chapter) premised on current boards not living up to the promise of good corporate governance. In this chapter, we critically assess modern board performance, with an eye on highlighting areas of weakness, and thus potential opportunity for our BSP proposal.

PUBLIC PERCEPTIONS

In the popular imagination, the board of directors is probably like the board of Hudsucker Industries in the Coen brothers' movie, "The Hudsucker Proxy." Seventeen fat, white, bald old men sitting around a glossy, oaken table in a sterile conference room taking orders from another fat, white, bald man called the CEO. (Thankfully, few CEOs do what the CEO of Hudsucker did – climb up on the table, run its length, and take a swan dive through a plate-glass window, only to plummet dozens of floors to the Manhattan pavement.) In the public's mind, we suspect, the board exists to collect a hefty paycheck for little work. They imagine directors attend occasional meetings in fancy places, and rubber-stamp the work of executives, who really call the shots. Occasionally, a board stands up and does the right thing, but so rarely as to make the phenomenon rival Halley's Comet.

This perception of boards as stocked with the CEO's toadies, like most stereotypes of business in American culture, has a substantial basis in truth but also a surprising degree of fiction. Admittedly, boards have been getting failing grades for centuries and, despite the rampant grade inflation witnessed in so many social institutions, all too many boards are still failing to

deliver.[i] In the eighteenth Century, Adam Smith famously complained that
one could not expect the directors of a joint stock company, "being the
managers rather of other people's money than of their own ... should
watch over it with the same anxious vigilance with which the partners in
a private copartnery frequently watch over their own."[1] Almost two centuries later, William O. Douglas complained that there were too many
boards whose members did "not direct"[2] and dismissed directors as "business colonels of the honorary type – honorary colonels who are ornamental
in parade but fairly useless in battle."[3] Still more recently, in the wake of
the 2008 financial crisis, numerous commentators posed "the same question: Where was the board?"[4] In the public mind, boards are sinecures of
the rich and famous (at best) and asleep at the wheel while driving around
with individuals' precious cargo (at worst).

EVEN GRADED ON A CURVE, BOARDS FAIL

Much of this criticism was and is merited. A well-known British judicial
opinion from the early twentieth century, describing the selection of
a rubber corporation's board, provides an amusing illustration of the basic
problem:

> The directors of the company, Sir Arthur Aylmer Bart., Henry William
> Tugwell, Edward Barber and Edward Henry Hancock were all induced to
> become directors by Harboard or persons acting with him in the promotion of
> the company. Sir Arthur Aylmer was absolutely ignorant of business. He only
> consented to act because he was told the office would give him a little
> pleasant employment without his incurring any responsibility. H.W.
> Tugwell was partner in a firm of bankers in a good position in Bath; he was
> seventy-five years of age and very deaf; he was induced to join the board by
> representations made to him in January, 1906. Barber was a rubber broker and
> was told that all he would have to do would be to give an opinion as to the
> value of rubber when it arrived in England. Hancock was a man of business
> who said he was induced to join by seeing the names of Tugwell and Barber,
> whom he considered good men.[5]

---

[i]   As we saw in Chapter 1, the history of boards has seen the evolution of the purpose of the board.
      A snapshot of board performance at any one point in time thus is likely to be misleading when it
      comes to asking what role the board should serve. If one believes a board should be providing
      monitoring services, for example, then the crony boards packed with insiders (of, say, the
      post–World War II era) were wanting, whereas if one believes a board should be providing
      strategic counsel, then today's boards would be flawed. Our focus in this chapter, however, is on
      the ways boards have failed in the generally accepted functions described in Chapter 2.

Unfortunately, such practices were the norm rather than the exception.

As a result of such practices, the hierarchy contemplated by corporate statutes was inverted. CEOs did not work for the board; the board effectively worked for the CEO. In his classic study of post–World War II General Motors, for example, management guru Peter Drucker described General Motors – then regarded as the paradigmatic US corporation – as a bureaucratic hierarchy dominated by professional managers. Indeed, he describes those managers as being essentially autonomous actors subject to no meaningful corporate governance constraints, because the firm's directors were figureheads and shareholders were irrelevant.[6] The former would never do anything to disturb the paycheck and prestige of position, while the latter were rationally apathetic and uninformed.

In the 1970s, however, a crisis of confidence threatened not just the comfortable world of the board of directors but the very foundations of corporate capitalism. The triggering event was the 1970 collapse of Penn Central, which occurred "amidst personality clashes, mismanagement, and lax board oversight."[7] Subsequent investigations revealed that Penn Central's board had been mere figureheads who were wholly unaware of the company's deteriorating financial condition. The board passively rubber-stamped such transactions as paying over $100 million in dividends to shareholders even as the company was going down the tube.[8]

The Penn Central debacle was followed in short order by the corrupt payments scandal of the early to mid-1970s, in which hundreds of prominent public corporations were implicated. The scandal was an offshoot of the Watergate investigations. The probes brought to light numerous illegal corporate contributions to the Nixon campaign. Investigation of those violations then revealed an even broader pattern of both domestic and foreign corporations making illegal campaign contributions, bribes to government officials, kickbacks on contracts, and so on. Eventually, the government targeted some fifty corporations for criminal prosecution or SEC civil litigation. Another 400 corporations voluntarily disclosed having made improper payments. By the end, it was clear that senior management at many of these companies had been fully aware of the corrupt payments, but their boards had been too far out of the loop to prevent them.

The cumulative effect of these scandals swept the legitimacy of the corporate form itself into the tumultuous political battles of the day. The period was one in which multiple progressive movements – including the antiwar, civil rights, feminism, gay rights, consumer protection, and environmentalist movements – intertwined in a constantly shifting flux of activism. Many of these groups came to see the institution of the corporation as being a root cause of social problems.

This view found its classic expression in Ralph Nader's philippic *Taming the Giant Corporation*.[9] Nader and his coauthors claimed that public confidence in American corporations was declining precipitously in the face of antisocial corporate behavior. They blamed myriad social ills – pollution, workplace hazards, discrimination, unsafe products, and corporate crime – on corporate managers who were effectively unaccountable to boards, shareholders, or society.

Consistent with the generally accepted diagnosis of the Penn Central collapse and the questionable payments scandal, Nader and his coauthors laid much of the blame at the feet of boards of directors. In turn, they blamed the board's impotence in large part on state corporate law, which purportedly had been "reduced to reflecting the preferences of the managers of the largest corporations."[10] Accordingly, Nader called for a federal corporation law, displacing state law, whose precepts would ensure greater management accountability both to shareholders and to society.

Among other things, Nader proposed a federal statute that would create a cadre of full-time professional directors. Only cadre members would be allowed to serve on boards. Incumbent managers would be prohibited from both sitting on their corporation's boards and nominating or selecting candidates for the board. Once elected, by way of cumulative voting, the board members would serve on a full-time basis, with no outside employment, and for no more than four two-year terms. Board members would be provided with staff and full access to corporate information. Each board member would be responsible for some specified aspect of the business, such as employee welfare or law compliance.

Although Nader was an outlier, at least in terms of the ferocity of his attacks and the radical nature of his proposals, many mainstream regulators and scholars of the period likewise concluded that state corporate law was moving away from, not toward, greater managerial accountability. Former SEC Chairman William Cary famously argued, for example, that competition among states for incorporations produced a "race to the bottom," in which shareholder interests were sacrificed.[11]

Leading mainstream figures like Cary believed that the race to the bottom, combined with the wave of scandals in the 1970s and the New Left's critique of corporate capitalism, as exemplified by Nader, had eroded public confidence in the modern business corporation and, as a result, had brought into question the very legitimacy of the economic system in which the corporation was the dominant actor. In order to arrest those trends, Cary urged adoption of a federal statute designed to promote greater management accountability to shareholders, although not going so far as to require federal incorporation. Like Nader's more ambitious scheme, Cary's proposal for partially federalizing corporation law ultimately went nowhere. Along with other similar proposals, however, they contributed to a shift in best practices and ultimately laid the groundwork for the creeping federalization of corporate law exemplified by SOX and Dodd-Frank.

BOARDS FAIL EVEN AT GRADING THEMSELVES

Letting Nader or even Professor Cary grade boards may not be fair or informative. After all, both were true outsiders with little or no real-world experience in the boardroom, and both were, to varying degrees, on a political mission. Instead of relying on outsiders whose goal it was to revamp corporate power, let us look at the grades board members give themselves. After all, they have the information and experience, and, if anything, are likely to bias their evaluations in a positive direction.

Since 2003, the NYSE has required the boards of listed companies to conduct an annual self-evaluation.[12] Commentators have endorsed such evaluations as being a critical corporate governance best practice, arguing that no one – not managers, shareholders, or regulators – has better information about how a board performs.[13] Outsiders are largely limited to evaluating board members based on outputs, such as firm performance, while board members are in the room and thus able to use a much broader set of metrics to evaluate both inputs and outputs.

In practice, however, boards are as bad at self-evaluation as they are most other tasks. Barely half of companies evaluate the performance of individual directors, as opposed to evaluating the board as a whole,[14] despite the obvious importance of determining whether individual board members are making effective contributions to the board's decision-making processes. Of those that do conduct individual evaluations, just slightly over one-third believe their company's evaluation of individual directors provides an accurate assessment of each individual's contributions.[15]

When board members do grade themselves, their GPAs aren't high enough to warrant their positions of influence and power. In their *Harvard Business Review* piece mentioned earlier, McKinsey head Dominic Barton and Canadian investor Mark Wiseman report shocking data from a set of surveys of board members. About one-third of directors self-report understanding their company's strategy; one in five said their boards understood how their firms created value; and about 15 percent reported having a "strong understanding of the dynamics of their firms' industries."

Boards also blamed themselves when it came to "organizations' over-emphasis on short-term financial results and underemphasis on long-term value creation." Half of corporate executives surveyed blamed their boards, but three out of four board members "pointed the finger at themselves."

SHOWING IMPROVEMENT

Despite these problems and the seemingly widespread view that boards are falling short, there are signs of some improvement in the boardroom.

As we saw in the previous chapter, regulatory responses to the series of corporate disasters – beginning with the Penn Central scandal and culminating in the financial crisis of 2008 – introduced a series of reforms designed to empower boards to be more effective, especially with respect to monitoring of the top management team. Modern public corporation boards now have majorities of independent directors, audit, nominating, and compensation committees composed exclusively of independent directors, and separate CEO and chairman of the board positions or, at least, an independent lead director. In addition, companies now promulgate corporate governance guidelines and codes of ethics, and routinely hold periodic private sessions at which no managers are present. Many of these reforms were controversial at the time they were adopted (and some still are), but whether or not SOX and Dodd-Frank deserve the credit, there has been some improvement in board performance.

In 1995, only one in eight CEOs was fired or resigned under board pressure. By 2006, however, almost one-third of CEOs were terminated involuntarily.[16] In addition, over the last several decades, the average CEO tenure has decreased, which has been attributed to more active board oversight.[17] As one commentator summed up these developments, boards of directors, "which once served largely as rubber stamps for powerful CEOs, have become more independent, more powerful, and under more pressure to dump leaders who perform poorly."[18]

Directors are also spending more time directing. The average number of board meetings per year increased from seven in 1998 to nine in 2008.[19] The average number of times board committees met per year likewise increased significantly after SOX became law in 2002. More meetings, of course, meant more time and, presumably, effort. A 2005 survey found that directors spent an average of more than 200 hours per year on firm business, which was a significant increase from the 100 to 150 hours per year typical of boards prior to SOX's passage.[20]

It is worth noting that this is really all we can say about board performance. There are no good measures of board performance because governance and operational performance are inexorably linked. One could look at overall corporate performance for an indication of boards doing better, but that obviously wouldn't tell us much. What we want to know is how well a particular company or companies would do if boards were performing better. There is currently no metric or way to estimate this. As we discuss further, one of the central benefits of the BSP proposal being adopted is that it would bring much greater transparency to corporate board costs and benefits. A market for BSPs would provide information about the value they provide, just as all market prices do. This alone might justify the move to BSPs.

BUT THERE'S STILL ROOM FOR IMPROVEMENT

Despite the admitted progress boards have made, research has identified some troubling findings that call into question board effectiveness. Only 64 percent of directors believe their boardroom dynamics are welcoming of new points of view. Less than half strongly believe that their boardroom dynamics encourage dissent. Just half strongly believe their board makes effective use of the talents of all board members.[21]

When added to the recent survey results mentioned earlier in this chapter, the picture for board members today is far from rosy. Boards are not yet consistently fulfilling the crucial role that the legal system has given them in mediating between shareholders and managers, and between corporations and the public at large. To make matters worse, the risks and complexity of business are only increasing, and the near future portends even more dramatic changes as the growth of passive investing, and the rise of activist investors, reshapes the governance landscape.

Notes

1. Adam Smith, *An Inquiry into the Nature and Causes of the Wealth of Nations*, 264–265 (Edwin Cannan (ed.), University of Chicago Press 1976) (1776).
2. William O. Douglas, Directors Who Do Not Direct, 47 *Harv. L. Rev.* 1305 (1934).
3. William O. Douglas, *Democracy and Finance* 46 (1940).
4. Ralph Ward, CEOs Got Grilled, but Let's Hear from Board Leaders, Too, *Detroit Free Press*, Dec. 10, 2008, at 15.
5. *In re Brazilian Rubber Plantations & Estates Ltd.*, [1911] 1 ch. 425.

6. See Peter F. Drucker, *Concept of the Corporation* 92 (rev. edn. 1972) (describing outside directors as figureheads). Instructively, the index to Drucker's classic analysis of General Motors does not contain an entry for shareholders. See ibid. at 318–319.
7. Brian R. Cheffins, Did Corporate Governance "Fail" During the 2008 Stock Market Meltdown? The Case of the S&P 500, 65 *Bus. Law.* 1, 7 (2009).
8. Jeffrey N. Gordon, The Rise of Independent Directors in the United States, 1950–2005: Of Shareholder Value and Stock Market Prices, 59 *Stan. L. Rev.* 1465, 1515 (2007).
9. Ralph Nader et al., *Taming the Giant Corporation* (1976).
10. Ibid. at 60.
11. William L. Cary, Federalism and Corporate Law: Reflections upon Delaware, 83 *Yale L.J.* 663 (1974).
12. NYSE, *Listed Company Manual* § 303.A09.
13. See, e.g. Jonathan F. Foster & Steven A. Rosenblum, The Importance of Director Self-Evaluations (Feb. 25, 2013), https://currentcap.com/2013/02/25/the-importance-of-director-self-evaluations; see also Frederick D. Lipman & L. Keith Lipman, *Corporate Governance Best Practices: Strategies for Public, Private, and Not-for-Profit Organizations* 12 (2006).
14. Taylor Griffin et al., How Board Evaluations Fall Short, www.TheCLSBlueSkyBlog.com. (Mar. 22, 2017), http://clsbluesky.law.columbia.edu/2017/03/22/board-evaluations-and-boardroom-dynamics. ("Only half (55 percent) of companies that conduct board evaluations evaluate individual directors ….")
15. See ibid. (reporting that "only one third (36 percent) believe their company does a very good job of accurately assessing the performance of individual directors").
16. Chuck Lucier et al., The Era of the Inclusive Leader, *Strategy & Bus.*, summer 2007, at 3.
17. Denis B.K. Lyons, CEO Casualties: A Battlefront Report, *Directors & Boards*, summer 1999, at 43.
18. Lauren Etter, Why Corporate Boardrooms Are in Turmoil, *Wall St. J.*, Sept. 16, 2006, at A7.
19. Report of the Task Force of the ABA Section of Business Law Corporate Governance Committee on Delineation of Governance Roles and Responsibilities, 65 *Bus. Law.* 107, 130–131 (2009).
20. Ed Speidel & Rob Surdel, High Technology Board Compensation, *Boardroom Briefing*, spring 2008, at 25.
21. Griffin et al., Board Evaluations.

4

Why Boards Fail

In Chapter 3, we gave today's boards low marks on the assignment they have been given to serve shareholders and society writ large in directing the business of America's large public companies. In truth, however, these marks are mere guesses, since we do not have good and effective ways to measure the value provided by a particular board or boards in general. Economists and finance scholars have tools for measuring the performance of companies, but no good ways of estimating the value of good governance. We are left with surveys and crude proxies from small data sets. But we think that the failing grades boards get from pundits fairly describe the reality we see in work we have done on corporate law and governance. In this chapter, we explain why we think boards are not measuring up.

INTRODUCTION

Although we do not have hard evidence, the consensus view seems to be that boards that work "listen, probe, debate, and become engaged in the company's most pressing issues."[1] They monitor management, but also provide advice and counsel. They act as cheerleaders, but also coaches. Companies blessed with such boards have a major competitive advantage. Their boards "help management prevent problems, sieve opportunities, and make the corporation perform better than it otherwise would" without them.[2]

Sadly, however, all too many boards still fail. At best, boards add value only rarely, typically in crisis situations that – as famed former Delaware Chancellor William Allen opined – "inevitably involve a CEO problem of some sort."[3] At worst, boards remain supine even in the face of such crises.

The reasons boards continue to struggle include inadequate time, misspent time, inadequate information, improper skill sets, and insufficient incentives.[i] Many of these problems are longstanding, of course, but they have been significantly compounded by the increased emphasis in recent decades on director independence. A combination of corporate best prac- tice guides, legislative and regulatory mandates, and stock exchange listing requirements has resulted in a huge increase in the percentage of board members who are independent. Boards today are thus dominated by part- timers, most of whom have full-time employment elsewhere, which com- mands the bulk of their attention and provides the bulk of their pecuniary and psychic income.

Let us turn now to a consideration of these reasons why boards continue to fail to measure up.

TIME CONSTRAINTS

The first reason why boards fail is the limited amount of time they spend on their jobs relative to managers, who work full-time managing the firm. The point is simple to see. Board members working a few days per year are hopelessly outmatched when sitting across the table from managers who work every day on the same matters.

Historically, directors did not spend much time together working as a group. In his 1871 treatise *Investments*, Robert Arthur Ward registered a complaint that continues to echo even today, writing that: "It is preposterous to suppose that a board of directors, few of whom attend regularly, and those few devoting only a few hours a week to the management of a gigantic concern, can, without the assistance of a very competent manager, prevent its drifting to ruin."[4]

Board meetings were few and short, a problem that persisted well into the next century. As corporate governance commentator Ralph Ward observes, for example, mid-twentieth-century boards gathered "every few months for a progress report and a good lunch."[5] When boards did get together, moreover, they spent very little time directing. According to one survey, during the 1980s the median board meeting lasted only three hours.[6]

Although the regulatory fallout from the financial crises of the last decade forced directors to devote considerably greater time to board service, two problems remain. First, directors remain outsiders who, by their very nature, are part-timers. This is a natural consequence of the push for independence,

---

[i] An additional problem faced by companies in emerging markets is the predominance of state- owned enterprises and controlling shareholders. The controlling shareholder's power to hire and fire directors without regard for the interests of minority shareholders significantly reduces board effectiveness. Simon C. Y. Wong & Dominic Barton, Improving Board Performance in Emerging Markets, *McKinsey Q.* 35 (2006), https://ssrn.com/abstract=899920.

which is based on a view that board members must be neutral arbiters of disputes among corporate stakeholders. But it necessarily means that the board will devote less time to important corporate matters than full-time employees, who by definition are not "independent." Second, as we shall also see, directors arguably are still spending too much time doing the wrong things.

The American Bar Association's prestigious Committee on Corporation Laws explains that this significantly affects "the board's ability to exercise its powers and discharge its obligations effectively":[7]

> Boards face a significant challenge in governing effectively given the part-time nature of board service. Most directors have competing demands on their time and attention, and most boards meet on average less often than once a month. Compounding this fact is that the board is comprised of a majority of independent directors who, by definition, have very limited relationships with the corporation outside of their board service. As a result, in addition to time constraints, independent directors have limited information sources about the company other than what management provides. Yet they must form objective viewpoints about the issues facing the company and the quality of the management team to perform fiduciary and other obligations.[8]

Boards outside the United States are subject to the same sort of time constraints. A survey of outside directors of companies in twenty-seven Eurasian countries found that their boards spent an average of less than three days per month on board service.[9] That average actually compares quite favorably to the eighteen hours per month directors of US corporations spent on average on board service prior to SOX. Post-SOX, US directors reported that their workload increased to as much as twenty-five hours per month, which is slightly higher than the twenty-two hours (assuming an eight-hour work day) the directors in emerging markets spend on average. In some of the studied emerging market companies, however, outside directors reported working the equivalent of ten days per month, which is unheard of in the United States outside of rare cases of extreme corporate distress. In fact, one wonders that if directors did work this much in US companies they would be considered independent anymore.

INFORMATION ASYMMETRIES

The second reason boards fail is because of large and persistent informational gaps between them and the managers they are tasked with overseeing or supporting. The law recognizes the problem of informational asymmetries, and permits board members to try to overcome them. Boards are entitled by law and best practice to access to the information they need to direct the company. As the ABA Directors' Guidebook explains:

Among the most important are the [board's] rights:

- to inspect books and records;
- to request additional information reasonably necessary to exercise informed oversight and make careful decisions;
- to inspect facilities as reasonably appropriate to gain an understanding of corporate operations;
- to receive timely notice of all meetings in which a director is entitled to participate;
- to receive copies of key documents and of all board and committee meeting minutes; and
- to receive regular oral or written reports of the activities of all board committees.

In addition, within reasonable time and manner constraints, directors generally have the right of access to key executives and other employees of the corporation and to the corporation's legal counsel and other advisors to obtain information relevant to the performance of their duties.[10]

Outside directors, however, typically do not have direct access to such information. Instead, they are reliant on a management that, as the old joke goes, treats the directors like mushrooms – that is, they are kept in the dark and routinely covered in manure.

It is conventional to blame board dysfunction on information shortcomings between independent directors and inside managers.[11] In fact, however, board dysfunction can be the result of having either too little or too much information. On some boards, directors are deprived of information. At other corporations, however, an "indigestible overload of information" is dumped on directors.[12] In either case, "outside board members" end up being "amazingly out of touch with the corporation for which they bear ultimate legal responsibility."[13] The same is true outside the United States, as shown by a survey of outside directors of companies in emerging markets, which found that a third of the respondents felt they were not sufficiently well informed to be able to fulfill their duties.[14]

In addition to concerns about the volume of information provided to boards, there is also concern about the type of information being provided. Most boards spend far more time learning about and discussing historical data than gathering information about current and future opportunities and problems. After all, historical data is easy to compile, might be expected to placate directors' need to see something, and is simpler to understand than forecasts or speculations about the future of the business.

The CEO is typically the bottleneck with respect to information, both in the United States and elsewhere. And this can bias the board in particular ways. At the very least, there is an irony in that the board is supposed to use corporate information to, in part, oversee the managers, but is dependent on these same managers for this information.

In some European countries, the corporate governance rules themselves are at fault. In the UK, for example, the corporate governance code provides that the chairman should gather information for the board, rather than empowering the board as a whole.[15] In France, only the CEO has the right to communicate directly with subordinate employees, depriving boards of access to an incredibly valuable source of information.[16] In many other European countries, corporate governance norms frown on outside board members communicating directly with employees other than the CEO.[17] Similarly, although many European corporate governance regimes theoretically allow boards to seek outside advice, in practice it is frowned upon as being unfriendly to the CEO.[18]

Even where neither law nor social norms impede board access to information, it is still in the CEO's interest to control the flow of information to the board. Sometimes this is so, of course, because the CEO is engaged in serious misconduct. In the notorious case of former Tyco CEO Dennis Kozlowski and CFO Mark H. Swart, for example, they were convicted of having stolen from the company by taking compensation that had received the required authorization by the compensation committee. "Allegedly, they stole more than $100 million in three 'bonus' larcenies in 1999 and 2000 and many millions more in other thefts until their enterprise began to unravel in January 2002, when Tyco's board learned that defendants had made a secret $20 million payment to a supposedly independent director."[19] They were able to do so because they concealed unauthorized bonuses and other financial benefits from Tyco's compensation committee.

Even where the CEO is not engaged in outright malfeasance, however, the board's power to hire and fire the CEO means the CEO still has an incentive to make sure the board gets only information that makes the CEO look good. In addition, because many CEOs resist board "meddling," it's in the CEO's interest to keep the board in the dark even with respect to positive information. Indeed, studies suggest that CEOs of companies with activist boards universally adopt strategies for manipulating the board.[20] The CEO's goal is to keep board involvement at a sufficiently high level of generality to permit the CEO to function largely free of board oversight.

Ideally, where the law allows, board members should respond by developing alternative information sources. In the United States, the law in fact mandates at least one such alternative, by requiring that the audit committee meet routinely with the company's independent outside auditor. Yet, many corporate scandals over the last several decades occurred because the independent auditors were just as much in the dark as the directors, if not more so.

The board therefore needs sources beyond the CEO and outside auditor, such as the other members of the C-suite, the company's internal audit office, and the company's principal outside law firm. Developing such relationships is time consuming and requires considerable effort, especially because many of these alternative information providers are themselves beholden to or vulnerable to the CEO.[i] Here again, the part-time nature of board work means that few, if any, directors have the time to build the necessary relationships of trust and confidence. As one experienced board member complained, in "eighty minutes, we were expected to absorb, react to, and approve a plan management has spent months putting together."[21]

Because most sources of information available to the board are in some way affiliated with the company's top management, they too have incentives not to rock the boat by giving the board information the CEO wants kept away from it. Accordingly, directors also ought to be taking the initiative. They should be doing independent research, reading analysts' reports and news accounts about the company, meeting key constituents and stakeholders, interacting with shareholders, attending trade association meetings, and so on. Put bluntly, boards need to spend a lot more time on the job and develop a lot

---

[i] As one of us has explained with respect to a firm's legal counsel, for example:

> Because it is management – not the board of directors – that hires outside legal counsel, it is management whom attorneys must please in order to retain or attract business. This pressure is especially true given the large number of capable firms and attorneys available for hire; law firms are something akin to fungible goods. In addition, legal counsel normally works far more closely with senior management than with the board of directors.

Stephen M. Bainbridge, The Tournament at the Intersection of Business and Legal Ethics, 1 *U. St. Thomas L.J.* 909, 918 (2004) (footnotes omitted). The net effect is that counsel typically have a close working relationship with the CEO and other members of the C-suite, while having little if any contact with the board:

> What happens is [the lawyers'] day-to-day conduct is with the CEO or the chief financial officer because those are the individuals responsible for hiring them. So as a result, that is with whom they have a relationship. When they go to lunch with their client, the corporation, they are usually going to lunch with the CEO or the chief financial officer. When they get phone calls, they are usually returning calls to the CEO or the chief financial officer.

Ibid. at 919 (quoting former Senator John Edwards).

more leverage if they are going to be fully informed. Whether directors have the skills and incentives necessary to do so, however, is quite doubtful.

TOO MANY GENERALISTS

The third reason boards fail is because they are composed of generalists, such as current or former CEOs of other firms, instead of experts in the range of fields needed by modern American businesses.

In contrast to insiders, who possess significant firm-specific human capital, independent directors tend to be generalists with little firm-specific knowledge, skills, or expertise. Modern boards thus tend to be "composed of individuals who are not qualified to assess the strategic viability of the corporations they direct."[22] Unfortunately, the rules mandating director independence virtually ensure that this problem will remain insoluble, because they effectively "rule out just about anybody who has firsthand knowledge of the company and its industry."[23] While independent directors can develop such knowledge over time, doing so can be a very lengthy process. Not only is there a mountain of information to be learned, but the relatively little amount of time independent directors spend on board business and the lengthy periods between board meetings make it difficult for board members to remember what information they've received. Many independent directors thus never "develop ... more than a rudimentary understanding of their companies' workings."[24] A survey of CEOs by corporate governance experts Colin Carter and Jay Lorsch strikingly found that barely half believed their boards have a clear understanding of the business.[25]

While at least some long-serving directors may develop a reasonable knowledge of the company's inner workings, long service can give rise to close friendships between nominally independent directors and the managers with whom they serve. This can compromise the director's ability to take strong action when management falters. In some cases, but not all, long-serving directors "may find it difficult to be truly independent in deciding what's in the shareholders' best interests."[26]

The problem is not just one of knowledge and information, of course. A board composed principally of generalists will typically lack the sort of specialized skills and expertise many board tasks require. The lack of such skills has been a major factor driving the rules governing audit committees, to cite but the most obvious example. Supervising the company's internal controls, financial disclosures, internal audit, and its relationship with the outside auditor is a complex task best left to individuals with strong backgrounds and training in finance and accounting. Ensuring that audit committees are staffed with such individuals drove the SOX and Dodd-Frank audit committee reforms and the resulting stock exchange listing standards. Yet, by all reports, recruiting qualified audit committee members has become difficult due to the high degree of effort the position requires and the perceived high liability risks.

The problem goes beyond the need for financial expertise on the audit committee. In the 1950s, polymath Herbert Simon – he was an economist, sociologist, psychologist, political scientist, and computer scientist – coined and popularized the term "bounded rationality."[27] Simon started with the standard economic premise that people are rational self-maximizers; in other words, they make rational choices designed to maximize their utility. Simon argued, however, that all humans are subject to varying limitations on their cognitive powers. To varying degrees, we all have inherently limited memories, computational skills, and other mental tools.

Bounded rationality becomes a particularly significant constraint on decision making under conditions of complexity and uncertainty. A problem may be complex either because it involves many options or because a limited number of initial options cascade into a decision tree with many branches. A closely related problem is that of ambiguity, or uncertainty, which exists when decision-makers are uncertain about the content of the alternatives available to them or otherwise lack the information necessary to make an optimizing choice. Under conditions of uncertainty and complexity, boundedly rational decision-makers are unable to devise either a fully specified solution to the problem at hand or to assess fully the probable outcomes of their action.

Like all humans, members of a board of directors are boundedly rational. As the monitoring model has increasingly dominated our understanding of the board's proper role, the problem of bounded rationality has become ever more serious. Granted, boards today have received some help from technology (such as information storage and analysis) and outside advisors, but corporations have become exponentially more complex than they were forty or fifty years ago when the monitoring model came into vogue. Companies are bigger and more geographically dispersed. Companies face far more complex risks and use far more complex tools to manage those risks. The regulatory landscape has become far more difficult to traverse. It seems increasingly doubtful that boundedly rational directors can keep up. Consider, for example, how prior to the financial crisis of 2007–2008 boards of financial institutions almost universally failed to understand the way their companies were using financial derivatives to manage risks or the new risks such devices created.

BAD INCENTIVES

The fourth reason boards continue to fall short of expectations is because of relatively weak incentives for excellence, especially relative to managers.

The most basic way of incentivizing people to do a good job is to pay them for doing so.[28] Unfortunately, the longstanding practice of paying directors substantial fees in cash, coupled with management's control of the board nomination process, acted in the past "to align the interests of the outside directors with current management rather than with the shareholders ... Directors whose remuneration is unrelated to corporate performance have little personal incentive to challenge their management benefactors."[29]

Corporate reformers responded by encouraging firms to pay directors "primarily in company stock that is restricted as to resale during their term in office."[30] Proponents of this approach believed that doing so would "create within each director a personally based motivation to actively monitor management in the best interest of corporate productivity."[31]

This approach to director compensation has now been adopted at many firms, but some commentators argue that it has not served to align director and shareholder interests sufficiently to motivate excellence by the board. There are two problems, which are different sides of the same coin. First, the amount of money paid to individual directors in stock is still extremely small – in the order of a few hundred thousand dollars per year, relative to market capitalizations in the billions and manager compensation in the tens or hundreds of millions of dollars. Board members own a trivial amount of the firms they manage, and therefore their incentives are still extremely weak, especially compared with board members of firms owned by private equity firms. As discussed later in this chapter, private equity firms use high-powered incentives to motivate board members, requiring them to put a huge portion of their wealth into the company's stock. We are not sure why public companies do not do this, but it is likely that it has to do with the perceived value of board members in the public company setting, including who they are, their role as "monitors," and the value they can provide within the confines of being a public-company director.

Second, the incentives of directors with substantial stock holdings or in-the-money options are more closely aligned with those of managers than with those of shareholders. As law professor David Skeel aptly observes, "[h]igh pay has a way of silencing dissent; and the use of options exacerbated this problem, since it gave directors the same upside without a corresponding downside, as was true for Ebbers and Lay" of WorldCom and Enron infamy, respectively.[32] Hence, if managers inflate the company's stock price by manipulating financial data or otherwise cooking the books, "directors may go along because they also stand to benefit."[33] There is thus an inherent tension between the competing goals of ensuring director independence and incentivizing them to perform at a high-quality level. One might overcome this objection by paying directors with even more equity and having them hold the shares for longer time horizons, but this is not the current practice, as it is in private equity.

Various nonmonetary incentives may also discourage boards from functioning at a high level. In a case involving the high fees paid to mutual fund advisers, for example, Judge Richard Posner argued that "boards of directors lack incentives to police compensation because directors are often executives of other companies who believe that executives deserve to be paid well."[34]

> Directors are often CEOs of other companies and naturally think that CEOs should be well paid. And often they are picked by the CEO. Compensation consulting firms, which provide cover for generous compensation packages voted by boards of directors, have a conflict of interest because they are paid not only for their compensation advice but for other services to the firm-services for which they are hired by the officers whose compensation they advised on.[35]

The same problem comes up when boards of directors are asked by shareholders to bring suit against CEOs or other managers who have allegedly breached their fiduciary duties. As the Delaware Supreme Court has observed, in such cases, a "question naturally arises whether a 'there but for the grace of God go I' empathy might not" incline the directors – even nominally independent ones – to lean on the side of management.[36]

BOARDS REFUSE TO LEAD

The fifth reason boards continue to fail is because board members do not aggressively assert their leadership authority when it comes to directing the business. Board members are generally followers, not leaders. This may be because of the act of delegation and the legal rules regarding independence and the like. Part-timers are rarely leaders in any field, and showing up a few times per year and trying to run the show would likely not go over well.

But it is an oddity of current board practice because most directors are leaders in their full-time jobs. They are CEOs, former high-ranking government or military officials, university presidents, business or law school deans, and so on. Yet, it is rare for boards to take on a leadership role. In part, this is because many of the best qualified individual board members decline to take on the role of lead director. Upon reflection, of course, this is not surprising, since "the task of board leadership is . . . a thankless one, increasingly burdensome, and legally dangerous."[37]

The reluctance of board members to take ownership of the leadership position is particularly problematic considering the stock exchange listing standards and best practice norms calling for routine meetings of the independent directors outside the presence of management (including the CEO). This time is potentially very valuable, as an opportunity for candid discussion and evaluation, especially when it is the CEO's job performance that is the chief agenda item. But somebody must call the meeting, set the agenda, and steer the discussion. In other words, someone must lead. If no one steps up, these meetings tend to devolve into bull sessions and vague chatter.[38]

To be sure, in ordinary times, it is often desirable for the CEO to have the primary leadership role. Too many cooks spoil the broth, as the saying goes. We might also invoke the old joke about a camel being a horse designed by committee. There are times, however, where it is critical that the board take the lead. CEO transition is an obvious example. Boards also need to lead when the firm is in financial distress, or is targeted in a takeover offer or other crisis situations.

Kodak's slow but steady decline into irrelevance offers a useful case study of the problem. As digital imaging changed photography forever, Kodak management simply failed to keep up and the board failed to step up:

> As the company approached the precipice of the most recent cliff, critics asked the question: "Where was Kodak's Board of Directors?" The board, as well as the company, was complacent. It put its faith in the CEO and did not help the company to successfully transition into the digital era. Kodak is one illustration of how boards could have averted corporate losses or even added value to their corporations had the directors been better situated to engage in nonprogrammed decision making . . ."[39]

Sadly, the question "Where was the board?" is all too often raised in the aftermath of corporate crises. In the wake of the 2008 financial crisis, for example, the cry went up again as critics "inquired about the nature and extent of the board's involvement in overseeing the risks associated with subprime lending and other activities" at many financial institutions.[40] All too often, due to a lack of leadership, boards fail to step up to the plate in times of crisis or transition.

This can be a particularly vexing problem when the board is faced by a domineering CEO who is also a substantial shareholder. The combination such executives wield of control via share ownership and the inherent power of the CEO position can often induce board passivity and even timidity in the face of these executives. This appears to have been a major contributing factor in the collapse of the Maxwell Group PLC in 1991, for example. Robert Maxwell famously disappeared at sea as his numerous peccadilloes were coming to light, ranging from misappropriation of funds to stock price manipulation to outright securities fraud. The disaster might well have been prevented if there had been "mechanisms in place mitigate the risks accrued to the governance process as a result of his inappropriate behavioural [sic] tendencies," which should have been the board of directors' primary concern.[41] But the board had been too timid to rein Maxwell in.

Board passivity and timidity have been to blame in numerous other infamous corporate scandals. Despite the fact that Enron's board of directors was composed of exceptionally talented individuals and that they possessed most of the necessary facts, for example, the board remained passive instead of actively restraining management's repeated misconduct. Another high profile corporate collapse of the same period, WorldCom, provides an even clearer example of a situation in which a board was dominated to the point of intimidation by the company's strong-willed CEO and CFO.

The problem of lacking leadership or boldness on the part of board members cannot be attributed to the nature or characteristics of board members, since, as noted, they are all high-achieving leaders outside of their board roles. Instead, the problem is the role boards have been assigned, and the current milieu in which board members operate. Timidity is linked to the natural person requirement and the fact that individual board members cannot team up to share information, risk, and expertise in a way that might level the playing field.

BOARDS LACK COHESIVENESS

The sixth reason boards fail is because of a lack of cohesiveness in board rooms and board operations.

Leadership is essential for organizational success, but even the strongest leader needs a cohesive team. As famed UCLA basketball coach John Wooden once observed, "the main ingredient of stardom is the rest of the team." Abraham Lincoln did not win the American Civil War on his own, for example, but by famously assembling a team of rivals that came together to win the war. Or, at least that is what historian Doris Kearns Goodwin says.

Almost all famous board successes happened because a unified and cohesive board of directors decided that it was time for a change in policy or, even more often, personnel. Harvard Business School professor Jay Lorsch thus notes that the legal framework provided by corporate law statutes and judicial opinions "really does little more than provide a board with legitimacy to govern."[42] The board's ability to do so effectively, especially in the face of a recalcitrant CEO, comes in very large part from "their cohesion as a group."[43]

Cohesive groups share more information. They develop high levels of interpersonal trust, which promotes mutual support when taking risks or facing crises. They more effectively utilize each member's strengths, while compensating for each member's weaknesses.

The trouble, of course, as always, is that a disparate group of part-timers who spend just a few days a year together are unlikely to develop the kind of cohesion necessary. Cases in which boards come together to successfully oust a CEO, for example, are newsworthy precisely because they happen so infrequently.

The problems faced by General Motors in the early 1990s are a frequently cited case study of how a lack of board cohesion allowed ineffectual top management to continue long after the need for change had become apparent. The board lacked an independent leader to bring them together, but also lacked a forum in which to consult with one another. The combined lack of leadership and group cohesion meant that it took a major financial crisis – the threat of a significant downgrading of General Motor's debt – for the board to finally act.[44] A more cohesive board likely would have stepped in much earlier.

Cohesiveness is also impeded by excessive board size. In many countries, twelve members is the typical board size.[45] This is far too many people to conduct effective meetings that last only a few hours, especially because board members tend to be high status individuals with healthy egos, who typically love to hear the sound of their own voice. (Just like professors!) The situation has improved somewhat on this score in the United States in recent years, as boards have shrunk in response to the demands imposed by SOX and Dodd-Frank, but board size remains a serious problem in many countries and in many firms in the United States.

SOX LOCKED BOARDS INTO A ONE-SIZE-FITS-ALL MODEL

A final reason boards fail is because law has stifled innovation by locking boards into a one-size-fits-all model that is necessarily under and over-inclusive.

We saw in Chapter 2 that monitoring is a key board function. Indeed, monitoring for a long time has been first among equals, as doubtless should be the case. Until quite recently, however, boards retained substantial flexibility to allocate their time between monitoring and their other functions.

This was also as it should be, because one size does not fit all. Firms differ. Every firm has a unique culture, traditions, and competitive environment.

A startup with inexperienced entrepreneurs needs an advisory board more than a monitoring one. A company in crisis needs board leadership more than oversight. A well-run, mature corporation staffed by managers with a penchant for hard, faithful work benefits most from a board that provides benevolent oversight and a sympathetic sounding board.

Likewise, different firms have differing arrays of accountability mechanisms. The monitoring board, after all, is not the only mechanism by which management's performance is assessed and rewarded or punished. The capital and product markets within which the firm functions, the internal and external markets for managerial services, the market for corporate control, incentive compensation systems, and auditing by outside accountants are just some of the ways in which management is held accountable for its performance. The importance of the board's monitoring role in a firm depends in large measure on the extent to which these other forces are allowed to function. For example, managers of a firm with strong takeover defenses are less subject to the constraining influence of the market for corporate control than are those of a firm with no takeover defenses. The former needs a strong monitoring board more than does the latter.

Directors themselves recognize that one size does not fit all. Instead, they understand their role to be much broader than mere monitoring. A survey by the National Association of Corporate Directors, for example, found that boards believe their key roles include such issues as planning for CEO succession, strategic business planning, and risk management.[46]

Accordingly, purported reforms that "reduce the board's role to monitoring and constrain a corporation's ability to choose a managing board threaten to deprive corporations of the full opportunity to utilize the board of directors as a resource."[47] Yet, that is precisely what SOX and Dodd-Frank do. None of the board provisions of either act contemplate any opportunity for private ordering. Neither contemplates allowing corporations to tweak the extent to which its unique board in its unique circumstances will allocate resources to oversight versus other functions.

Overemphasizing Monitoring Has Costs

As we have seen, information is the coin of the realm in the world of corporate boards. The more information boards have, the better they are able to carry out their quasi-managerial functions such as advising senior managers, making major policy decisions, and providing networking services. More and higher quality information, of course, also empowers directors to be more effective in their oversight capacity.

As we also saw, however, because information can be used to management's detriment in the board's oversight capacity, management has an incentive to use its position as an informational chokepoint strategically. By overemphasizing the board's monitoring function at the expense of its other roles, SOX and Dodd-Frank have compounded the problem by pushing the board toward an adversarial relationship with management, which further incentivizes the latter to exercise discretion with respect to the information allowed to reach the board. Obviously, managers will be loath to pass on bad news. Even good news, however, will be massaged, phrased, and packaged not so as to aid the board in making decisions but to cast management in the best possible light. Ironically, the adversarial relations potentially arising from adherence to the monitoring model thus not only make it more difficult for the board to carry out its managerial and service functions, but they also make it harder for the board to serve as an effective monitor.

The aggressive oversight contemplated by the monitoring model may have even more deleterious effects on the management–board relationship than just the perpetuation of information asymmetries. A certain amount of cognitive tension in the board–top management team relationship is beneficial to the extent that it promotes the exercise of critical evaluative judgment by the former. Groups that are too collegial run the risk of submitting to groupthink and various other decision-making errors.[48]

If aggressive monitoring fosters an adversarial relation between directors and managers, however, this beneficial form of conflict may transform into more harmful forms. At best, rigid adherence to the monitoring model may transform a collaborative and collegial relationship into one that is cold and distant. At worst, it can promote adversarial relations that result in destructive interpersonal conflict. Adversarial relations between two groups tend to encourage each group to circle the wagons and become defensive vis-à-vis the other. They encourage zero sum gamesmanship rather than collaboration. They divert energies into unproductive areas. They descend into a simple "us versus them" mentality. Cohesion disintegrates. As Peter Wallison thus observes, the "congressional imprimatur" SOX put on the monitoring model "may have set up an adversarial relationship between managements and boards that will, over time, impair corporate risk-taking and thus economic growth."[49]

Boards Spend Too Much Time Doing the Wrong Things

A 2006 survey found that before SOX became law, 66 percent of board members reported they worked less than 200 hours per year on firm business. Post-SOX, matters have flipped 180 degrees, as 65 percent of board members reported working more than 200 hours per year and 30 percent claimed to work more than 300 hours per year on firm business.[50]

While the data do not establish a causal relationship, they do suggest at least a correlation between SOX's passage and the time commitment required of board members. Much of the additional time appears to be devoted to oversight activities, which is consistent with the assumption that SOX reinforced the monitoring model's influence. If so, as we just saw, the additional time and effort being expended by directors may have important costs.

Even if a firm's board and management maintain an appropriately balanced relationship, moreover, the additional time and effort elicited by SOX may not be directed productively. Indeed, Wallison argues that boards today "are more focused on compliance with standards and regulations than they are on obtaining a competitive advantage."[51] A McKinsey report likewise observed that boards "spend the bulk of their time on quarterly reports, audit reviews, budgets, and compliance – 70 percent is not atypical – instead of on matters crucial to the future prosperity and direction of the business."[52] As a result, the report continued, many directors are so "[d]istracted by the details of compliance and new regulations" that they "simply don't know enough about the fundamentals and long-term strategies of their companies to add value and avoid trouble."[53] This is so despite the fact that boards, as we saw in Chapter 1, are the unit within the corporation that ought to be spending the most time looking forward and anticipating change.

It therefore is not unreasonable to speculate that the unrelenting need to focus on compliance post-SOX contributed in some measure to the 2008 financial crisis. Financial institution directors distracted by the emphasis on internal controls and disclosure reportedly let slide tasks like risk management oversight. Two leading UK commentators, for example, opine that:

> The commercial sector was remiss in its stewardship. Evidence suggests that: boards spend too little time on examining the worsening economic conditions and their implications for the business and its strategy; . . . [and] board agendas allowed too little time for the big decisions and too much time for the minutiae of governance compliance, driven by a box-ticking mentality.[54]

Thanks to SOX, the same was even truer of US corporations – especially but not exclusively banks and other financial services firms – whose leaders had "become mired in the minutiae of SOX compliance."[55] As such, the law of unintended consequences claimed a truly epic victim.

Boards of companies in emerging markets face a similar problem with board focus, even though they are free from the regulatory constraints of US law. In many emerging markets, there is a shortage of management talent.

As a result, boards often lack confidence in their managers and therefore take on short-term operational matters instead of providing the long-term strategic focus that is the mark of effective boards. The problem is compounded in some markets by unclear divisions of labor between boards and management and poor prioritization. Cultural patterns can also impede board effectiveness, such as norms mandating that younger board members defer to more senior ones.[56]

Notes

1. Ram Charan, *Boards at Work: How Corporate Boards Create Competitive Advantage* 3 (1998).
2. Ibid. at 5.
3. William T. Allen, Free Markets Focus on Corporate Governance, *Directorship*, Jan. 1991, at 11.
4. Robert Arthur Ward, *Investments* 18 (1871).
5. Ralph Ward, *The New Boardroom Leaders: How Today's Corporate Boards Are Taking Charge* 4 (2008).
6. Jeremy Bacon, *Membership and Organization of Corporate Boards* 25 (1990).
7. The Corporate Laws Committee, ABA Section of Business Law, Corporate Director's Guidebook—Sixth Edition, 66 *Bus. Law.* 975, 1002 (2011).
8. Ibid.
9. Ralph de Haas et al., The Inner Workings of the Board: Evidence from Emerging Markets 8 (Jan. 23, 2017), https://ssrn.com/abstract=2904663.
10. Corporate Director's Guidebook, at 988–989.
11. See, e.g. Michael P. Dooley & E. Norman Veasey, The Role of the Board in Derivative Litigation: Delaware Law and the Current ALI Proposals Compared, 44 *Bus. Law.* 503, 533 (1989) (making the point that, as part-time outsiders, independent directors inherently have less information and take longer to persuade than full-time insiders).
12. Ralph D. Ward, *Saving the Corporate Board: Why Boards Fail and How to Fix Them* 1 (2003).
13. Ibid. at 123.
14. Haas, *Inner Workings*, at 9.
15. Paul L. Davies & Klaus J. Hopt, Corporate Boards in Europe—Accountability and Convergence, 61 *Am. J. Comp. L.* 301, 333 (2013).
16. Ibid.
17. Ibid.
18. Ibid.

19. *People* v. *Kozlowski*, 846 N.Y.S.2d 44, 45 (2007), aff'd, 11 N.Y.3d 223, 898 N.E.2d 891 (2008).
20. Philip Stiles & Bernard Taylor, *Boards at Work: How Directors View Their Roles and Responsibilities* 31 (2001).
21. Charan, *Boards at Work*, at 102.
22. Nicola Faith Sharpe, Rethinking Board Function in the Wake of the 2008 Financial Crisis, 5 *J. Bus. & Tech. L.* 99, 109 (2010).
23. See Colin B. Carter & Jay W. Lorsch, *Back to the Drawing Board: Designing Corporate Boards for a Complex World* 45 (2004).
24. Ibid.
25. Ibid. at 23.
26. Ibid. at 49.
27. See Herbert A. Simon, *Rationality and Administrative Decision Making, in Models of Man* 196, 196–198 (1957).
28. For an application outside the common practice, see M. Todd Henderson & Frederick Tung, Pay for Regulator Performance, 85 *S. Cal. L. Rev.* 1003 (2012).
29. Charles M. Elson, Director Compensation and the Management-Captured Board—The History of a Symptom and a Cure, 50 *SMU L. Rev.* 127, 162–164 (1996).
30. Ibid. at 165.
31. Ibid.
32. David Skeel, *Icarus in the Boardroom: The Fundamental Flaws in Corporate America and Where They Came From* 165 (2005).
33. Carter & Lorsch, *Drawing Board*, at 48.
34. John Baumann, Isn't This Where We Came in?: An Examination of the Turbulent History and Divergent Economics Underlying Section 36(b) of the Investment Company Act of 1940 and a Proposal to Finally Put the Law to Use, 85 *S. Cal. L. Rev.* 917, 937 (2012).
35. *Jones* v. *Harris Assocs. L.P.*, 537 F.3d 728, 730 (7th Cir. 2008) (Posner, J., dissenting).
36. *Zapata Corp.* v. *Maldonado*, 430 A.2d 779, 787 (Del. 1981).
37. Ward, *Boardroom Leaders*, at 40.
38. Ibid. at 43.
39. Nicola Faith Sharpe, *Questioning Authority: The Critical Link between Board Power and Process*, 38 *J. Corp. L.* 1, 33 (2012).
40. Amy L. Goodman & Gillian McPhee, Director Compensation in Turbulent Times, Corp. Gov. Adv. 10920226 (C.C.H.), 2008 WL 10920226.
41. Ngozi Vivian Okoye, *Behavioural Risks in Corporate Governance: Regulatory Intervention as a Risk Management Mechanism* 113 (2015).
42. Jay W. Lorsch, Empowering the Board, *Harv. Bus. Rev.*, Jan.–Feb. 1995.
43. Ibid.

44. Carter & Lorsch, *Drawing Board*, at 99.
45. Ibid. at 27.
46. Nat'l Ass'n Corp. Directors, *Public Company Governance Survey* (2008).
47. Jill E. Fisch, Taking Boards Seriously, 19 *Cardozo L. Rev.* 265, 268 (1997).
48. See generally Stephen M. Bainbridge, Why a Board? Group Decision Making in Corporate Governance, 55 *Vand. L. Rev.* 1 (2002).
49. Peter J. Wallison, Capital Punishment, *Wall St. J.*, Nov. 4–5, 2006, at A7.
50. Peter D. Hart Research Associates, *A Survey of Corporate Directors* (Feb. 2006).
51. Wallison, *Capital Punishment*, at A7.
52. Christian Casal & Christian Caspar, Building a Forward-Looking Board, *McKinsey Quarterly* (Feb. 2014).
53. Ibid.
54. Neville Bain & Roger Barker: *The Effective Board: Building Individual and Board Success* (2010).
55. Cheryl L. Wade, Sarbanes-Oxley Five Years Later: Will Criticism of SOX Undermine Its Benefits? 39 *Loy. U. Chi. L.J.* 595, 597 (2008).
56. Wong & Barton, Board Performance, https://ssrn.com/abstract=899920.

PART II

THE BOARD SERVICE PROVIDER

In this part, we present our idea for reconceptualizing the board of directors. We first describe the basic concept, and then consider the ways in which BSPs would offer improvements at delivering corporate governance services compared with traditional boards. We then look at some of the detailed ways in which BSPs might operate and how their incentives would be superior to the current board model.

5

Board Service Providers
The Basic Idea

In the first four chapters, we set the stage for our proposal, showing the historical origins of the current board model, describing what boards actually do in practice, and grading and evaluating their performance. The key lesson from this first part of the book is that boards are not well suited to the evolving governance demands of modern firms. We've seen the political origins of boards are an odd fit with modern use, but how innovation at the broad level has been a hallmark of corporations over the years. Boards have changed (slowly) as times have demanded. Yet, the modern trend toward a monitoring board is subject to increasing stress from both the limits of the current board model in terms of performance and the changing nature of the business environment. Federal law is increasingly forcing boards into a one-size-fits-all approach at the same time as the demands on boards to innovate and adapt to new circumstances – increased risk, changing investor dynamics, and so on – are increasing. In this chapter, we begin to set out our proposal to solve this problem.

INTRODUCTION

In 1964, Sidney Poitier became the first black man (specifically, Bahamian-American) to win an Academy Award for Best Actor. He became the biggest box-office draw in America by 1967, appearing in great and consciousness-raising movies, like "In the Heat of the Night" and "Guess Who's Coming to Dinner." Poitier is to film what Jackie Robinson is to baseball. But, for those of us interested more in corporate governance than films, Poitier is most famous for his role in the lawsuit about how much the Walt Disney Company paid a failed executive.

It all started with a helicopter crash. The accident killed Disney president Frank Wells, forcing CEO Michael Eisner to replace him at short notice.

(Eisner's emergency quadruple bypass surgery increased the hurry.) Eisner turned to his long-time friend, super-agent Michael Ovitz. At the time, Ovitz earned over $20 million per year as the head of Creative Artist Agency, and his 50 percent ownership stake was worth upward of a hundred million more. He was one of the most powerful people in Hollywood. Eisner won a bidding war with another suitor, the Music Corporation of America, and ultimately persuaded Ovitz to become his number two at Disney.

But boards, not CEOs, hire company presidents and set their pay. Here is where Poitier entered the scene. Disney's board was famously populated with Eisner's cronies, including the principal of the elementary school Eisner's children had attended and the architect who designed one of Eisner's homes. Poitier was on the board too. In fact, he was on the four-member Compensation Committee, one of the key committees. This was curious. Poitier was a distinguished gentleman of Hollywood, but his command of the Black-Scholes pricing model for options probably was less than that of the typical American executive. Thus, his role on the important Compensation Committee suggested the Disney board was more about personality than expertise or directing.

The Compensation Committee needed expertise – even experienced business people need help understanding modern compensation packages, the incentives they create, and the potential for misuse hidden within them – so it contracted with Graef Crystal, one of the nation's leading experts on executive compensation. The Committee and full board reviewed various presentations about Ovitz's proposed pay package, but Poitier (and another independent director named Lozano) participated only briefly and without receiving written reports from Crystal and others that made clear the payments Ovitz would receive under various scenarios. Ovitz got the generous deal he wanted.

Ovitz was not a good fit at Disney, and after slightly more than a year, he was terminated. He got north of $140 million for his efforts. A lawsuit followed in which the shareholders tried to recover some of that payment from the personal wealth of the Disney directors. The Delaware court that reviewed the case found Poitier's actions to be "casual" and "uninformed," but ultimately found neither him nor the other directors personally liable.[1] Such is the state of corporate governance.

There are many lessons about boards and governance to be gleaned from the hundreds of pages of court opinions in the Disney litigation, but for the purpose of setting the stage for our proposal, let us highlight three.

First, the board of Disney, like all corporate boards in the United States, is composed of individual humans offering their governance services independently. Sydney Poitier sold Disney board services to Disney, and he did so as a sole proprietor. Or, looking at it the other way, Disney hired Sydney Poitier to provide board services, and, as required by state law (Delaware in this case), Poitier was obligated to provide the services as a sole proprietor. As we have seen, he could not have created Poitier LLC, in which he was the sole owner and employee, and had that entity provide the board services. He also could not have associated with others to provide the services. This means that he and Lozano and the other directors could not have created an entity in which they were all owners or employees (call it Boards-R-Us Inc.) to provide their services to Disney. This is strange, because this is exactly what Disney did when it needed legal or accounting or consulting services – it routinely hired "firms" or associations of individuals under a corporate banner to provide those services.

Second, and following from this first point, if Poitier wanted to cooperate with anyone else to provide board services, he had to enter into a contractual relationship with them. For instance, when Poitier and the others on the Compensation Committee needed advice about the details of Ovitz's proposed contract, they had to hire Graef Crystal, another independent contractor, to provide that advice.* As we discuss in the chapters that follow, if board services were provided by a business, instead of an unaffiliated group of sole proprietors, more experts and better information would be available at lower cost to those providing board services. Consultancies, accounting firms, and law firms are all associations of many individuals who interact with each other to solve particular problems in this more efficient way. If state law weren't in the way, we suspect board services would be provided this way too.

Third, the individual nature of board service provision impacts the way in which law interacts with corporate governance. The Disney board, like all other boards, is composed of separate people who must bear all the risk of directorship individually, meaning their personal assets (including their wealth and reputation) are at risk as individuals. To see what this means, consider again the Ovitz case, and imagine that the board actions in paying Ovitz were illegal – that is, they did not comport with accepted governance practices. (This is what the court more or less found.) Faced with this, the court had two choices: to hold the individual directors liable or to excuse them of their liability. The former choice would mean sending each of the directors a bill for over ten million dollars, while the latter would risk setting a dangerous precedent for other boards in that it would send a message that

---

* Crystal may have provided these services through a firm in which he was the sole person involved (a personal service corporation) or as an employee of a larger consulting firm. Board members that contract, or perhaps subcontract, for expertise may hire firms or individuals.

they could skirt their duties without consequence. The court opted for the latter, but tried to shame future boards with its harsh rhetoric about the shortcomings of the Disney board's conduct. Whether or not this will be effective remains to be seen. But, however effective it is, imposing liability would unquestionably offer greater deterrence against future violations by boards.

It should be clear from this discussion that we imagine something else that would address these features of modern corporate governance, and offer what we think is a better approach. So, what do we imagine instead? In the rest of this chapter, we set out the basic idea. In later chapters, we will consider it in greater detail.

THE BOARD SERVICE PROVIDER

When Michael Eisner asked Sydney Poitier to serve on the board, Poitier joined fellow board members as a single voice and vote among many. Each of them had been asked by Eisner too, and approved by the vote of shareholders, albeit a vote that looked more like an election in North Korea or the old Soviet Union instead of an American one. The board met a few times per year, heard various reports from management, asked questions, and voted. They all then flew home and put aside the troubles of Disney until called upon to consider them again. It is unlikely that any of the Disney directors spent this time building expertise in the particular areas they would be asked to consider, knowing that they could always buy such expertise in the market. While all of the Disney directors brought considerable business acumen and experience to the table, they did so as individuals working together as a team, not as a team itself. The Disney directors were a loosely affiliated group, composed of individuals without any formal affiliation.

Instead of such a board comprising individuals, we propose allowing corporations to hire another business entity to act as the board of directors. Poitier and Lozano and their other board members might still be involved, but as employees of an *entity* hired to do the work. The business hired to be the board of Disney could be any kind of business entity – a partnership, LLC, corporation, or other type of association. We call this new business entity a "board service provider" or BSP. The board would be an "it," not a group of individual men and women. Instead of nominating and electing a slate of unrelated individual independent contractors to serve as board members, a BSP would be chosen to provide director services.

To be clear, we are not proposing that each individual director be permitted to form their own professional corporation through which they would provide board services (or some other limited liability entity). Such a regime would bring only whatever benefits there are from reduced director liability, by allowing the individuals to shield their personal assets from liabilities that result from their work as a director, but none of the other benefits we think arise when a single firm replaces the entire board. (For instance, as we discuss in this chapter, better access to information, better risk sharing, more oversight of directors, etc.)

The directors would not be corporations, but would cooperate together in the form of a corporation. This sounds like a small change, maybe even trivial. But to think that would be to deny the incredible power and benefits of cooperating through the corporate form. After all, individuals can try to do everything themselves or by contracting with others as individuals, as boards do today. But the past century has taught us that we can do much more when individuals form corporations instead. As we discuss in the chapters that follow, merely changing the nature of the way individuals associate – moving from teams of individuals to a corporate form under which teams of individuals operate – has enabled society to increase its wealth to levels unimaginable to our ancestors. In fact, it is not too bold to say that the corporation is one of mankind's greatest inventions. And, we argue in this book, that deploying it to provide board services would improve them, just as it has in so many other areas of our lives.

We imagine specialty board services providers – BSPs – being formed to provide these services. Consider Disney again. Disney, or rather Disney's shareholders and other stakeholders, demand corporate governance services be provided by people outside of Disney – some people who do not work at Disney day-to-day are needed to bring expertise, independence, critical judgment, a set of fresh eyes and perspective, reputation, insurance (in the form of potential liability for the failure to prevent losses), and so on to the management of Disney. This structure is legally required, but we suspect that the law here follows what would be investor demand for an agent to watch its other agents.

The BSP – we call it "Boards-R-Us" for simplicity – would be a company, like Disney itself. Disney is merely the name for the thousands of people who cooperate to make the entertainment experiences we consume under that brand. This cooperation could be done by virtue of contracts among these many thousands of people, just as the Disney board cooperates. But that model is clearly less efficient than using the corporate fiction to organize that activity.

The economist Ronald Coase pointed this out in a famous article, "The Nature of the Firm," in 1937. Coase asked why firms exist, or, rather, why individuals working with others do not simply use a variety of contracts to organize their economic activity. Imagine Alice and Bob want to start a business selling cakes. They need the input of bakers, designers, cashiers, accountants, and a variety of other workers. They could create a corporate entity, and then hire all of these people to work for it. Then, as bosses, they could simply command them to do certain tasks. Or, instead, Coase imagined, they could simply write individual contracts with these people, as strangers, to provide specific tasks, like baking, designing, and so on. The choice is always "build" versus "buy." Given these two choices, Coase asked why most economic activity is done through the former option, that is, through firms.

His answer was profound, yet simple: There are costs and benefits of using contracts (the buy option), and when the costs exceed the benefits for a particular activity, that is, where it is easier and less costly to simply order someone in a hierarchy to do something rather than writing a new contract to have them do it, then a firm will arise. Consider something simple, like getting a photocopy made. A boss could ask her assistant to make the copy, or could put out a request for a bid from FedEx-Kinkos and other suppliers of copying services. There are benefits of the first approach – simplicity and speed – and potential benefits of the second approach – price and quality, perhaps. Whether it makes sense to have the assistant do the work depends on these tradeoffs. The huge decline in secretarial jobs over the past few decades demonstrates that the boundaries of the firm can change as these costs and benefits change. The optimal firm size is thus not a matter of logic or design, but experience. As the relative cost of inputs changes with the costs and benefits of hierarchy (build) versus contracting (buy), the size of the firm will adjust. If contracting becomes more expensive, say because the court system is not reliable to adjudicate disputes or because the technology of searching for and monitoring contracting partners degrades, then firms will grow in size, all else being equal, and vice versa.

This approach logically applies to the provision of any good or service, including corporate governance or board services.

We do not know the optimal size of the board services provider, but, as we explore in later chapters, we doubt the optimal firm size for providing board services is one person, which is what a legal requirement that directors be sole proprietors implies.

If firms providing board services were permissible, a competitive market for the provision of these services would arise, just as happened for legal, accounting, and consultancy services for companies. In fact, we can imagine many of the firms that currently provide these other services offering board services. The specialty BSPs we imagine being created to provide governance could be in competition with the Boston Consulting Group (a consultancy), Sidley

Austin (a law firm), Towers Watson (a compensation consultancy), Aon (an insurer of directors), and KPMG (an accountancy), each of which could expand its operations to include providing director services. Many of these firms already provide strategic and management advice to large corporations, a role that used to be provided by boards. Many of them also serve compliance and monitoring functions as a complement to or substitute for board actions. Our proposal is simply a natural extension of these activities to a full recognition of statutory board functions provided by outside firms.

Could the Boston Consulting Group have been a better board than the Disney board or the Enron board or any of the other boards we've seen that have failed? We cannot know for sure, but we have reason to believe that the market for corporate governance would result in superior board services, all else being equal. This is not to say that BSPs will be perfect or that governance failures will not happen. We are sure they won't be and that they will. Rather, our argument is that the level of overall corporate governance could be improved, and the overall cost of governance could be reduced, if BSPs were used.

But maybe they won't. Sometimes experiments fail. Even failed experiments are valuable. After failing with about a thousand ways of creating a filament for an electric lightbulb, Edison was asked about the failure. He declared that he hadn't failed, but rather figured out a thousand things that won't work as a filament. We think it is high time that such a spirit be brought to the stale world of corporate governance.

The best way to understand how the BSP model differs from the current board model is to compare the differences along the key dimensions of board activity. These include how directors are appointed, who they are, what functions they serve, how they make decisions, how they are elected and removed, and what liability rules govern their conduct.

APPOINTMENT AND ELECTIONS

A central feature of any system of board governance is how directors get their jobs on the board in the first place, and then how they keep or lose them. First, let's look at how they get their jobs. Under the current approach, a company's initial board members are either its incorporators or are named in the corporate charter. Thereafter, the firm's shareholders or the shareholders' agent (for example, the CEO) nominate individual directors to run for election. For exchange-listed public corporations, the nominating committee of the board of directors is tasked with selecting new directors and nominating the directors to be elected at the annual shareholder meeting.

If BSPs were permitted, this initial stage would likely look quite similar. The promoters of the firm would choose a BSP (instead of individual directors) to serve until the first meeting of shareholders, or name the first BSP in the corporate charter. The BSP would serve until the next annual meeting. Many venture-backed startups already appoint several members of the venture capital fund to serve on the board to advise the company and validate it to outsiders; a BSP would be a professional board service that could also help provide both these values – advice and reputation. As we discuss later, BSPs could also accommodate having input from particular individuals, such as representatives of management and certain other stakeholders, like venture capital investors. These people could serve as employees or independent contractors (again, the build versus buy decision) of the BSP.

Today, after the initial board is chosen, shareholders vote to elect board members each year.[2] Directors are submitted as a group (known as a "slate") to shareholders via the company's proxy voting materials, but they run as individuals. This means that directors appear as a group proposed by management – the management slate – but that shareholder cast their votes for or against ("withhold") for individual directors. Because directors generally run unopposed – there is not a rival slate offered – the shareholder vote is more advisory than anything else. Indeed, under traditional plurality voting rules, a vote of less than 50 percent suggests only shareholder dissatisfaction, because directors with even a single vote can continue to serve.[3] Although these elections resemble political ones, the closest political analog for these elections is North Korea, not North Dakota.

The only sure way to remove a director is through a proxy contest, in which a rival pays, win or lose, the full costs of distributing ballots to shareholders and convincing them to vote for the rival. Firms pay incumbents' costs no matter what, and incumbents are effectively spending shareholders' money to maintain their jobs.[4] Given the asymmetry of costs and benefits of this strategy, proxy contests are exceedingly rare and are seen primarily in cases in which the benefits of winning a board seat include gaining control of the entire board, and thus the economics of the entire firm.[5] There is no market for corporate governance, only a market for corporate control.

How would things look different with a BSP? A virtue of permitting BSPs to challenge the monopoly sole proprietors currently have on providing board services is that if the current process for selecting and electing directors is a good one (either at a firm level or economy-wide level), then little would have to change if firms were permitted to use BSPs. In other words, a particular company, like Disney, could choose to pick a BSP instead of its current directors, and change nothing else about the election process. Or, a new startup could opt to have a BSP board, and otherwise follow the traditional approach to choosing the board.

A BSP thus could be chosen initially, then renominated and reelected indefinitely, as is the case today with individual directors. As with current directors, a BSP would be subject to removal by the shareholders. Shareholders could vote out the BSP and vote in another BSP or a slate of individual directors, if one was offered as an alternative, in a proxy contest or at the initiative of management. In later chapters, we will consider how BSPs would impact the economics of proxy contests, concluding that without any other changes, competition for board control would be greatly enhanced. (We will also note how, if this is not ideal, either for a particular company or for all companies, the rules can be tweaked slightly to accommodate more stability.)

For existing firms with existing boards wanting to hire a BSP, there are a variety of processes that could be used. The firm, by the nominating committee, by a special committee appointed solely for the purpose, or by the CEO, could choose a BSP to run against the current board or as the sole option for shareholders. Two or more BSPs could be chosen to run against each other, creating real competition and shareholder choice about governance. Or, perhaps most alluringly, a BSP could simply challenge the existing board to a proxy contest, giving shareholders the choice of governance model. These approaches could be formalized by statutory command or, preferably, by the choice of individual firms. These and other options for the nomination and election procedures, including ones that could reduce board turnover, are discussed later in the chapter.

What might this look like? Imagine a company is flying high but badly governed. The stock is doing well, but there are substantial risks lurking in the balance sheet. Maybe the company has evolved from making tractors to selling derivatives, and it is ill equipped in terms of systems, people, and knowledge to manage the new risks. Some outsiders think they could do a better job managing the company at the board level – setting a new tone at the top, bringing in needed expertise in finance and strategy, and helping to install more rigorous compliance and oversight. These outsiders could try to take over the entire company (in a hostile takeover or private equity-style investment) or, if that risk is too much to take on, say because of some frictions in the capital markets, they could mount a campaign to install new directors through a proxy fight.

As noted earlier, unless these outsiders are well known to shareholders, this will be a costly battle. And, because of the asymmetry in compensation for the battle – the incumbents charge the shareholders, the insurgents pay their own way – the gains from the takeover must be significant. The result of this state of affairs is very few takeovers, and none that we know of that are predicated solely on improvements in board governance, as distinct from operational performance.

Instead, a well-known company with a national reputation, say, McKinsey & Company or Boards-R-Us, could decide that it could govern the company better in its current state. Not run the day-to-day, but provide the needed expertise in oversight, strategy, and so on. For McKinsey or Boards-R-Us to wage a battle to take over the board would be much less costly, since it could trade on its national reputation, as well as spread the costs of the battle across many such battles in a portfolio approach. The end result, we suspect, would be more battles for control of the board than we currently see, without a rise in hostile takeovers. The labor market for boards would be thicker, in a way, without causing disruption to core operational activities of firms.

Of course, it might be desirable for BSPs to be regarded as pure service firms rather than activists or corporate raiders. Instead of launching proxy contests, BSPs could offer their services both to incumbent boards and the increasingly large group of hedge fund activists. The first decade of the new millennium saw repeated efforts by corporate governance activists to extend the shareholder franchise and otherwise empower shareholders to take an active governance role. In response, the major stock exchanges adopted new listing standards expanding the voting rights of investors. Likewise, the DGCL and the Model Business Corporation Act (MBCA) were amended to allow corporations to require a majority vote – rather than the traditional plurality – to elect directors.

In 2008, the activists' efforts gained renewed impetus with the election of Barack Obama as President of the United States, the expansion of Democratic majorities in both houses of Congress, and the installation of a Democratic majority at the Securities and Exchange Commission. Echoing such constituencies as unions and state and local government pension plans, Washington Democrats blamed the financial crisis of 2008 in large part on corporate governance failures. Accordingly, much of their response took the form of new shareholder entitlements, such as say on pay and expanded ability to use shareholder proposals under Rule 14a-8 to effect changes in corporate election procedures. At the state level, DGCL § 113 codified a Delaware Supreme Court decision recognizing a right for shareholders to unilaterally adopt bylaws governing the process by which corporate decisions are made, specifically including those requiring reimbursement of expenses of certain proxy contestants. Section 112 of the DGCL was adopted to authorize bylaws allowing shareholder access to the company's proxy materials to nominate directors.

In addition to the activists' political gains at both the federal and state levels, an important change is that significant amounts of new capital have flowed into activist funds, especially hedge funds, giving them greater financial firepower. Another important factor is that many firms have disarmed, abandoning poison pill and classified board defenses.

As a result, activists have had increasing success in influencing corporate management through proxy contests and other interventions. Today, even the largest and most successful companies are no longer immune to shareholder activism, as illustrated by hedge fund manager David Einhorn's campaign to force Apple to change its capital structure.

The combination of activist funds and BSPs could be a major game changer in corporate governance. A well-established and experienced BSP would make an activist proxy campaign more credible, because the BSP could not be dismissed as mere cronies of the activist.

COMPOSITION AND FUNCTION

Another dimension along which we can compare and contrast the current board model and our proposed alternative is the composition and function of the board. Today, board members are most commonly current or former CEOs of other companies, as well as high-profile individuals from business, science, law, academia, accounting, politics, and other fields.[6] Consider, for instance, the board of Walmart. As of June 2013, it has sixteen members, twelve of whom are not otherwise employees of Walmart. These include two business professors, three former CEOs, three current CEOs, the former head of an accounting firm, the former head of an advertising firm, the former head of the Small Business Administration, and the general partner of an investment fund.

The choice of directors is undoubtedly based on many factors and is highly situational. For early stage companies, directors with access to key fundraising connections or with industry expertise may be highly prized, while for later-stage companies, directors with political connections or leadership positions at firms in complementary industries might be more valuable. Boards going through a crisis might need the help of an expert in risk management, someone with government connections, or someone who has led an organization through a crisis. Other factors, such as personal relationships and diversity considerations, may also be involved in choosing directors. Some of these reasons may be desirable from the perspective of shareholders, including access to lower-cost capital, business connections, political influence, and strategic vision. Others may not be, including the personal satisfaction of the CEO, in terms of quid pro quos or rubbing elbows with great figures.

Consider, for example, Barry Diller's media conglomerate, IAC/ InterActiveCorp. IAC appointed then thirty-one-year-old graduate student Chelsea Clinton to the board.[7] Perhaps this makes business sense, since political connections are (unfortunately) valuable for firms. But it also created a way for IAC's chairman, Barry Diller, to maximize his utility, as opposed to IAC's shareholders – Diller is a big donor to the Democrats, and helping Ms. Clinton is an obvious way to continue that practice. There is reason to suspect the latter, since former board members of IAC then included Diller's wife, the fashion designer Diane von Furstenburg, and General Norman Schwartzkopf, and since the current board also includes von Furstenburg's son, Alex.

Our idea is to do away entirely with having individuals sitting on the board. Just as a firm outsources much legal work to a law firm rather than a committee of lawyers and its external audit function to an accounting firm rather than a committee of CEOs, the board function would be outsourced to Boards-R-Us and its ilk.

To be sure, there would be individuals serving as the point of contact between the corporation and the BSP, just as individual partners serve as the contact point between the corporation and its law firm and auditor. Where the board is called upon to make a decision, such as whether to approve a merger, the CEO would meet with the contact person at the BSP, who would then bring the full resources of the BSP to bear on making the decision. The precise composition of a decision-making team within the BSP might vary with the type of decision at hand, just as law firms put together different teams to handle a given client's varying matters.

Under the BSP approach, the type of individuals providing board member-like services could more or less be what they are today or they could be completely different, depending on how the BSP developed over time to meet the needs of its clients. A BSP could hire the exact mix of individuals that currently serve on corporate boards – current and former CEOs, politicians, lawyers, and so on. These contractual relationships could be permanent or temporary, meaning some individuals might have a relationship with one BSP or for one particular board service contract, while others might offer their services on a freelance basis. If the current composition of board members is optimal, there is nothing about our proposal that would upset this. Some additional contracting might be necessary to form coherent firms out of a changing mix of individuals, but this is a rather small cost.

One benefit of the BSP model, however, is that it would discourage, on the margin, the hiring of individual board members as window dressing or because of the CEO's domination of the board. As famed management guru Peter Drucker once observed, a truly "effective board member has to be a professional director. Indeed, board membership should be recognized as a full-time profession for a really first-rate man."[8] Current boards still all too often include, say, the child of a president or famous actor. A BSP hired to provide such services is less likely to include such individuals because it has a profit motive in selecting the best candidates. If having the relatively inexperienced daughter of a former president and former secretary of state on the board will improve governance for a particular firm, then a BSP would have an incentive to hire that person to be part of a board services team. This "value" could include reasons that aren't about shareholder or firm value, such as pleasing the individual or group making the decision on which BSP to hire.

Some might believe that appointing board members is a fringe benefit of the CEO, in which case the move toward a BSP that makes idiosyncratic appointments less likely might require compensating the CEO, either with additional compensation or with some other power. There are, however, reasons to doubt the importance of the work done by our proposal in this regard. CEOs are already less closely involved in board appointments, given the rise of the independent nominating committee, which is now required by law for public companies. Insofar as it remains an issue for CEOs, the move to a BSP may make this issue less salient and less important. In other words, once CEOs no longer think about board seats as theirs to fill and instead think about firms to hire to provide service to the company, the importance of this power will likely be lower.

The analogy to law firms and accounting firms may seem imperfect. A BSP would, at least in theory, have vastly more power than an accounting firm or law firm, since the latter render only advice. In practice, however, the analogy may be fairly tight. While accounting firms and law firms are generally under the authority of other decision-makers in the firm, this is not true for certain classes of extraordinary firm actions. Accountants and lawyers are bound by professional responsibility rules and statutes to bind their clients in certain ways that cannot be overridden or to withdraw from representation in ways that raise costs for their clients. The same could be true of BSPs – the bulk of their work could be analogized to providing a professional service to the CEO and the firm generally, while in some extraordinary cases, like approving a merger, the BSP would have significant powers.

Importantly, our approach does not prevent the use of mixed boards. Consistent with our emphasis on providing enabling rather than default rules, we believe that companies should have the ability to have a BSP serve as part of a larger board that also includes individuals chosen via the traditional model. The most obvious case for a mixed board would be where the firm wished to continue having inside directors (that is, current or recently retired employees, especially the CEO) serve on the board. Large shareholders may demand a board seat as well. Indeed, investors with large stakes in particular firms often seek influence over firm policies by nominating (either directly or with the consent of management) directors to represent their interests. The government also occasionally asserts its interest in particular firms through the appointment of a board member, as it did in when retired Admiral Mike Mullen joined the board of Sprint after it agreed to merge with Japanese conglomerate Softbank. Mullen joined the board to oversee the new entity's compliance with a national security agreement Sprint entered into with the US government. If valuable in a particular case, this tactic could continue to be used, either by convincing the BSP (through management) to add a particular individual to the team for a particular firm or by expanding the board to include individual members in addition to a BSP's role.

COMPENSATION

Another dimension of comparison is in how directors are compensated for their work. Directors of large, publicly traded American firms are paid a mix of cash and equity grants in the corporation. The latter, a relatively recent innovation, are designed to align the wealth of directors and shareholders so that director incentives are improved from the perspective of the firm's residual claimants.

In the BSP model, we expect that the BSP would bill client corporations a basic annual fee for services, just as law firms and external auditors do. Unlike the latter types of service providers, however, we anticipate that client corporations may wish to pay part of the BSP's compensation in equity – such as restricted stock – so as to align the interests of the BSP with those of the client's shareholders. Nothing prevents firms from owning stock in other firms, and the stock holding requirements and restrictions currently applied to director compensation could be readily transferred to the BSP. Although some professional services firms did not historically take equity stakes in their clients, in recent years consultancies, law firms, and other service providers have increasingly done so. We see no reason why this trend could not be expanded to include BSPs.

Although a greater ownership stake by the board has the potential to improve incentive alignment, there are two barriers to this with the current board structure. The first is that giving boards large upside stakes with limited downside risks skews decision making in a socially undesirable fashion. The second is that individual, part-time board members are not well positioned to bear this kind of risk, and their work does not routinely justify such large stakes. Hiring a BSP could help address these concerns. Because of risk pooling, greater reputational stakes, greater efficiency, and so on, a BSP could hold a much larger stake in its client than the sum of the stakes held by individual board members.

LIABILITY

In the BSP model, liability for board misconduct or breaches of fiduciary duty would reside at the entity level, instead of the individual level. In the event of alleged director misbehavior, the shareholders of the company would sue the BSP derivatively for breaches of fiduciary duties. Liability for any violations would be borne by the BSP as an entity, rather than the individual directors being jointly and severally liable for the total damages. Entity liability would not preclude individual liability as well under extraordinary circumstances. As with any case of entities facing liability, individual agents may also be held liable if there are facts and circumstances suggesting the policy undergirding the legal rule would be furthered by individual liability.

We think this simple change has the potential to transform corporate governance law by making courts *more likely* to intervene in cases, like Disney's dispute with Ovitz, in which there is fairly clear evidence of a corporate governance failure. The logic is straightforward. As noted earlier, directors are independent amateurs without deep pockets, but face enormous potential liability for the decisions they make. For instance, the sloppy approval of a merger could subject directors, including individual directors, to multimillion-dollar liability, not to mention the significant risk to their personal reputations. Courts seem reluctant to impose liability on directors, perhaps increasingly so in recent years.[9] This could be because of institutional competency concerns, worries about hindsight bias, the potential chilling effect on risk-taking, the reluctance to hold individuals (some of whom are not extremely rich) liable for potentially huge damage awards, and the potential impact of increased liability on the supply of individuals willing to provide director services. Whatever the reasons, if directors form associations to share risk, this reduces the potential negative cost on individuals, and thereby may increase the willingness of courts to impose liability. We take up this point in greater detail in Chapter 7.

SUMMARY

In this chapter, we have set out the basic idea and features of our proposal to permit corporations to hire other entities to provide corporate governance services. When we put it this way, it seems rather obvious. Just as corporations hire law firms and accounting firms, it seems straightforward that they should be permitted to hire corporate governance firms. We call firms like these Board Service Providers, or BSPs.

But, the idea is not as simple and the argument for it not so easy. In making our case, we are up against several hundred years of history of individuals serving as board members, independent of each other. We are also fighting against a legal mandate and the accepted practice of all of America's corporations. We will therefore take up the argument as to why this is a good idea in the remainder of the book.

Our goal in this chapter was merely to acquaint the reader with the basic contours. We set out the basics of what a BSP might look like in terms of composition, compensation, and operation. There is an enormous amount of variation possible in how a BSP might operate, and we would not presume to be able to predict what is the optimal approach of a BSP to structuring its business. Thus, we start our argument with the most barebones version of the idea, imagining no changes to the world of corporate governance other than that an entity serves as the board instead of a loose affiliation of individual directors. We will relax some of these restrictions in later chapters, but for now, have in your head just this simple transformation. Instead of the board of Disney or Boeing or Alphabet being a group of individuals, imagine it as an entity. The same individuals could work for the entity, and they could be the only employees, or there could be many more experts and others supporting them. Instead of shareholders monitoring and evaluating and voting for individual directors (based on information they don't actually get in practice), shareholders would do this for an entity acting as an entity. Instead of courts reviewing the actions of individual directors, courts would do this for an entity acting as an entity.

As we will consider next, this simple change has the potential to transform corporate governance in a number of positive ways.

Notes

1. See *In re Walt Disney Co. Derivative Litigation*, 907 A.2d 693 (2005).
2. See D.G.C.L. § 211(b) (providing that an annual meeting of stockholders shall be held for the election of directors on a date and at a time designated by or in the manner provided in the bylaws).
3. Until recently, state law merely required a plurality shareholder vote. DGCL § 216(3) formerly provided, for example, that "Directors shall be elected by a plurality of the votes of the shares present in person or

represented by proxy at the meeting and entitled to vote on the election of directors." Stephen M. Bainbridge, *Mergers and Acquisitions* 153 (3rd edn. 2012). Today, however, state law permits – but does not require – firms to adopt various schemes having the effect of requiring director candidates to receive a majority of the votes cast in order to serve. See ibid. at 154–157 (discussing state law developments).

4. See, e.g. *Rosenfeld* v. *Fairchild Engine & Airplane Corp.*, 128 N.E.2d 291 (1955), reh'g denied, 130 N.E.2d 610 (1955) (describing reimbursement rules for proxy contests).

5. Bainbridge, *Mergers and Acquisitions*, at 177 (discussing rarity of proxy contests and reasons therefor).

6. See Board of Directors, WALMART, http://corporate.walmart.com/our -story/leadership/board-of-directors (last visited Jan. 4, 2014).

7. Brett Pulley, Chelsea Clinton to Join Board of Directors at Diller's IAC/ InterActiveCorp, ***Bloomberg***, (Sept. 26, 2011, 11:29:48 PM), www .bloomberg.com/news/2011-09-26/chelsea-clinton-joins-board-of-directors -at-iac-interactivecorp-.html.

8. Drucker Institute, *Farming Out the Directors* (Aug. 26, 2013).

9. See, e.g. Tamar Frankel, *Trust and Honesty: America's Business Culture at a Crossroad* 183–184 (2006) ("There are some departures from the historical strong protection of corporate boards. For example, in the past two decades, the Delaware courts ... were reluctant to make corporate directors liable for the wrongs committed by their corporations. The courts respected the directors' business judgment and, with a few notable exceptions, shielded the directors from the claims of shareholders."); Lisa M. Fairfax, Spare the Rod, Spoil the Director? Revitalizing Directors' Fiduciary Duty through Legal Liability, 42 *Hous. L. Rev.* 393, 409 (2005) ("[T]he tremendous deference courts grant to board decisions means that courts hold directors liable for only the most egregious examples of director misconduct.").

6

How BSPs Address the Pathologies of Modern Corporate Governance

The central claim of this book is that BSPs could deliver, at least in some instances, better corporate governance at lower costs. In this chapter, we try to demonstrate the first part of that claim by mapping the BSP model to the functions played by the modern board. As we saw in Chapter 2, modern boards have three basic functions: monitoring, management, and service. In this chapter, we argue that BSPs have the potential to make improvements or at least do no harm in all of these board functions.

Instead of simply rehashing the monitoring, service, and managerial functions, however, we map the BSP to the prevailing business school theories of the board's role and purpose. Business schools teach several theories about the contributions boards make to corporate success, all of which are to varying degrees both normative and descriptive. Put another way, these theories purport to explain what boards do, why they do it, and whether they should be doing it. Specifically, we focus here on five theoretical frameworks that are widely used in the literature: managerial hegemony, resource dependence, stakeholder, stewardship, and agency.[i] Taken together, our analysis of the BSP within each of these frameworks confirms our belief that they can provide superior corporate governance at lower cost than present boards.

MANAGERIAL HEGEMONY THEORY

Managerialist theorists view the board of directors as essentially a figurehead. Preeminent management guru Peter Drucker perfectly captured this view

---

[i] One purpose in focusing on the business school literature in this chapter is that doing so further illustrates the essentially nonideological nature of the BSP model. With one exception – that is, the largely discredited managerial hegemony theory – the BSP makes sense no matter which of the prevailing business school theories one chooses to adopt.

when he dismissed "the board of directors" as "an impotent ceremonial and legal fiction."[1]

As Drucker's derisive comment suggests, managerialists posit that although the corporation statute may assign ultimate authority to the board, that authority has long since been irrevocably delegated to – or usurped by, in some accounts – the CEO and the top management team. As a result, boards are mere creatures of the CEO, rubberstamping the CEO's decisions.[2] The board's function in this model is to provide a veneer of legitimacy for unelected industrial autocrats. Both supporters and critics of this state of affairs accepted the basic thesis that managers ran the show rather than either directors or shareholders. "Pro-managerialists asserted that expertise necessitated this; anti-managerialists asserted that the power arose due to the absence of market constraints."[3]

It has been a long time since anybody (except perhaps CEOs) viewed the managerial hegemony theory as a legitimate normative claim about how boards ought to behave. Indeed, to the contrary, managerialism, with its key idea of the corporate statesperson acting in a responsive and responsible manner, is increasingly obsolete and embarrassingly irrelevant. To paraphrase Robert Reich, the corporate statesperson is "dead, gone the way of the Edsel."[4]

In large part this is so because managers typically do not act as the Platonic kings described by managerialist theory, selflessly putting the organization ahead of their own interests, but as normal rationally maximizing humans who wish – consciously or subconsciously – to enhance their own wellbeing. Instead, they are – as some managerialist theorists themselves posit – "a new, privileged class of elites whose interests focus on maximizing their wealth and power and using corporate assets for personal gain."[5] As such, managerialism does not paint a particularly attractive normative picture.

Although managerialism was an accurate description of how corporations worked for much of the twentieth century, power is shifting from managers toward boards and, some would say, shareholders. Managers today are far more constrained by a variety of internal and external governance mechanisms than were their mid-twentieth-century predecessors. Among other things, even when modern boards lack information or proper incentives, they still retain the ability to set limits on managerial discretion through their power to hire and fire and to set compensation. Managerialism thus no longer has as much descriptive validity as it once did.

In our view, widespread adoption of the BSP model would further undermine the managerialist theory both descriptively and normatively. By improving managerial accountability through more effective board oversight, the BSP would undermine the claim that the board is simply a Potemkin village behind whose façade management does at it pleases. At the same time, if we are correct that BSP-led companies will outperform their non-BSP competitors, the normative claims that managerialism is the optimal way of organizing the corporation will be disproven.

One could, one of us thinks (Todd), make an arguable case that firms run by CEOs without boards would, at least in some cases, be superior to firms with boards: at least the boards that we have today. After all, the performance of an individual in charge of a firm is likely much more transparent and that individual is likely much more accountable than a group of unaffiliated board members as we've described them.

But, for the reasons we've explored to this point, the combination of a motivated, informed, and capable board and a CEO is likely to be a superior option in most instances. It is for that reason that we advocate permitting the board to evolve through the BSP approach. By deploying a BSP, we think firms can get more out of firms than if they were managed by a lone CEO or by the current board model. But, we are open to the possibility that in a particular case a CEO alone would be superior, or, perhaps, the current board model. There is nothing about our proposed reform that precludes these options. In short, we'd like to see more experimentation than the current legal regime tolerates.

CLASS HEGEMONY THEORY

Class hegemony theory is a variant of managerialist theory that focuses on the shared interests, objectives, and preferences of top managers as a sociological class that stretches across the C-suites of most, if not all, major corporations. Noting that the boards of major corporations are often interlocked, with executives of one company serving on the board of other corporations whose executives in turn serve on still more boards, class hegemony theorists claim that managers can trade favors and protect one another's interests.[6] As with managerialism, this is not an especially appealing normative conception, and seems less accurate as board independence rules have started to break up some interlocks.[i]

In any case, class hegemony theory – like managerialism – would be far less descriptively apt with respect to BSPs. We expect BSPs to be staffed with a cadre of professional advisors, like those found at consultancies of various

---

[i] "An interlock is the social relation that is created between two corporations when one person is a member of the governing boards of both organizations." Humphry Hung, A Typology of the Theories of the Roles of Governing Boards, *Corp. Gov.*, April 1998, at 101, 104.

kinds that support current board members. Because the BSP board will not necessarily comprise executives of other operating companies, the logrolling essential for class hegemony to prevail will be eliminated.

But, even if our prediction is incorrect, and current board members continue to provide governance services as employees of a BSP, the market for BSP services will serve as a check on the worst forms of backscratching abuse. As discussed later in this chapter, a market for corporate governance will discipline BSPs in ways that will reduce the gains from employing individuals that do not deliver value for shareholders, who will choose the BSP. Shareholders will have more options in annual elections, more transparency about the performance of boards, and more access to expert information directly without the need for figurehead intermediaries.

RESOURCE DEPENDENCE THEORY

Another popular b-school theory of boards is about resource dependence. Resource dependence theory is a networking story. Directors are chosen because of their potential to create interlocks with potential resources. The board's function is to "enhance a firm's ability to raise funds, to add to the reputation of the company through recognition of their name in the community, and to deal with threats in the external environment."[7] By interlocking multiple boards of directors the board facilitates access to mission-critical resources by providing introductions, creating formal and informal communication channels, and helping coordinate ongoing relationships.

As both a normative and descriptive theory, resource dependence is incomplete. To be sure, providing access to resources is part of the board's service function, but it is only part of that function. It thus fails to acknowledge that advising the CEO is a critical part of the board's service function. In addition, resource dependence entirely overlooks the board's managerial and monitoring roles.

At the same time, of course, resource dependence is clearly part of what boards do. As boards are currently structured, however, they may not do it well. Resource dependence theory implies that large and diverse boards are preferable, to maximize the number of potential interlocks and the size of the resulting networks. A considerable body of research, however, suggests that larger boards are less effective.[8] Best practice guides commonly recommend boards have between four and ten members.[9]

In any event, BSPs should be far better at building a network of resources on which the firm can draw than are individual directors. There is considerable current pressure on directors to reduce the number of boards on which they sit, which is premised on the sensible view that directors only have so much time and effort to devote to such a demanding job and therefore should not spread themselves too thin across multiple boards. As a result, each director now provides fewer interlocks, and thus fewer connections and less access to valuable resources. In contrast, a large service entity with dozens or even hundreds of professionals serving many different companies in many different industries will be positioned to provide access to a diverse network. If the goal of a board is to build connections, BSPs will be a clear upgrade.

In any case, let us consider the possibility that particular BSPs will not be able to provide as diverse a set of networks as can a multimember board of unrelated individuals. For some firms, the importance of, say, access to a network of investors, may be sufficient to outweigh the benefits of hiring a BSP. If the network is available only through a single individual, and that individual cannot be hired or retained by the BSP, then this may mean that individual directors are a superior option for that firm at that particular time in its life cycle.

But, crucially, there is nothing in our proposal that requires the use of a BSP. If a particular firm would be better served by the status quo board model, then shareholders could make that choice. In fact, we expect that for most firms the use of a BSP may be optimal only when they reach a certain maturity. Large, public companies are probably better served by our proposed board than start-up companies, companies in distress, or smaller, private firms. But, again, we could be wrong about this too. We think the market should decide. And, in our approach, shareholders would implicitly select the board model every time they choose a board. For instance, as we consider later, every year a BSP might run against an incumbent slate of directors, and the shareholders could choose to hire the BSP or opt for the traditional model. If one is more efficient and valuable at a particular time, there is no reason why the shareholders could not switch between models as needed to maximize the value of the business.

Moreover, we see no obvious reason why a BSP would not be able to provide these networking or access services. For one, modern-day consulting firms and investment banks provide important networks of information and access for companies without relying on individual contracts as in the board model. Large BSPs comprising hundreds or thousands of professionals, including many individuals currently serving as board members, could likely do the same thing. If current or former CEOs are valuable members of companies' decision-making processes, their services will be demanded by BSPs, which could hire them on a permanent or ad hoc basis. Finally, where this is not feasible, a BSP could serve as a matchmaker between clients, just as investment banks often do.

One final point is worth mentioning. Opening up new possibilities through the BSP innovation may reveal previously unappreciated benefits. The BSP may be superior to current boards at advising CEOs, since the BSP will have better information, better incentives, and specialists on call. While one might object that if this were the case, companies would already be deploying them, as we note in this chapter, the current situation may be an artifact of law and the stickiness of the status quo more than a conscious reflection of a first-best equilibrium.

STAKEHOLDER THEORY

Stakeholder theory is sometimes described as a variant of resource dependence theory that focuses on the role of the board in maintaining relationships with key corporate constituencies.[i] Some commentators in the resource dependence school argue that a key purpose of corporate interlocks is to assist the corporation in coopting or diffusing threats or uncertainties posed by other corporations. By interlocking the company with other corporations that are the firm's key competitors, suppliers, customers, and so on, the board allows the company to communicate with and credibly commit to relationships with the crucial external actors in the firm's environment.

Stakeholder theory focuses more on the board's role vis-à-vis constituencies such as "employees, customers, suppliers, stockholders, banks, environmentalists, government and other groups who can help or hurt the corporation."[10] As a normative claim about how boards ought to behave, stakeholder theory has been highly controversial in both the legal and business literature.[11] As a descriptive claim, however, it appears to have some – albeit arguably limited – validity. A now somewhat dated 2000 survey by Korn/Ferry, for example, found that although directors most frequently ranked shareholder interests as their primary concern, a substantial number of directors also expressed a responsibility toward stakeholders.[12]

Where a firm wants its board of directors either to liaise with stakeholders or, assuming it is legally proper for the board to do so,[13] to consider stakeholder interests in making corporate decisions, a BSP can do so at least as well as a

---

[i]   As applied to corporate governance, the term "stakeholders" reportedly originated in a 1963 Stanford Research Institute memorandum as a descriptive term for "those groups without whose support the organization would cease to exist." R. Edward Freeman & David L. Reed, Stockholders and Stakeholders: A New Perspective on Corporate Governance, 25 *Cal. Mgmt. Rev.* 88, 89 (1983).

board comprising autonomous individuals. When it comes to negotiating and liaising with stakeholders, the BSP presents a single face to the relevant constituencies rather than multiple interlocutors. If the BSP can make better managerial decisions than a board composed of individuals, as we have argued, they can do the same when tasked with taking into account stakeholder interests.

Consider, for instance, a firm that wants to better manage relationships with labor or commit to greater stewardship of the environment. This is likely to be most effective when done through the management team, but since we are considering a theory about the role and value of *boards*, we should compare how a BSP would do at this compared with the status quo board. For the traditional board to manage these stakeholder interests, it will have to have a board member with labor or environmental expertise. Some boards may have these people, but perhaps not. Since the range of potential stakeholders is large, it is unlikely that a firm will have a board member that can claim expertise or networks in all the areas in which a firm may want to deploy the board. After all, boards already need a range of expertise in areas like accounting, finance, strategy, the particular industry, compensation, and a host of other topics.

Even if there is an expert on labor or environmental issues on the board, there is a potential weakness in relying on an individual board member to be solely responsible for managing this process. Although boards routinely delegate authority to committees or subgroups of the board, there is additional risk from having a single individual board member be the only person on the board with the information, expertise, and authority to handle the management of an important stakeholder relationship.

In contrast, a BSP would not have these problems. With a larger stable of employees and experts at its disposal, the BSP is likely to have an expert or teams in every area where improved stakeholder relationships may be needed. After all, firms may not be able to predict these in advance, and the needs may vary over time. Labor might be a key constituency at one point in the company's life, while at another time it might be the government, the local community, the environment, and so on and so on. If it is valuable for shareholders to have the ability to access to, communicate with, and credibly engage with these various communities over time, the BSP will have incentives to build up capabilities to do so. While boards today might buy these services in the market, the stakeholder theory assumes there is something valuable about having the people on the board that can do so directly. On these terms, the BSP would be superior.

Team Production Theory

Team production theory was introduced in the legal literature by Margaret Blair and Lynn Stout. They contend that directors act not as hierarchs charged with serving shareholder interests, but as referees – "mediating hierarchs," to use their term – charged with serving the totality of interests of in a corporate entity. In turn, those interests are defined as the "joint welfare function" of all stakeholders who make firm-specific investments.[14] While we are skeptical of the merits of the team production model both as a descriptive and normative matter,[15] in this context it suffices to point out that a BSP would be superior to a board comprised of autonomous individuals at mediating the competing interests of corporate stakeholders. Although multi-member panels are some-times used as mediators, mediation "is predominantly a one-person show. For the most part, a single mediator facilitates negotiations between parties."[16] The BSP speaks with one voice, while the traditional board speaks with many. And, insofar as the board as an entity today is informed by the various perspectives of the individuals that comprise the board, this would be true, or could be true, of the BSP as well.

STEWARDSHIP THEORY

Stewardship theory is premised on a benign view of human nature in which directors seek not wealth or power but rather satisfaction from a job well done. Directors enjoy dealing with intellectually challenging tasks. They seek recog-nition and admiration for having done a good job, exercising authority responsibly, and being "good stewards of corporate assets."[17] Our guess is that this theory describes the motivations and behaviors of all directors some of the time and some directors all of the time, but for most directors it is just one of many competing and conflicting motivations. Nevertheless, it is a theory that is normatively attractive to many, and therefore is an aspiration that may be valuable to assert for a particular firm or board.

Insofar as the theory is true as a descriptive matter or desirable as a norma-tive matter, there is no reason why the members of the BSP team working for a client would not have similar motivations to serve the client capably. Consultancies, accounting firms, and law firms use similar high-minded ideals to describe what they do and to motivate their employees to do good work. For instance, McKinsey & Company, a leading strategy consultancy, describes its work as "serving its clients" and "cultivating client relationships," rather than "pitching" or "selling." Consultants are chosen for their love of solving intellectual problems, not on their desire to maximize any particular bottom line. And the ethos and culture of stewardship (of client assets) is reinforced on a daily basis through firm lore, training, and language. Presumably, McKinsey does this because it is valuable for its work and its brand in serving its clients on strategy or other projects. We see no reason why this would be any different if McKinsey or any other firm were providing board services.

In fact, given the mythology built up over the generations about the sanctity of the board and the importance of board members acting like Platonic guardians of corporate assets, we would expect that the values of selfless service inherent in the stewardship theory would be emphasized and reinforced even more at a BSP than at a consulting firm or accounting firm. After all, the first BSPs will find themselves competing with incumbent boards for the govern-ance work, and they will have to be able to credibly convey their integrity and stewardship value (if shareholders do indeed value it) to shareholders in order to win the election.

AGENCY THEORY

Agency theory makes a 180-degree swing in the assumptions about human nature and motivations from those underlying stewardship theory. It is pre-mised on a model of humans as boundedly rational actors seeking to maximize their own wellbeing.[18] As one of us has observed elsewhere:

> Neoclassical rational choice theory assumes that individuals act so as to maximize their expected utility. Typically, it acknowledges no cognitive limits on their power so to do. New Institutional Economics accepts that economic actors seek to maximize utility, but takes into account limits on cognition. Those limits, in turn, are posited to result in decisions that often fail to maximize utility. Hence, the phrase "bounded rationality," which posits decision makers who are subject to inherent limits on their ability to gather and process information. To varying degrees, all humans have inher-ently limited memories, computational skills, and other mental tools.[19]

In that work, the model of boundedly rational actors was deployed to try to explain the behavior of judges, and it has become the standard tool in that world, as it has in many others. The model has become the basic theoretical frame for corporate governance scholarship in the legal literature[20] and is "regarded as the Bible of corporate governance" by most management theorists.[21]

In the corporate setting, agency cost economics focus on the principal-agent problem created by the separation of ownership and control characteristic of public – and even many large privately owned – corporations. The necessity for locating control in a single office within the firm rather than in the shareholders' hands inevitably arises out of the need for efficient, rapid, high quality decision making. Corporations exemplify the governance mode Nobel laureate economist Kenneth Arrow referred to as "authority," which he contrasted to "consensus." The latter is characteristic of organizations in which each member of the organization has comparable information and interests. Under such conditions, assuming the firm's structure creates no serious collective action problems, the organization's members can all participate in the decision-making process at low cost. In contrast, where an organization's members have differing interests and asymmetric information, and the organization is large or complex enough for participatory democracy to be plagued by collective action issues, efficient decision-making requires a central agency to which all relevant information is transmitted and which is empowered to make decisions binding on the whole organization.[22]

The corporation is a paradigmatic example of such an organization. Imagine trying to find a space big enough for several hundred thousand shareholders, with differing interests and knowledge, to come together for decision-making sessions. It simply is not practicable. Of course, the problem is far thornier. With stocks trading hands every few minutes and shareholders from around the world moving in and out at random, even identifying the people to invite into the consensus process would be impossible. Recognizing the need for corporations to separate ownership and control, so as to assign the bulk of decision-making to a smaller, more cohesive body, corporate law created the board of directors.

While separating ownership and control was thus essential for the corporate form to succeed, doing so produced – in the words of New Deal era corporate governance scholars Adolf Berle and Gardiner Means – "a condition where the interests of owner and of ultimate manager may, and often do, diverge and where many of the checks which formerly operated to limit the use of power disappear."[23] Economists Michael Jensen and William Meckling later formalized this concern by developing the concept of agency costs.[i]

---

[i] Jensen and Meckling defined agency costs as the sum of the monitoring and bonding costs incurred to prevent shirking by agents, plus any residual loss from undeterred shirking. Michael C. Jensen & William H. Meckling, Theory of the Firm: Managerial Behavior, Agency Costs, and Ownership Structure, 3 *J. Fin. Econ.* 305 (1976). In turn, shirking is defined to include any action by a member of a production team that diverges from the interests of the team as a whole. As such, shirking includes not only culpable cheating, but also negligence, oversight, incapacity, and even honest mistakes. In other words, shirking is simply the inevitable consequence of bounded rationality and opportunism within agency relationships.

As we have seen, of course, as corporations evolved and become more complex, the board's role morphed from that of central decision-making agency to monitor of the management to whom decision-making had been delegated. Agency theory posits that monitoring is essential because managers have powerful incentives to shirk.

As presently constituted, boards of directors struggle to deal with the principal-agent problem. As we have seen, boards often fail to act as effective monitors of management.

Part of the problem, of course, is the time constraints under which individual directors currently function. A large organization providing multimember teams to carry out the BSP function inevitably will be able to devote more person-hours to gathering and processing information and exercising evaluative judgment on the basis of that information than can an individual, part-time director. Full-time directors would, by definition, be able to devote more time than part-time ones, and the BSP model provides a mechanism to create professional directors with no other employment. In addition, a BSP would allow professionals to leverage support staff to increase the time spent on any matter, all else being equal. Professional services firms in other areas, like accounting, law, and consulting, deploy pyramidal structures with multiple levels of full-time professionals, allowing them to spend considerably more time on a given project than if a single, part-time individual were working on the same project alone. In addition, because of the economies of scale achievable by a BSP, it can do so at a lower cost per person-hour.

Another part of the problem is the information asymmetry between management and the board. As just noted, a BSP will be able to devote more time – and, of course, other resources – to gathering information and at lower cost. In addition, a single BSP wielding the full powers of the board may be in a better position to demand forthrightness by the top management team than would a

---

A simple example of the agency cost problem is provided by the bail upon which alleged criminals are released from jail while they await trial. The defendant promises to appear for trial. But that promise is not very credible: The defendant will be tempted to flee the country. The court could keep track of the defendant – monitor him – by keeping him in jail or perhaps by means of some electronic device permanently attached to the defendant's person. Yet, such monitoring efforts are not free – indeed, keeping someone in jail is quite expensive (food, guards, building the jail, etc.). Alternatively, the defendant could give his promise credibility by bonding it, which is exactly what bail does. The defendant puts up a sum of money that he will forfeit if he fails to appear for trial. (Notice that the common use of bail bonds and the employment of bounty hunters to track fugitives further enhances the credibility of bail as a deterrent against flight.) Of course, despite these precautions, some defendants will escape jail and/or jump bail. Hence, there will always be some residual loss in the form of defendants who escape punishment.

single, lone-wolf director acting alone. Even a subgroup of individual directors acting in concert would have less bargaining power vis-à-vis top management than a BSP acting as the entire board. Although the information asymmetry between a top management team and the BSP could never be fully eliminated, just as there are persistent information asymmetries between top management and the firm's outside lawyers and accountants,[24] we would expect BSPs to have better access to information than do individual directors. Not only is the BSP likely to have better information about the firm it is serving, but it will also have much more information about the particular questions it is considering, whether they be about compensation, strategy, finance, or other areas. As we shall see, moreover, BSPs will enable much greater general knowledge and information to be brought to bear on a firm's decisions and at much lower cost.

Perhaps the biggest part of the problem, however, is that board members themselves are agents (in the economic sense, if not the legal sense of the word) with incentives to shirk. A BSP solves this problem by having internal mechanisms that incentivize team members to be effective monitors of management.

Consider, for instance, a CEO manipulating accounting returns in an attempt to mislead shareholders and other stakeholders. The behavior serves the interests of the CEO, who's pay and job may depend on the stock price, but not shareholders who buy at inflated prices. A board wanting to discover and deter any manipulation will have to collect information about the true financial returns of the firm, to interpret the real returns and compare them to the reported returns, and to develop an approach to remedying the situation and putting in place systems to deter future violations. This will require attention, hard work, expertise, and state-of-the-art technologies. While some of this can be brought to bear by directors, either directly or by purchasing it from outsiders, such as consultants of various kinds, BSPs may be able to do the work at lower costs. If there is a difficult accounting issue, the BSP can easily bring its accounting experts onto staff to look at the problem and suggest a plan of action. This may be at a lower cost than having to hire an accounting firm or expert to do the same work.

As noted earlier, this is the argument Ronald Coase made about firms generally. We see individuals cooperating through firms, as opposed to through contracts in a market, where the returns to adding individuals or functions to the firm exceed the costs. This applies in the case of BSPs engaged in monitoring functions. If it is cheaper or more efficient for an incremental monitoring function (watching, collecting information, processing information, developing a remediation plan, installing systems to detect wrongdoing, etc.) to be done through command rather than through a negotiated contract, then that function should be brought inside of the firm providing the monitoring. In the case of directors, the size of the firm is a single person – all additional functions beyond that of a single director are done through contract. It is difficult to believe that this is the optimal firm size for monitoring.

Associating with other professionals in a multimember firm, for example, allows individuals to develop and invest in specialized knowledge and expertise. Service professionals are routinely organized as business associations comprising managers, who have decision-making authority and supervise other professionals, who provide support services. The typical law firm or consultancy fits this model. The pyramidal structure of such firms allows professionals to become experts in particular areas, and then to be deployed as needed as part of a team. Consider a typical management consulting firm. These firms deploy experts with particular skills or knowledge of different industries or fields, technical experts in certain areas (for example, econometrics, finance, and so forth), lawyers, accountants, scientists, psychologists, and countless other professionals, as well as generalist consultants. Just as directors currently are required by law to buy all of their support services, either from the company they serve or from the market, one could imagine consultants, lawyers, or accountants being required to do so as well. But the Coasean equilibrium for these professional services firms is larger than for one-person firms, and we expect the same is true of directors.

To see how this might translate into the market for BSPs, imagine a BSP vertically integrating with some or all of the experts that currently provide board members with information and advice. In the pure BSP model, one or more of the BSP's senior managers act as a liaison between the BSP and client, just as a lead law firm or accounting partner often acts as the primary liaison between such firms and their clients. Alternatively, the individuals currently serving the client as directors could be hired by the BSP and thereafter continue functioning as the client's board. In either case, the BSP would be a large firm that vertically integrates the BSP function with all board advisory services, except those provided by lawyers and accountants, compensation consultants, management consultants, and others serving in support roles. The economies of scale and scope described earlier would allow the partners in this model to have board services as their full-time occupation.[i] The result would

---

[i]   Management consultants, for instance, use their large firm size to invest heavily in training consultants, to produce knowledge and expertise, to allow specialization, and to permit deployment of talent at the optimal point across time and space. For an account of how the industry works through the lens of one of its most successful firms, see Duff McDonald, *The Firm: The Story of McKinsey and Its Secret Influence on American Business* (2013). These firms

likely be not only an improvement in the quality and incentives of directors (or those now serving in that role) but also the creation of a new profession, that of professional director. Professions, as such, are thought to be valuable because they develop codes of conduct and engage in self-regulation to encourage profession-specific reputation.[ii]

SUMMARY

In this chapter, we have examined in some detail the various roles that boards play in modern American corporations. These include monitoring management, helping make good business decisions, and providing services to the company, be it access to capital, information, or otherwise. A quick history of the roles played by boards shows that different roles have been paramount at different times, and that boards have adapted their role to the circumstances of the era to be maximally valuable to their companies. Today, unquestionably this is to provide monitoring of corporate management.

The BSP approach has the potential to do no harm to the supply and efficiency of these roles, at a minimum, and, we believe, offer significant opportunities for improving existing functions and providing new ones at the same costs as at present. The efficiencies inherent in the BSP model should allow boards to be better monitors, as well as offering new opportunities for providing additional managerial support, while still providing (and even expanding) the relevant service

have hundreds if not thousands of professionals, some of whom provide front-line services, but many of whom provide those employees on the front line with research, expertise, support services, technology, and so on. Having front-line professionals under the same corporate umbrella as these ancillary functions allows services to be provided at lower cost because of the ability to allocate them across a wider asset base. This allows specialization and cost savings from shared services.

[ii] Our proposal for BSPs is thus a potential mechanism for achieving Ronald Gilson and Reinier Kraakman's dream of professional directors. In *Reinventing the Outside Director: An Agenda for Institutional Investors*, they proposed creating a class of professional directors who would serve on a portfolio of boards as their full-time job. Ronald J. Gilson & Reinier Kraakman, Reinventing the Outside Director: An Agenda for Institutional Investors, 43 *Stan. L. Rev.* 863 (1991). These professionals would know their portfolio companies better because they would be able to devote more time to following those companies, and they would be more dependent on institutional shareholders for their position. They recommended the use of a central clearinghouse to take care of the logistics of helping institutional shareholders select professional directors to serve on their companies' boards. The Gilson and Kraakman proposal went nowhere, perhaps because the idea of turning over the governance of a company to a clearinghouse was a step too far for corporate managers. Our proposal for BSPs is a more modest step, in that it could achieve the same goal but within the current power structure of firms. Yet we can imagine this simple change leading to a new profession, just as envisioned by Gilson and Kraakman.

networks. Simply put, the BSP approach allows different types of decision making and governance to be tailored to a particular company's needs, offering the possibility that one approach (say, a team of equals) could be used to provide one type of board service, while another approach (say, a unitary overseer) could be used to provide another type.

Notes

1. Peter Drucker, The Bored Board, *Wharton Mag.*, Fall 1976, at 19.
2. Philip Stiles & Bernard Taylor, *Boards at Work: How Directors View Their Roles and Responsibilities* 19 (2001).
3. William W. Bratton, Jr., The New Economic Theory of the Firm: Critical Perspectives from History, 41 *Stan. L. Rev.* 1471, 1480 (1989).
4. John Danley, Beyond Managerialism: After the Death of the Corporate Statesperson, 1988 *Bus. Ethics* 21.
5. Xavier Baeten et al., Beyond Agency Theory: A Three-Paradigm Approach to Executive Compensation, 10 *IUP J. Corp. Gov.* 7, 13 (2011).
6. Stiles & Taylor, *Boards at Work*, at 17–18.
7. Stiles & Taylor, *Boards at Work*, at 16.
8. Sanjai Bhagat & Bernard Black, The Non-Correlation between Board Independence and Long-Term Firm Performance, 27 *J. Corp. L.* 231 (2002) (finding a negative relationship between increasing board size and various performance measures); Mark J. Roe, German Codetermination and German Securities Markets, 1998 *Colum. Bus. L. Rev.* 167, 170 (1998) ("American studies find that smaller boards are more effective than big ones … "); David Yermack, Higher Market Valuation of Companies with a Small Board of Directors, 40 *J. Fin. Econ.* 185, 189 (1996) (reporting that increasing board size negatively impacts firm performance).
9. See, e.g. Frederick D. Lipman & L. Keith Lipman, *Corporate Governance Best Practices: Strategies for Public, Private, and Not-for-Profit Organizations* 14 (2006); see also Corporate Director's Guidebook Third Edition, 56 *Bus. Law.* 1571, 1592 (2001) ("The emerging consensus is that, except perhaps in the very largest and most complex corporations, smaller boards (those with nine or fewer members) function more effectively than larger boards.").
10. Humphry Hung, *Typology*, at 101, 106.
11. For good summaries of the corporate social responsibility debate, see John Hendry, Missing the Target: Normative Stakeholder Theory and the Corporate Governance Debate, 11 *Bus. Ethics* 159 (2001) (focusing on the management literature); Andy Lockett, Jeremy Moon & Wayne Visser, Corporate Social Responsibility in Management Research: Focus, Nature, Salience and Sources of Influence, 43 *J. Mgmt. Stud.* 115

(2006) (same); C. A. Harwell Wells, The Cycles of Corporate Social Responsibility: An Historical Retrospective for the Twenty-First Century, 51 *U. Kan. L. Rev.* 77 (2002) (focusing on the legal literature). For a useful collection of essays focusing on corporate social responsibility from the perspective of business ethics, see *Corporate Social Responsibility: A Research Handbook* (Kathryn Haynes et al., eds., 2013).

12. Korn/Ferry Int'l, *27th Annual Board of Directors Study* 33–34 (2000).
13. For overviews of the law of corporate social responsibility, see Reuven S. Avi-Yonah, The Cyclical Transformations of the Corporate Form: A Historical Perspective on Corporate Social Responsibility, 30 *Del. J. Corp. L.* 767 (2005); Jonathan R. Macey, Corporate Social Responsibility: A Law & Economics Perspective, 17 *Chap. L. Rev.* 331 (2014); David Millon, Two Models of Corporate Social Responsibility, 46 *Wake Forest L. Rev.* 523 (2011).
14. See, e.g. Margaret M. Blair & Lynn A. Stout, A Team Production Theory of Corporate Law, 85 *Va. L. Rev.* 247 (1999); Margaret M. Blair & Lynn A. Stout, Team Production in Business Organizations: An Introduction, 24 *J. Corp. L.* 743 (1999).
15. See Stephen M. Bainbridge, Director Primacy: The Means and Ends of Corporate Governance, 97 *Nw. U. L. Rev.* 547, 592–605 (2003) (criticizing the team production model on both normative and descriptive grounds).
16. Lee A. Rosengard, Learning from Law Firms: Using Co-Mediation to Train New Mediators, *Disp. Resol. J.*, May–July 2004, at 16, 17.
17. Stiles & Taylor, *Boards at Work*, at 16.
18. The term "bounded rationality" was coined by Herbert Simon. See Herbert A. Simon, Rational Choice in the Structure of the Environment, in *Models of Man* 261, 271 (1957).
19. Stephen M. Bainbridge & G. Mitu Gulati, How Do Judges Maximize? (The Same Way Everybody Else Does–Boundedly): Rules of Thumb in Securities Fraud Opinions, 51 *Emory L.J.* 83, 100–101 (2002).
20. Kent Greenfield, The Place of Workers in Corporate Law, 39 *B.C.L. Rev.* 283, 295 (1998) (describing the principal-agent problem as "the fundamental concern of corporate law").
21. Morten Huse, *Boards, Governance and Value Creation: The Human Side of Corporate Governance* 45 (2007).
22. Kenneth J. Arrow, *The Limits of Organization* 68–70 (1974).
23. Adolf A. Berle & Gardiner C. Means, *The Modern Corporation and Private Property* 6 (1932).
24. Cf. Stephen M. Bainbridge, Corporate Lawyers as Gatekeepers, *UCLA J. Scholarly Persp.*, Fall 2012, at 5, 13 ("[I]n many of the recent corporate scandals, the misconduct was committed by a small group of senior managers who took considerable pains to conceal their actions from outside advisors, such as legal counsel.").

7

Incentivizing the BSP

In this chapter, we delve a bit deeper into the details of how BSPs might work. We note at the outset that we believe the optimal approach to operating and managing a BSP will be learned only over time and through experimentation in the market. Therefore, we focus in this chapter not on prescription or predicting what will work, but on the various tradeoffs and considerations when it comes to trying to get the best out of a BSP.

We consider a variety of ways in which the BSP model could provide improved incentives that would help ameliorate some of the dysfunctions of the current board model. Directors, like everyone else, are motivated by compensation, the threat of liability, reputation, and various other competitive forces in the markets in which they operate. We consider each of these in turn.

Although directors are well paid for the work they do, their monetary incentives to work hard and do well are fairly limited since they capture so little of any gains and suffer so little of any losses from the decisions they make. In light of this fact, reputation plays an important role in the incentive calculus. But, as discussed previously, the reputational gains and losses are also highly attenuated from performance. This creates the possibility of large welfare gains from improved incentives for directors.

In addition, the move to BSPs would, we argue, increase judicial oversight through lowering the costs of holding boards to account for wrongdoing. In short, courts are more likely to enforce fiduciary duties against a BSP than against individual human directors. More generally, we will argue that BSPs' exposure to market forces will enhance the incentives for BSPs to engage in good work.

COMPENSATION INCENTIVES

Large, publicly held corporations generally pay directors a few hundred thousand dollars annually for their work and require directors to hold a fairly trivial amount of the corporation's stock. Microsoft is typical of very large, publicly held corporations. In 2011, Microsoft had a ten-member board, and each director was paid $100,000 in cash and granted stock worth $150,000. This mix of cash and stock is designed to give board members a stake in the outcome of their decisions, while compensating them for the time they spend preparing for and in board meetings. Although the stockholding requirement undoubtedly gives board members some incentives to care about firm value, the amounts are routinely so small that critics believe they do little to optimally align shareholder and board incentives.[1]

Under the BSP approach, compensation may look much as it does today or could be quite different. For instance, if a BSP assigns a number of individuals to serve as permanent board members, the firm might simply replicate the current pay structure of the underlying client company, paying a fixed salary (equal to the company's current annual retainer) and requiring individual employees of the BSP to hold equity in the client, as in the Microsoft example. If instead the BSP deployed a variety of professionals to a particular client depending on the situational needs, then one might expect the stock in the client to be held at the BSP level, and the payment to board members to be based on an algorithm tied to individual performance as a director for one or more firms. If the BSP and client opted for the full BSP model, with one or two liaison managers interfacing between client and BSP and the BSP itself serving as the board, we would expect compensation structures within such BSPs to resemble those of other consultancies.[i]

But there are some possibilities for innovation that could improve the incentives of board services providers. One option would be for the BSP to take a much larger stake in the client company. A greater ownership stake by the board has the potential to improve incentive alignment, but there are two barriers to this within the current board structure. The first is that giving boards large upside stakes with limited downside risks skews decision making in

---

[i] For instance, professional services firms, like consultancies or restructuring firms, typically pay executives two components: a "salary" based on work performed, and a "bonus" tied to the overall profitability of the firm. The former is based on work done on specific projects, successful pitches, and any management or supervisory work; the latter is based on a share of the residual based on overall value to the firm. For lower-level employees, a mix of salary, performance-based incentives, stock ownership, and other forms of compensation is used depending on the firm and the situation.

a socially undesirable fashion. The potential solution to this is discussed in this chapter. The second is that individual, part-time board members are not well positioned to bear this kind of risk, and their work does not routinely justify such large stakes. Hiring a BSP could help address these concerns. Because of risk pooling, greater reputational stakes, greater efficiency, and so on, a BSP could hold a much larger stake in its client than the sum of the stakes held by individual board members.

Indeed, we expect that as the market evolves and the initial design and conflict issues are resolved, there will be movement in the direction of giving BSPs greater stakes in the residual corporate claims. One possibility would be for companies to hold an auction for board services on a periodic basis (for example, annually or biennially), in which rival BSPs would compete to win the work. In an auction model, the company looking to hire a BSP would write a board services contract specifying the financial and other terms of the deal. For instance, the company might offer the winner of the auction a portion of the residual claim on the firm's assets, such as a guaranteed dividend or number of shares. BSPs would then submit bids for the minimum amount of dividend or shares they would take in order to perform the work. This would have the dual virtues of giving BSPs greater incentives to perform by making them hold residual claims on firm value and making BSPs compete in a transparent way for the board role.

Another potential change to the compensation structure was alluded to in the discussion of vertical integration of the board services industry. Firms pay a lot more for board services than simply the cash and stock issued to directors. Firms buy directors' insurance, self-insure for certain claims against directors, and, as noted previously, hire various consultants, accountants, lawyers, and other experts to assist the board in fulfilling its duties. Consider again the case of Microsoft. For a company of Microsoft's size and industry, directors' and officers' (D&O) insurance costs about $4 million, or about $400,000 per director. In addition, Microsoft's corporate charter, like that of most firms, contains a provision indemnifying directors against breaches of the duty of care. This self-insurance is difficult to quantify, but is likely a significant cost as well. Additionally, boards routinely hire experts of various kinds, including management and compensation consultants, law firms, and other service providers. While there are no good estimates of these costs, there is reason to believe they are in the range of several million dollars per firm per year. All told, for example, Microsoft pays at least $2.5 million for board services, plus a minimum of several million more for insurance and other services, making the total cost of director services nearly $10 million per year. If Microsoft's costs are typical, this means the director services market – for just the Fortune 500 firms – is a $3- to $4-billion-per-year industry. Costs for smaller firms are probably lower, but given that there are about 15,000 publicly traded firms in the United States, if the average publicly traded firm has just $1 to $2 million in direct and indirect director costs, there is the potential for a $15- to $30-billion-per-year BSP industry.

That this huge industry is delivered entirely through the actions of a group of part-time, sole proprietors is surprising. As noted earlier, there are likely significant gains to be had from industry consolidation across the supply chain. This could mean that BSPs would house some combination of decision-making, insurance, and support in one corporate body. In terms of compensation, the payment for board services could reflect this combination of services, with BSPs bidding on multi-million-dollar contracts. There are a few potential positive effects of this. First, the significant size of these payments would likely be sufficient to justify the creation of BSPs and to generate competition among them for a given board services contract. The size of those fees would also help create a vibrant market for corporate governance by raising the stakes of taking over the board. Indeed, the introduction of potentially more efficient competitors in this space might have the effect of driving down board costs, while holding constant or improving corporate governance. Second, this model would increase the transparency of board costs for shareholders, who currently do not have good information on the total costs of boards.

LIABILITY-BASED INCENTIVES

We think the use of BSPs may also have salutary effects on the quality of corporate governance through improved judicial supervision of board activities. Courts may be more willing to hold BSPs liable than individual directors, and this could help make fiduciary duties more robust. The logic is straightforward. As noted earlier, directors are independent amateurs without deep pockets, but face enormous potential liability for the decisions they make. For instance, the sloppy approval of a merger could subject directors, including individual directors, to multimillion-dollar liability, not to mention the significant risk to their personal reputations. Courts seem reluctant to impose liability on directors, perhaps increasingly so in recent years.[2] This could be because of institutional competency concerns, worries about hindsight bias, the potential chilling effect on risk-taking, the reluctance to hold individuals (some of whom are not extremely rich) liable for potentially huge damage awards, and the potential impact of increased liability on the supply of individuals willing to provide director services. Whatever the reasons, if directors form associations to share risk, this reduces the potential negative cost on individuals, and thereby may increase the willingness of courts to impose liability.

To see the point, consider the impact that the availability of D&O insurance has on judicial enforcement of board duties. In the absence of any insurance, courts would be significantly less likely to find individual board members liable for breaches of their fiduciary duties. In this way, third-party insurance can, at least in theory, be a mechanism for enhancing compliance with law. Sharing risk (in this case through insurance contracts) reduces the costs of liability for individual directors, and therefore may make a finding of liability more likely, all else being equal. The downside of insurance – the moral hazard or shirking problem – can be reduced through monitoring (both ex ante and ex post) and some risk-bearing, in the form of deductibles or the like.

Self-insurance in the form of organizational choice is simply an extension of this idea to areas of liability beyond those currently covered by contractual insurance. Directors who are able to pool their risk through a business form we call the BSP can reduce their risk. The ability to share, and thus reduce, risk is one of the most powerful reasons for forming a business association. A single individual running a business faces all of the risk if the business fails or generates liabilities that exceed its assets. If all businesses were required by statute to be run by an individual acting as a sole proprietor, risk alone would work a serious impediment to the provision of all sorts of products and services. By forming a business association in which risk is shared among various owners, the business can take on more risk than could or would a sole proprietor. This is because some individuals will have greater risk tolerances than others, and these tolerances may not line up with other attributes that can be put to use by a firm.

The additional liability would be doing work primarily in cases in which potential damages exceed liability coverage, since this is the extensive margin where courts are most likely to feel whatever pressure they feel to take it easy on misbehaving directors. The existence of insurance for breaches of certain fiduciary duties already reduces the downside for directors, and therefore makes judicial supervision more robust than it would likely be in the absence of insurance. The additional risk reduction from operating as a business association would therefore act mostly in those cases in which the expected liability exceeds the insurance coverage. This could be either for large damage awards or for certain actions usually not covered by insurance, such as breaches of the duty of loyalty.

The risk sharing of organizational choice may also do some work in cases in which the conduct is completely covered by insurance. There is reason to believe that the D&O insurance market does not work optimally,[3] and adding self-insurance or replacing the D&O model with self-insurance could help make corporate liability more effective. While one would expect insurance costs to discipline firms, it is not obvious this translates readily into the market for director talent, since liability is so rare that it is not often linked with necessarily bad behavior, and, in any event, the labor market for directors is thought to be so dysfunctional. Directors do not bear the liability personally, except in the rarest and most extreme circumstances, and there is some evidence that directors' reputations, which we expect to provide most of the discipline, are not highly correlated with past performance. There is also some evidence that insurance prices do not obviously respond to incidents of director liability. Bringing the insurance function within the firm providing the service (either through vertical integration of the D&O function or simply through risk-pooling inherent in providing services through firms) may improve the pricing of risk and the judicial treatment of defendants.

Not only might the BSP model make courts less reluctant to impose fiduciary duties on boards, but the corporate model for boards is also likely to generate more fiduciary duty litigation. Every allegation of serious board misconduct is likely to result in multiple suits: one by the company against the BSP and one by the shareholders of the BSP against the directors of that firm. The addition of the second type of suit could work as an additional deterrent to board misconduct, malfeasance, and gross negligence. Of course, if one believes that the current amount of litigation is optimal (or even excessive) because directors face the perfect incentives to behave well, then additional liability may add costs in excess of the benefits.

REPUTATIONAL INCENTIVES

Another benefit of our model is that it will *increase* the reputational stakes of every board decision, meaning more incentive for good work, all else being equal. Reputation is already an important element of the corporate governance regime. Harnessing the reputation of directors to prevent cheating and shirking is a vital element of effective corporate governance. Lawsuits, whether settled or reduced to judgment, alleging disloyalty or insufficient care by directors can harm directors' reputations. This can cost directors their position on the board in question or seats on other boards, either now or in the future. Since directorships are lucrative given the little work involved, and one done well usually leads to another, a director's reputation could be worth several hundred thousand dollars per year or more. In addition, lawsuits may result in more general losses to directors' reputations in their other endeavors, be they in business, law, academia, politics, or other fields. Modern corporate boards often have directors who have made large investments in their reputations, and these directors can be expected to act in ways to minimize the col-lateral damage from misbehaving as a director. For instance, the Enron board famously included the former dean of the Stanford Graduate School of Business, three CEOs of other companies, political luminaries from the United Kingdom, and the former head of the M. D. Anderson Cancer Center. These are important positions that these directors worked very hard to achieve, which adds to the reputational hit for director wrongdoing.

Some scholars believe reputation is the most important constraint on director behavior and that it alone can induce efficient board conduct.[4] Others, pointing to failures by boards filled with individuals with seemingly valuable reputations, note that the evidence suggests reputation is not doing all the work necessary to ensure good governance.[5] Of course, the existence of some corporate failures does not mean directors are engaging in suboptimal care levels or that reputation is not sufficient; the optimal level of governance failure is not obviously zero.

But we need not resolve this debate to demonstrate the value of BSPs. Reputation and legal sanctions are complementary mechanisms for policing corporate decision making, and as noted previously, there is reason to believe legal sanctions are likely ineffective at inducing optimal actions by directors. The business judgment rule may be the optimal rule, but it surely lets some sloppy and self-serving transactions happen without scrutiny. Accordingly, the more work that reputational sanctions can do, the less work that law needs to do or the less we need to worry about judicial enforcement of director duties. From the current baseline of whatever work reputation is doing, greater reputational stakes can only improve governance, especially since they can relieve pressure on courts to police corporate decisions.

In theory, the size of reputation, and therefore the work done by reputa-tional assets in disciplining behavior, is correlated with the number of indivi-duals whose reputations are influenced by a particular decision. This is because for associations providing services, "the reputation of the entire firm is at stake whenever a single [service] is sold."[6] If an individual makes a decision, then only the individual's reputation is at stake; if a firm of one hundred individuals makes the same decision, the reputation of the entire firm is at stake. If each of the individuals has the same amount of reputation, the stakes are one hundred times greater in the case of a firm making the decision. Of course, the full reputation of each person in a large organization may not be reduced in the event of a failure, but the net impact of reputational losses is likely increasing with the number of individuals comprising the decision-making entity. Therefore, a significant advantage of creating large business associations to provide services is that they can generate greater reputational assets than the sum of the individual reputations at stake for a given transaction.

The greater reputation at stake for a given transaction means higher-quality services. Reputation is a way of bonding the quality of a product or service, and, for a given level of legal scrutiny, the greater the firm's reputation, the more likely the product or service will be of high quality. The bonding theory of reputation holds that "[t]he more [services] sold, all things equal, the more valuable is a reputation for high quality, and thus the stronger is the reputational bond to provide high quality."[7] Therefore, as a matter of reputation theory, there is reason to believe BSPs will be able to provide higher-quality services than individual board members acting as a group of sole proprietors. Associations of individuals can better commit to quality than individuals acting alone or as a loosely affiliated group.

Our friend, the late corporate and partnership scholar Larry Ribstein, applied this bonding argument to the law firm setting,[8] which is closely analogous to the board services model we propose. Ribstein argued that there was a strong relationship between reputation and the size of a professional services firm: the larger the firm, the greater the cost of reputational losses, and therefore the stronger commitment to quality. Applying the insight of Ronald Coase, Ribstein noted, however, that increasing size also adds organizational costs. Accordingly, professional services firms will increase the number of professionals until the point at which the marginal cost of monitoring an additional professional for quality equals the reputational gain from adding the professional. It is highly unlikely that this equilibrium point is a single professional, as state corporation statutes require for the provision of board services.

Edward Iacobucci extended Ribstein's work, pointing out some additional downsides of size. Although Iacobucci started from the position that business associations "are better able to commit to providing high quality for reputational reasons than sole proprietors,"[9] he noted that size has an additional cost beyond monitoring – large size "increases the short-run profits from sacrificing reputation and providing low-quality service" in an individual case.[10] For large firms, the negative effects from cheating fall on a per-service basis as the size of the firm grows. In addition, the transparency of cheating is reduced across a very large firm, as clients in one part of the world may not learn about poor performance in another part of the world, as they would for much smaller firms. Iacobucci resolved this tradeoff by providing conditions in which the reputational gains from scale outweigh the potential for reputational opportunism. For instance, the long-term gains are greater than the short-term opportunism where services are provided nonsimultaneously, such that each sale risks the reputation of the entire firm, but the gains from cheating are limited to a single product or service. Giving partners in the association an equal stake in the outcome also ameliorates the potential risk of short-termism. Applying this model to professional services firms, in his case law firms, Iacobucci concluded: "To the extent that the firm adopts profit sharing, a partner's incentives to provide low quality are weaker than a sole proprietor's. This in turn makes a larger firm, all things equal, better able to commit to maintaining a reputation for high-quality legal service."[11]

The conclusion that size leads to higher quality because of investments in reputation is supported by empirical evidence in the case of law firms. Profits per partner, a standard measure of law firm quality, are generally higher for larger law firms. Larger law firms also perform better along other metrics of quality. For instance, Marc Galanter and William Henderson found that ethical violations are more common for sole proprietors and small firms than for larger law firms.[12] Other work by Henderson found more equal sharing of profits by more prestigious law firms,[13] which is consistent with Iacobucci's claim about profit sharing being an important check on opportunism. As Iacobucci concluded, all of these "findings are consistent with larger law firms having better reputations, and thus consistent with the theory" about reputation increasing with firm size, but subject to limits that can be reduced through incentive structures.[14]

The theory of reputations, subject to the caveats provided by Ribstein and Iacobucci, is as applicable to the provision of board services as it is to the provision of legal, accounting, or consulting services. One can easily imagine a BSP of similar size to the large professional services firms in these other industries. As noted previously, the director services industry may consist of as many as 15,000 firms spending tens of billions of dollars per year on hiring, insuring, and otherwise supporting directors. If even 10 percent of those firms switched to a BSP, one could imagine an industry arising with numerous large BSPs, each employing hundreds or thousands of professionals serving as corporate decision-makers and support staff. This is not even considering the other industries that are related to director services or provide services to directors that could easily be integrated into a larger BSP. For instance, companies or their boards routinely hire consultants or experts in tax, compliance, internal controls, auditing, strategy, and other areas. Many of these are billion-dollar industries, and BSPs could theoretically provide some or all of these services, either directly or indirectly. In short, the potential for the creation of large, multibillion-dollar firms with significant reputational assets is not far-fetched. BSPs with numerous professionals, serving as directors, researchers, experts of various kinds, and so forth, would have a large reputation at stake in each transaction, and this would lead to higher-quality services, all else being equal.[i]

EXPOSURE TO MARKET FORCES

Effective corporate governance depends on ensuring directors are accountable for corporate decisions. This is done through several mechanisms, some internal and some external to the company. Businesses use incentive contracts and the power to reappoint directors, as well as reputational sanctions and legal liability.

A related benefit of the BSP model is that BSPs would be more accountable than the group of individuals currently providing board services; indeed, we believe that the accountability of the whole would be greater than the sum of the liabilities of the parts. We have already identified a variety of ways in which the BSP model would likely increase accountability: reducing the impact of personal liability through risk pooling, and thus increasing the robustness of fiduciary duties; providing a second-order accountability regime through the threat of suits by two distinct sets of corporate owners (both the shareholders of the client firm allegedly mistreated by the BSP and the shareholders of the BSP); and increasing the reputation at stake in each transaction. Beyond these, however, there is at least one additional way in which BSPs would likely be more accountable for bad performance than individual directors.

Currently, there is a mismatch between decision-making authority and the mechanisms of accountability. Although board members vote individually on all corporate decisions, their actions are made and recorded as a group. This

---

[i] We should be clear that we do not believe this means there will be no governance failures or even the optimal number of such failures. This is also not to say that we agree with those scholars who believe that reputation alone is or, under our model, would be sufficient to provide optimal incentives for directors. Our more modest claim is that there are improvements to be had in corporate governance from the deployment of the reputational assets of large BSPs. And this additional benefit of BSPs supports permitting companies to hire boards that are not natural persons.

On the other hand, we acknowledge that a BSP could have incentives to pursue a particular course for a company not because it is the right decision for that company, but because of the BSP's need to develop a favorable reputation. For example, a BSP might consent to certain governance reforms, not because the reforms are right for a particular company, but because it needs to build a reputation of being concerned with governance in order to win board appointments. The question is not whether a BSP eliminates agency costs, however, but whether it reduces them relative to natural person directors. For the reasons discussed in this chapter, we think the net reputational effect will be beneficial.

has the potential to undermine the efficiency of the market for corporate directors. The votes of an individual director are not made public, and therefore the ability of shareholders or other corporate observers to hold directors accountable for their decisions is limited. Directors may get reputations in the market for director talent, but information is extremely limited, and the incentives of decision-makers (for example, CEOs) may be misaligned with those of shareholders. Partly for this reason, critics have pointed out that the market for independent directors is not well functioning. There is effectively no robust market for board seats based on externally measured performance. This means that internal metrics, like the CEO's preferences, will determine who sits on the board.

There is some evidence suggesting that the market for directors is not functioning as robustly as possible. Steven Kaplan and David Reishus examined whether the performance of CEOs influences their ability to earn and retain seats on the boards of other companies.[15] They found that CEOs of companies with large dividend cuts (as a proxy for poor performance) are less likely to serve on the boards of other companies, although they cannot distinguish between a theory of labor market constraint and a theory of choice by managers to spend more time on their own firms. Importantly, however, they find that while negative performance is correlated with serving on fewer boards, it does not result in board members losing their current board seats very often. The data show that over 80 percent of directors who are CEOs of poorly performing firms continue to retain their board seats at other firms four years after the poor performance, as measured by a dividend cut.[16]

The use of BSPs has the possibility to improve accountability by identifying a single entity as the decision-maker, and by creating a more robust market for board services. Rival board services firms will likely compete for the work, creating a competitive market for governance that exists outside of and beneath the market for corporate control. As discussed later, for example, BSPs could offer their services to shareholders in a competitive election. If a BSP is providing director services to Acme and rival Board Services Inc. believes it can do the work better or at lower cost, it could bid for the work, either by convincing the individual responsible for nominations of its superiority or by going directly to shareholders in a proxy contest.

Importantly, rival BSPs might have the financial incentive to compete for board positions in ways that individual directors currently do not. Currently, individual directors run as a slate, and any competition for individual places on the board happens behind the scenes, through networks, headhunters, building relations with management, and so on. This state of affairs has been criticized as leading to too much deference to management, since board members only get seats by pleasing the choosers. The competition does not happen in the open because it is not feasible or cost-effective for an individual board member or group of board members to run as a rival slate or for a particular seat in a proxy battle. Although it is theoretically possible for an individual wanting to serve on the board of Acme to communicate with all the shareholders of Acme urging them to vote to put that person on the board, the cost of identifying the shareholders, convincing them to support the candidate, and then obtaining their proxies would be prohibitively expensive. This is why the current model of board services generates competition only when votes for board members are linked to an economic stake in the firm. Running for a board seat or seats makes sense only when the economic gains from taking over the firm, and thereby having a claim on operational profits, generate sufficient benefits to offset the (large) costs of a proxy vote. In other words, the market for board seats is inexorably tied to the market for economic control of the firm.

The BSP approach would delink these to a certain extent. The BSP model would reduce the costs of multiple board members coordinating to take control of a board, and would perhaps lower the costs of providing board services sufficiently to make it economically feasible to win a board election without needing an economic stake in the firm. Large BSPs could have economies of scale and a brand that would lower the costs of communicating their value to shareholders. It is not difficult to imagine a BSP becoming sufficiently well known, like a prominent law, auditing, or consulting firm, such that the costs of communicating with and persuading shareholders would be dramatically lower than for individual board members. If Boards-R-Us is the incumbent BSP, and Board Services Inc. believes it can perform board services more efficiently (that is, better governance for the same cost or the same governance at lower cost), then it could inform shareholders of its intention to run for the job and stand for election at the annual meeting.

Our approach would create market competition, in a sense, for board services without the need to change the economic structure or ownership composition of the company. So, if Boards-R-Us is the incumbent board, and Board Services Inc. displaces it in a shareholder election, this would not have any impact on the underlying ownership of Acme's shares. It would be similar to Acme changing its accountants from KPMG to Ernst & Young. Although board members control the corporation in ways that accountants do not, this does not necessarily turn a contested board election into a battle for control of the firm in the way we think of what is at stake in today's market for corporate control. Today, because board elections are not competitive in the absence of an economic stake giving voting control to a corporate raider, changing the board and controlling the economic fate of the corporation are inexorably linked. In other words, if one wants economic control of the corporation, one takes a large enough economic stake to be able to control the election of the board. But in our imagined world, board elections would be competitive, even in the absence of insurgents taking large equity stakes in the firm. Board services would be awarded based on a majority (or supermajority or whatever voting rule the firm thinks makes the most sense) vote of the shareholders. Then, once board members (or, in this case, a BSP) are elected, they owe fiduciary duties to the firm's shareholders, which is true regardless of the associative type of the board.

Another benefit of using a BSP is that it may make measuring board-governance quality more straightforward. A significant problem in reaching the goal of improved corporate governance is our inability to measure governance quality at particular firms. This is because "governance" is not something that can be measured precisely in the abstract, since it is conflated with operational performance. Firms are valued based on their operational performance – that is, their ability to generate cash, not on whether they have "good" or "bad" governance. Although governance and performance might be correlated in some cases, this is not necessarily the case; some "good" performing firms could improve their governance, and some "bad" performing firms undoubtedly have great governance.

Shareholders, academics, and other corporate observers try to measure governance in a variety of ways, all of which have limitations. First, we can attempt to measure the quality of firm governance or a particular governance change (for example, the appointment of a board member or the declassification of a board) by estimating the impact of the announced change on the firm's overall value. The use of event studies is a widely accepted technique for doing this, but these studies are also subject to many criticisms, not least of which is that they will not work for small changes to governance that would not be material to shareholders. In addition, there may be confounding variables, and the results may be noisy and subject to design criticisms. For individual firms, operational performance may make governance less salient or important for shareholders.

Second, most of the studies of governance do not consider the value for a particular firm or director, but rather involve the decisions by many firms on a particular issue, like whether to have a classified board, whether to separate the role of chair and CEO, and so forth. These studies, while valuable, suffer from the same problems identified in this chapter, as well as endogenous factors and causation-direction concerns, and the possibility that they cannot identify local maxima in broad trends.

The use of BSPs could help us better measure board performance separate from the operational performance of the underlying firms. This would be possible, for example, if a group of BSPs provided director services to multiple companies. The stock price of the BSPs would reflect the market's judgment about the quality of these services for a basket of companies. Assuming that the operational performance of these companies was not perfectly correlated, it would be possible to get a better estimate of the quality of governance. Of course, this metric would be imperfect, as governance and operational performance may be impossible to untangle perfectly. But market-traded BSPs would give us more information about governance quality than the current "market" for director services, which is not transparent and not priced directly by the market. To be sure, directors occasionally serve many firms, and one could try to estimate the market value of directors who do so. But the trend is against multiple directorships, and, in any event, there is no market pricing in the way that publicly traded BSPs would be priced.

Notes

1. See Lucian A. Bebchuk & Jesse M. Fried, Tackling the Managerial Power Problem: The Key to Improving Executive Compensation, *Pathways*, Summer 2010, at 9, 11–12.

2. See, e.g. Tamar Frankel, *Trust and Honesty: America's Business Culture at a Crossroad* 183–184 (2006) ("There are some departures from the historical strong protection of corporate boards. For example, in the past two decades, the Delaware courts ... were reluctant to make corporate directors liable for the wrongs committed by their corporations. The courts respected the directors' business judgment and, with a few notable exceptions, shielded the directors from the claims of shareholders."); Lisa M. Fairfax, Spare the Rod, Spoil the Director? Revitalizing Directors' Fiduciary Duty through Legal Liability, 42 *Hous. L. Rev.* 393, 409 (2005) ("[T]he tremendous deference courts grant to board decisions means that courts hold directors liable for only the most egregious examples of director misconduct.").

3. For a general discussion of the incentive effects of insurance on corporate conduct, see Tom Baker & Sean J. Griffith, *Ensuring Corporate Misconduct: How Liability Insurance Undermines Shareholder Litigation* (2010). With regard to failures of the D&O insurers, see ibid.

at 109 (explaining that "D&O insurers do almost nothing to monitor the public corporations they insure.").

4. See Frank H. Easterbrook & Daniel R. Fischel, Mandatory Disclosure and the Protection of Investors, 70 *Va. L. Rev.* 669, 675 (1984) (discussing the reputational concerns of managers); David M. Phillips, Principles of Corporate Governance: A Critique of Part IV, 52 *Geo. Wash. L. Rev.* 653, 673, 682 (1984) (arguing that reputational concerns can displace the need for legal sanctions).

5. See, e.g. Yaniv Grinstein, Complementary Perspectives on "Efficient Capital Markets, Corporate Disclosure and Enron," 89 *Cornell L. Rev.* 503, 505 (2004) ("Enron's board members had lots of reputation at stake, but concern for reputation and legal punishment failed to provide adequate incentives for board members of Enron to demand explanations for questionable deals.")

6. Edward M. Iacobucci, Reputational Economies of Scale, with Application to Law Firms, 14 *Am. L. & Econ. Rev.* 302, 303 (2012).

7. Ibid. at 303.

8. See Larry E. Ribstein, Ethical Rules, Agency Costs, and Law Firm Structure, 84 *Va. L. Rev.* 1707–1708 (1998).

9. Iacobucci, *Reputational Economies*, at 304.

10. Ibid. at 305.

11. Ibid. at 327.

12. Marc Galanter & William Henderson, The Elastic Tournament: A Second Transformation of the Big Law Firm, 60 *Stan. L. Rev.* 1867, 1908 (2008).

13. William D. Henderson, An Empirical Study of Single-Tier Versus Two-Tier Partnerships in the Am Law 200, 84 *N.C. L. Rev.* 1691, 1696 (2006).

14. Iacobucci, *Reputational Economies*, at 324.

15. Steven N. Kaplan & David Reishus, Outside Directorships and Corporate Performance, 27 *J. Fin. Econ.* 389 (1990).

16. Ibid. at 390. For similar data, see Stuart C. Gilson, Bankruptcy, Boards, Banks, and Block-holders: Evidence on Changes in Corporate Ownership and Control when Firms Default, 27 *J. Fin. Econ.* 355, 356 (1990).

PART III

LEGAL ISSUES

The major barrier to our proposal is law – the BSP is currently legally impossible for the publicly traded corporation in the United States. In this part, we discuss how BSPs are currently prevented by various legal rules and regulations, and consider how these rules might be changed to permit the use of BSPs. We also survey the law of various advanced economies to see what changes, if any, would be needed to permit experimentation with BSPs. Finally, we look at the emerging and growing field of federal corporate law in the United States, and whether and how BSPs could comply with it.

8

BSPs and the Law

BSPs are against the law at present and in the United States. But this is not universally true. In the United Kingdom, for example, until quite recently the law only required that a company "have at least one director who is a natural person."[1] In this chapter, we first discuss the various ways in which law in the United States currently prohibits BSPs. We then review the law in other selected major economies. Finally, we discuss the doctrinal – as opposed to the policy – case for changing the law to permit BSPs.

Current law provides numerous obstacles to effecting our proposal, which therefore requires rethinking if our proposal is to get off the ground. The most basic hurdle is the requirement of state corporation law that directors be natural persons. The DGCL, for example, flatly states that each member of the board of directors "shall be a natural person."[2] The MBCA effects the same result in a somewhat more roundabout fashion. Section 8.03 states that a board "must consist of one or more individuals,"[3] while section 1.40 defines individual as "a natural person."[4] Accordingly, under the DGCL and MBCA, nonnatural legal persons – such as corporations and other forms of business organization – therefore cannot serve as either members of a board or as a replacement for the board in its entirety.[5]

The number of reported judicial decisions dealing with the issue is small and most rely on express statutory commands such as those contained in the DGCL and the MBCA. Not surprisingly, they thus uniformly hold that directors must be natural persons. In *National Football League Properties, Inc.* v. *Superior Court*,[6] which involved a small discovery dispute ancillary to a lawsuit brought by the Oakland Raiders football club against the National Football League and various NFL-affiliated entities, for example, the Raiders claimed that they were a "member, director, and shareholder" of NFL Properties and, in this capacity as a director, the club was entitled to inspect NFL Properties' corporate books and records under a somewhat unusual California statute giving a corporation's directors such inspection rights. The court rejected the Raiders claim because "[a] director of a corporation must be a natural person, pursuant to [California] Corporations Code section 164."[7]

The listing requirements of the various stock exchanges do not directly address the issue, but implicitly appear to follow state law by assuming directors are natural persons. For instance, the NYSE Listed Company Manual requires the board of any listed company to be composed of a "majority of independent directors,"[8] and the independence test requires each director to have "no material relationship with the listed company (either directly or as a partner, shareholder or officer of an organization that has a relationship with the company)."[9] In addition, the listing rules require boards to have compensation, audit, and nomination committees, all composed entirely of independent directors.[10] The rules also seemingly contemplate that directors shall be natural persons by drawing a distinction between "persons or organizations."[11] Taken together, these rules seem difficult to reconcile with a model in which an entity serves the entire board function.

Federal law also seems to presume that boards of directors consist exclusively of natural persons effectively acting as sole proprietors. Although no federal statute specifically requires directors to be natural persons, the implicit premise of recent reforms following the accounting scandals of the early 2000s and the financial crisis of the late 2000s is board service by natural persons acting independently. For instance, SOX requires that a majority of each public corporation's audit committee consists of independent directors. In turn, the definitions of independence adopted by the exchanges in response to SOX all seem to envision natural persons.[12]

A similar approach was taken in Dodd-Frank in response to allegedly irresponsible compensation practices at publicly traded firms during the run up to the financial crisis. For instance, section 952 of Dodd-Frank requires the SEC to direct the stock exchanges to adopt listing rules requiring greater independence for board members serving on compensation committees.[13] Again, the relevant provisions implicitly assume that boards consist exclusively of natural persons.

Must Boards Be Multi-Member?

Until quite recently, state law also required that boards of directors have more than one member. Indeed, most states specifically required that boards consist of at least three members, who had to be shareholders of the corporation and, under some statutes, residents of the state of incorporation.[14] Such requirements would not preclude the use of BSPs, because BSP employees could be appointed to the board (assuming they met the residency and stock ownership requirements), but the rules would have prevented using a BSP as the sole member of the board.

Today these requirements have largely disappeared. DGCL § 141(b) authorizes boards to have one or more members and mandates no qualifications for board membership. MBCA §§ 8.02 and 8.03 are comparable.

Some relevant regulations, however, still seem to at least implicitly assume multi-member boards. The NYSE's Listed Company Manual provides, for example, that "[t]o empower non-management directors to serve as a more effective check on management, the non-management directors of each listed company must meet at regularly scheduled executive sessions without management."[15] The listed company's Form 10-K must disclose the identity of the independent director who chairs the mandatory executive sessions. Although the rule does not indicate how many times per year the outside directors must meet to satisfy this requirement, emerging best practice suggests that there should be such a meeting held in conjunction with every regularly scheduled meeting of the entire board of directors.[i] These rules only make sense in the context of multi-member boards.

THE LAW IN OTHER COUNTRIES

In many countries besides the United States, what are often referred to as "corporate directors"[ii] are also effectively banned, but a few permit them. We begin with the United Kingdom, where there have been several interesting recent developments in this area. In the following section, we more briefly review the status of corporate directors in some other major economies.

---

[i] The NASDAQ and AMEX standards are substantially similar. One wrinkle is that NASDAQ expressly states an expectation that executive sessions of the outside directors will be held at least twice a year. Note that all three exchanges exempt controlled companies – those in which a shareholder or group of shareholders acting together control 50 percent or more of the voting power of the company's stock – from the obligation to have a majority independent board.

[ii] Because corporate director appears to be an accepted term of art in the UK and certain other countries and appears often in the relevant statutes, case law, and legal literature of those countries, we use it in this section in lieu of BSP. Unless the context indicates to the contrary, we use the term herein to include any legal entity that serves as a director.

The Law in the UK

Prior to 2006, the UK had no statutory restrictions on the use of corporate directors. Indeed, a widely cited 1907 Chancery Division decision held that under the then in force Companies Act of 1862 there was "nothing . . . which in any way makes it incumbent on a company . . . to have directors who shall be individual persons and responsible as individuals to the shareholders."[16]

As noted at the beginning of this chapter, however, since adoption of the U.K. Companies Act (2006), § 155(1) has required that a company have at least one director who was a natural person. This provision was understood to permit corporate directors to serve on company boards so long as at least one member was a natural person. In practice, however, the use of corporate directors seems to have been limited to private companies, as stock exchange listing standards were seen as effectively requiring directors to be natural persons.[17]

A related issue arises under § 251 of the Companies Act (2006), which recognizes the so-called shadow director and defines them as "a person in accordance with whose directions or instructions the directors of a company are accustomed to act." A corporation or other legal entity may be deemed a shadow director of another company where the latter's de jure directors act in accord with the former's instructions.

Although our full-blown proposal would now be unlawful in the UK, British law currently presents no obstacle to a BSP being *a* member of the board, although that may be about to change (as discussed later). The BSP simply could not be *the* board. But this restriction presumably could be circumvented by appointing BSP employees as the board, in which case the BSP itself likely would be deemed a shadow director. Although plausible, the gains we think would arise from a market for BSPs would be diluted in such cases.

Setting aside the case of shadow directors, the corporate director option is rarely used, although the exact numbers are difficult to find. A 2013 survey of UK companies found that approximately 38,000 companies (1.2 percent of all UK companies) had one or more corporate directors.[18] In contrast, however, a 2014 government report reported that there were 67,000 companies with corporate directors (2.1 percent of all companies).[19] In either case, the vast majority of companies with one or more corporate directors were nonpublic and small in size.[20]

Interestingly, a survey of fifty-five companies having at least one corporate director reported that "31% saw no advantage to having one, and 11% responded that they did not know what the advantages of having one were."[21] While the small size of the sample relative to the tens of thousands of UK companies with corporate directors makes it difficult to draw firm conclusions from the survey, it is interesting that so many of the surveyed firms were unable to offer a legitimate reason for using entities as directors. As it turns out, perhaps they were unable to do so because corporate directors were often used for purposes at or over the edge of the law.[i]

Despite the low frequency at which UK companies used corporate directors, the Serious Fraud Office estimated that corporate directors figured in a quarter of the cases it investigated.[22] A 2014 Parliamentary assessment of the need for reform concluded that:

> Corporate directors – one company (or legal person) as the director of another – are inherently opaque with respect to the natural person in fact controlling a company. Where someone controls an appointed director – who might be acting irresponsibly as a "front" for them – there is also scope for opacity and a lack of accountability. . . . The use of irresponsible "front" directors who allow themselves to be controlled by another can similarly introduce opacity with respect to that control and lead to reduced effectiveness of corporate oversight.
>
> Since all appointed directors have the same status under the law, there is no means of identifying how many appointed directors are acting irresponsibly as a front for another, nor how many people are seeking to control them. But we do know that international organizations and UK law enforcement consider such arrangements high risk in terms of facilitating crime such as money laundering.[23]

This changed in 2015 with the passage of the Small Business, Enterprise and Employment Act, which now provides that "a person may not be appointed a director of a company unless the person is a natural person."[24] Existing nonnatural person directors of UK companies were originally to be phased out by October 2017, but in September 2016 the UK government indefinitely postponed implementation of the ban.[ii] It did so in order that the government could consider permitting exceptions in limited circumstances, as authorized by the statute.[25] As of this writing (late spring 2017), the government has not yet

---

i   This inference is perhaps further supported by the survey's further finding that only 42 percent of surveyed companies would replace a corporate director with a natural person if the former were banned. U.K. Dep't for Business, Innovation, & Skills, Final Stage Impact Assessments to Part A of the Transparency and Trust Proposals (Companies Transparency) 180 (2014).

ii Once implemented, the law makes it an offense by the company purporting to appoint a corporate director, the nonnatural person so appointed, and any "officer who is in default" of both companies. 14 Halsbury's Laws of England ¶ 526 (5th edn. 2016). "Officer" is defined for this purpose as a director, manager, secretary, or any other person who is treated by the company in question. Ibid. at ¶ 316. An officer is "in default" if he/she authorizes, permits, participates in, or fails to take all reasonable steps to prevent the violation. Ibid.

defined the scope of such exceptions or the situations in which they will be granted, but action was expected in the near future.[26]

Some UK government discussion of the issue suggests that large companies – a category into which all public companies fall – may be more likely to win exceptions:

> It should be noted that large companies might reasonably be thought to pose a lower risk of being used as a shell company for illicit activity (since larger companies might be more likely to be employing staff and producing goods, while those seeking to use a company as a vehicle for illicit ends need only establish a small one to do so). At the same time, they might be more likely to gain business benefits, for instance efficiency within large group structures, from the use of corporate directors.
>
> Circumstances where corporate directors are used to increase efficiency often coincide with situations of extensive regulation and transparency and high standards of corporate governance.[27]

Considering the UK experience, it may be desirable to likewise limit implementation of our proposal to public corporations, which have much the same size and regulatory constraints of large UK companies.

Having said that, however, we believe the UK overreacted by presumptively banning corporate directors. As we explain in other chapters, corporate directors that function as BSPs can add considerable value by expanding corporate networks, providing management with expert advice and specialized knowledge, and improving decision making. All of these functions were cited by UK companies surveyed as to the advantages of corporate directors. As noted, 31 percent of the surveyed companies could not state any advantage provided by corporate directors, but 24 percent stated that corporate directors broadened the skill sets and knowledge possessed by the board. Nine percent state corporate directors provided greater continuity; 5 percent cited improved efficiency; and access to a wider network, access to finance, and better decision-making were all cited by 2 percent of survey respondents.[28]

Concerns about transparency and accountability could be addressed through disclosure without sacrificing those benefits. In the words of US Supreme Court Justice Louis Brandeis's famous aphorism, "[s]unlight is said to be the best of disinfectants; electric light the most efficient policeman."[29] In April 2016, the UK government implemented enhanced disclosure requirements with respect to most company's beneficial owners.[30] All persons with significant control (PSCs) – defined as an individual who owns or controls more than 25 percent of the company's stock – who are known to the company must be placed on a PSC register that includes the PSC's identity, date of birth, address, and other pertinent information. In addition, companies have a "positive duty to take 'reasonable steps' to identify its PSCs."[31]

> A practitioner reviewing the new requirements described the issue this way:
> Clearly what constitutes reasonable steps will vary in each case, but the Government guidance makes it clear that a company will have to demonstrate significant efforts in this regard. For example, if a company believes that it has a PSC, but has been unable to identify them by direct contact, a company should consider serving notices requesting information on anyone they know or have reasonable cause to believe knows the identity of the PSC, or could know someone likely to have that knowledge. This could include intermediaries or advisers known to act for them, such as lawyers, accountants, banks, trust and company service providers or any other contacts such as family members, business partners or known associates.
> Further, if the suspected PSC has a relevant interest in the company, but the company is unable to obtain the required information, a company must "seriously consider" whether it is appropriate to impose restrictions on any shares or rights they hold in the company.[32]

As with the ban on corporate directors, the new requirements were justified as necessary to improve corporate transparency and accountability. Similar disclosure requirements could be imposed on corporate directors, so that regulators and, if desired, the public would know the identities of the corporate director's own directors, officers, and major beneficial owners of its shares. To further promote accountability and transparency, such requirements could include a similar positive duty on the part of both the company appointing the corporate director and the company serving as the corporate director to ensure that all relevant information is fully disclosed.

The Law in Selected Major Economies

In view of how basic the choice to limit director qualifications by personhood appears, it strikes us as surprising that in some countries the law remains unsettled.[i] The laws of most major economies in which the issue is settled, however, ban corporate directors. We review the law of several major economies in the next few sections.

---

[i] See, e.g. Jae Yeol Kwon, The Internal Division of Powers in Corporate Governance: A Comparative Approach to the South Korean Statutory Scheme, 12 *Minn. J. Global Trade* 299, 318 (2003) ("The academic view ... is unsettled on whether a legal person such as a corporation is eligible to be a director under the South Korean Commercial Code.").

Where BSPs Would Be Banned

The Commonwealth of Australia. The Corporations Act (2001) provides that "[o]nly an individual who is at least 18 may be appointed as a director of a company."[33] This provision is understood as banning corporate directors.[34] In *Grimaldi* v. *Chameleon Mining NL and Another,* for example, the defendant corporation had made use of incorporated consulting entities in the conduct and management of the business.[35] The court explained that the terms "director" and "officer" were given an expansive interpretation in Australian corporate law to "enlarge the classes of persons concerned in the management and affairs of a corporation, upon whom legislative standards and liabilities ought be imposed."[36] Under that expansive definition, the incorporated consulting entities had been acting as directors. In turn, the court noted that, "[un]like § 155(1) of the Companies Act 2006 (UK) ..., § 201B(1) of the Corporations Act provides that '[o]nly an individual ... may be appointed as a director.'"[37] The entities in question thus were not valid directors but were nevertheless de facto directors by virtue of their involvement in the management of the business. Finally, the court held that under Australian law, "the liabilities, statutory and fiduciary, of a director" could be imposed upon such de facto directors despite their irregular legal status.[38]

Somewhat related to the status of the de facto directors at issue in *Grimaldi* is the status of "shadow directors." As in the UK, Australian law provides that someone who has not been formally appointed to the board may nevertheless be treated as a director – commonly called a shadow director, although the term does not appear in the statute – if the corporation's properly appointed directors "are accustomed to act in accordance with the person's instructions or wishes."[39] Despite the general ban on corporate directors, Australia law does permit incorporated entities to serve as shadow directors.[40] Indeed, in *Buzzle Operations Pty Ltd (in liq)* v. *Apple Computer Australia Pty Ltd.,* the court expressly rejected an argument that the limitation contained in § 201B(1) requiring a director to be a natural person applied equally to shadow directors, stating that "I do not think there is any implication ... that for a person to be a de facto or shadow director that person must be capable of being validly appointed as a director."[41] To the contrary, despite the prohibition in § 201B(1), the court held that "[t]here is nothing inherently incongruous with a body corporate being a de facto or shadow director."[42]

Canada. Section 105 of Canada's Business Corporations Act disqualifies any "person who is not an individual" from serving on a corporate board of directors.[43] In addition, the individual nominated to serve as a director may not do so if the individual is less than 18 years old, mentally unsound, or bankrupt.[44]

The People's Republic of China. Chinese corporate law lacks both blanket authorization or prohibition of corporate directors.[45] The Mandatory Provisions for the Articles of Association of Companies to be Listed outside the People's Republic of China ("Mandatory Provisions"), however, prohibit "a non-natural person from being a director of a company listed outside the PRC."[46] It's suggested that this prohibition indicates that the relevant Chinese "authorities have considered this issue and hold a negative position."[47]

The Realm of New Zealand. The Companies Act (1993) provides that only a "natural person" who is not otherwise disqualified "may serve as a director."[48] In *Commercial Management Ltd.* v. *Registrar of Companies,* New Zealand's Court of Appeal observed that amendments to the prior Companies Act of 1955 had likewise prohibited a "body corporate" from serving as a director and explained that:

> The provisions that a body corporate shall not be capable of being appointed or holding office as a director or secretary were introduced by the Companies Amendment Act 1982 following the Macarthur Report (1973) para 305. There were consequential amendments to § 200(2) deleting the reference to a corporation as a director and transitional provisions for the termination of existing appointments of a body corporate as a director or secretary. The Act having been amended to exclude a body corporate as either a director or a secretary of a company left only natural persons 18 years of age or over within the criteria of eligibility competent to be appointed or to hold office as a director or secretary.[49]

Counsel for the company argued that the statute only prohibited corporations from serving as directors, but did not prohibit other legal entities, such as the partnership seeking to serve in that capacity for the company, from doing so. The court acknowledged that a partnership is not a legal entity under New Zealand law, but rather an association of two or more persons conducting a business jointly. The court further acknowledged that the Companies Act – as then in force – did not expressly prohibit such an association from serving as a director. The court nevertheless concluded that a partnership could not serve in that capacity. The court explained that several key provisions of the Act implicitly "envisage[d] the office of director as being held by one individual and not held jointly by two or more persons."[50] Among other such concerns, the court seemed particularly worried that allowing a partnership of which a corporation was a member to serve as a director would permit all too easy circumvention of the statutory ban on corporate directors. In addition, the court inferred from the Act a policy that "the office of director ... calls for individual judgment and responsibility," which would be confounded if two or more persons acting jointly were to serve as a director. Presumably, the drafters of the 1993 Companies Act had this precedent in mind when they made explicit the prohibition on anyone but a natural person serving as a director.

Obviously, we defer to the New Zealand court's reading of its statutes. It is not at all obvious to us, however, that the office of director necessarily requires individual judgment and responsibility. To the contrary, of course, it is our fundamental thesis that collective judgment and responsibility are preferable to that of an autonomous individual.

The Republic of Ireland. Ireland has long prohibited corporate directors.[51] A Company Law Review Group (CLRG) was established in 2000 to evaluate, inter alia, a change in that prohibition. "In its first report, the CLRG was very clear that a move to permit corporate directors would not be well received generally."[52] The report argued that a primary goal for any reforms should be enhanced personal accountability for corporate directors and that permitting corporate directors would reduce director accountability. Accordingly, the CLRG recommended that the ban on corporate directors be continued.

The Republic of Singapore. The Singapore statute states "[n]o person other than a natural person who has attained the age of 18 years and who is otherwise of full legal capacity shall be a director of a company."[53] The prohibition has been justified by local commentators on the ground that "[o]nly an individual is able to exercise discretion in moving forward actions for the company, given that the company itself is inanimate,"[54] but this argument errs by reifying the corporate director. A 2011 report by Singapore's Ministry of Finance justified continuing the ban "in view of the difficulties in determining the person who is actually controlling the company and accountability of corporate directors."[55] Again, this explanation strikes us as overbroad, since those concerns could be addressed through an adequate disclosure regime.

Where BSPs Would Be Permitted

The Hong Kong Special Administrative Region of the People's Republic of China. Hong Kong's company law is somewhat like that of pre-2015 Great Britain. A private company may have one or more corporate directors, but must have at least one director who is a natural person.[56] Private company is defined for this purpose as one that "restricts the right to transfer its shares, prohibits public subscription for its shares or debentures, and limits the number of shareholders to 50."[57]

In contrast, public companies may not have corporate directors.[58] A 1997 consultant's report to the Hong Kong Government and its Standing

Committee on Company Law Reform on possible comprehensive changes to Hong Kong's company law explained that restriction on grounds that allowing corporate directors "cuts directly across preoccupations of proper exercise of directors' discretion and accountability."[59] As with the comparable justification advanced in the UK for its pending ban on corporate directors, it is our view that such concerns may mandate greater disclosure but do not justify a complete prohibition.

Professor Hui Huang of the Faculty of Law, Chinese University of Hong Kong, informs us that the number of Hong Kong companies with corporate directors is relatively small. Among the firms where they are used, one common justification is that foreign investors outside Hong Kong may require corporate service providers or financial institutions to provide nominee director services to cope with such business matters as signing documents promptly in Hong Kong. In addition, many companies use corporate directors for convenience reasons. Where directors must travel frequently, for example, Professor Huang suggests that a corporate director provides flexibility by allowing other officers of the corporate director to sign necessary documents. Finally, he also notes that a parent company in a corporate group can act as a director of its subsidiaries or associate companies, which he believes may facilitate the management process and thereby save internal costs.[60]

Other Jurisdictions. In addition to the UK and Hong Kong, other jurisdictions in which corporate directors are permitted at least under some circumstances include Luxembourg, the Netherlands, Guernsey, and the British Virgin Islands. Jersey permitted their use until 1991.[61]

Summary

The foregoing does not purport to be a comprehensive global survey, of course, but it nevertheless seems reasonable to draw certain conclusions. First, developed economies generally do not permit corporate directors. Second, those that do so to some extent tend to limit their use to private companies. Third, the trend is toward abolishing corporate directors. Finally, bans on corporate directors are typically justified on grounds of transparency and accountability.

In our view, as noted earlier, these justifications are unpersuasive. The obvious solution to transparency concerns is disclosure of the desired information, not a prohibition of the conduct in question. As for accountability concerns, so long as the identity of the natural persons who own and control the corporate director are disclosed and means provided for service of process on those individuals, there is no practical difference between natural and legal persons as directors.

To be sure, corporate directors have the shield of limited liability. In effect, however, so do natural persons serving as directors. Indeed, "in practice the number of cases in which directors are actually held liable for violation of their duty of care is very small. A major factor explaining this result is de jure or de facto the business judgment rule, which exists in many countries."[62] Natural persons serving as corporate directors are further insulated from liability in many countries by procedural obstacles to shareholder lawsuits.[63]

In fact, as argued previously, we believe that corporate directors functioning as BSPs can offer greater accountability than natural persons. By allowing a director to pool risks and thus reduce the impact of personal liability, the BSP enhances the robustness of fiduciary duties. By providing a second-order accountability regime through the threat of suits by two distinct sets of corporate owners – that is., both the owners allegedly mistreated by the BSP and the owners of the BSP – and increasing the reputation at stake in each transaction, the BSP model further assuages director accountability concerns relative to the current natural person only model. Finally, a multi-member board disperses accountability, making it harder to identify the truly responsible actors, whereas a single BSP will stick out like the proverbial sore thumb.

THE CASE FOR CHANGING THE LAW

Admittedly, the task of amending myriad state laws, federal laws and regulations, and stock exchange listing rules seems daunting.[i] Fortunately, many of the relevant statutes and rules are sufficiently interlinked to make the task somewhat more manageable than may appear at first glance. If state corporate laws were amended to allow firms to serve as directors, for example, the change would cascade through much of the rest of the corporate governance legal system. After all, state law creates the foundation upon which the federal and stock exchange regimes are constructed.

The task is further eased because unlike many areas of the law, in which the federal nature of the US political system means that legal change must take place in most or sometimes all fifty states to be effective, corporate law is so dominated by Delaware that a change in Delaware's statute would mean more than half the battle was already won. Although the precise numbers vary slightly over time, Delaware long has been the home for anywhere from 50

---

[i] We return in this section to the US context, although we believe our arguments also apply to the laws of other countries.

to 60 percent of the Fortune 500 companies, as well as the companies listed for trading on the NYSE and NASDAQ.

Assuming the mechanical process of effecting the requisite legal changes can be managed, the case for effecting the necessary changes is straightforward. State corporation statutes consist mostly of default rules that can be changed by firm owners.[64] State law thus provides an off-the-rack set of default rules regarding basic corporation law, but generally allows firms to vary widely in their approach, so long as the divergences are set forth in the corporate charter and are effectuated in ways consistent with law (for example, done with shareholder consent).[65] For instance, the DGCL provides that a board of directors shall manage firms, "except as may be otherwise provided in . . . its certificate of incorporation."[66] It is curious that Delaware thus allows corporations to substantially modify the role of the board of directors – and even to opt out of the board model – but mandates that boards consist solely of natural persons. In contrast, our reform brings the statutory rules governing boards even closer into alignment with the fundamental enabling principle of state corporate law.

The reluctance of lawmakers to authorize entities to serve as directors becomes even more curious when one turns from the fundamental policy of corporate statutes to the rules applicable to other business enterprises. In many other legal entities, corporations and other business organizations are permitted to serve as the functional equivalent of a board of directors.

The most obvious of these analogies is that of unincorporated business organizations such as the partnership – in all its myriad forms – and the limited liability company (LLC). Partnership law, for example defines a partnership as an association of two or more persons who are carrying on as co-owners of a business for profit.[67] In turn, person is defined for this purpose to include "an individual, business corporation, nonprofit corporation, partnership, limited partnership, limited liability company," as well as numerous other minor organizational forms.[68] In a partnership with one or more incorporated members, those members have the same management rights as a natural person.[69]

In a limited partnership, there are two classes of partners. The limited partners generally have no managerial rights. Instead, those rights are exercised exclusively by the firm's general partner. Indeed, the control rights of a general partner in a limited partnership are even broader than those of a board of directors in a corporation, since limited partners generally have even fewer voting rights than do shareholders. In contrast to the ban on entities serving as directors, however, state law uniformly permits corporations or other business entities to serve as a limited partnership's general partner.[70]

The Delaware Limited Partnership Act defines a "general partner" as "a person who is named as a general partner in the certificate of limited partnership,"[71] for example, and then defines "person" as "a natural person, partnership . . ., limited liability company, . . . corporation, . . . or any other individual or entity."[72] Many limited partnerships in Delaware and elsewhere take advantage of this flexibility to use firms as board equivalents. This suggests that there is a latent demand for governance to be performed by business entities, instead of individuals, for some companies.

Much the same rules apply for other unincorporated entities, such as limited liability companies and business trusts. Indeed, the Delaware Limited Liability Company Act and the Delaware Statutory Trusts Act are based on the Delaware Limited Partnership Act and, like the latter, permit business associations of all sorts to serve in a role analogous to that of corporate managers and boards of directors.[73]

Mutual funds and similar investment companies offer another pertinent example of businesses operating under a legal regime permitting entities to serve as (or, at least, on) a board of directors. The Investment Company Act of 1940 (ICA) includes incorporated entities within the scope of persons who may serve as directors. Specifically, ICA § 2 defines a director as "any director of a corporation or any person performing similar functions with respect to any organization, whether incorporated or unincorporated."[74] In *Chabot v. Empire Trust Co.*,[75] the Second Circuit held that an incorporated investment company manager was a director for the purposes of the ICA.[76] In so holding, the court noted that Empire, the corporate entity in the case, was empowered by the trust certificate to act with all the powers of a typical director, and this therefore brought it within the definition in the ICA.[i] The fact that Empire was a corporation was not a barrier to it acting like or,

---

[i]   In reaching its conclusion that Empire had all the powers of a typical director, the court considered the following:

> Empire is responsible for the entire management of the fund, except the purchase and sale of the portfolio securities. Empire is empowered "to do all acts, take all proceedings and exercise all such rights and privileges relating to any property at any time held by it as Trustee as could be done, taken or exercised by the absolute owner thereof, except as expressly restricted herein." (Trust Agreement § 8.5.) "At any time the Trustee may take such action as it in good faith may believe to be required for the benefit of the trust property." (§ 8.8) Empire is charged with responsibility for selecting a successor investment advisor (§ 10.2) and must consent to the creation of any new series of shares (§ 11.1). It is unnecessary to describe in detail all of the many aspects of authority granted to Empire by the instrument. It is clear that the functions exercised by it as trustee are "similar" to those exercised by a director; indeed they are identical in many respects.

Chabot v. Empire Trust Co., 301 F.2d 458, 460–461 (2nd Cir. 1962).

for purposes of the ICA, being treated as a director. What mattered to the court was function, not form, and so long as the corporation was acting as a director would, the law would consider it a director.

Third, the Supreme Court has construed portions of federal securities laws broadly to include corporations within the meaning of the term "director" for purposes of those statutes. In *Blau v. Lehman*,[77] the Supreme Court held that for purposes of liability under the short-swing profit rule in section 16(b) of the Securities and Exchange Act of 1934, a corporation may be treated as a director if it effectively deputizes a natural person to perform its duties on the board.[78] The court explained that whether a company is a director by deputization is "a question of fact to be settled case by case and not a conclusion of law."[79] The takeaway from this case is that if the policy rationale behind a particular law would be served by treating a corporation as a director, then courts will be willing to look at what the entity was doing rather than whether it was an individual.

Fourth, as already noted, policy considerations have led most states to abandon the requirement that boards have multiple members, thus opening up the possibility of corporations or other business associations serving the board function through a single seat. Until 1969, Delaware required that the board of directors of corporations with more than three shareholders have a minimum of three members. In that year, however, the DGCL was amended to permit all corporations to have single-member boards.[80] The MBCA likewise permits single-member boards.[81] The shift to permitting single-member boards was driven by concerns about the governance of close corporations. As the drafters of the MBCA explained, requiring close corporations with one or two shareholders to have a minimum of three directors could "require the introduction" to the board "of persons with no financial interest in the corporation."[82] But we think the application of this logic could easily be extended to accommodate our proposal for BSPs. Since states are willing to forego the advantages of multi-member boards by allowing single-member boards, they ought to be willing to allow a BSP to serve as that single member.

Finally, the Bankruptcy Code permits corporate entities to serve in roles analogous to the board of directors. Trustees are empowered by the Code to represent and manage the estate as would the board of directors.[83] Section 321 then sets forth the eligibility requirements for trustees: "A person may serve as trustee in a case under this title only if such person is an individual ... or a corporation authorized by such corporation's charter or bylaws to act as trustee, and, in a case under chapter 7, 12, or 13 of this title, having an office in at least one of such districts."[84] In fact, "the contract between a debtor or a debtor in possession and a management company [brought in to assist with the reorganization often] provides that the management company, rather than any individual consultant, will serve as an officer or director of a debtor or debtor in possession."[85]

As these examples suggest, hiring a firm to provide board or board-like services is not as radical a change as it may appear at first glance. To the contrary, this precise model is permitted in many related areas. The inescapable conclusion from this set of examples is that legislators, courts, and other regulators are willing to accept or even encourage corporate entities to act as directors or boards when the firms are serving director functions and the policy rationale for a particular application (such as the insider trading rules) warrants such treatment. In short, where there are good policy reasons to tolerate BSPs, we see the law tolerating them. We see no reason why the same should not be true for BSPs of corporations.

Notes

1. U.K. Companies Act § 155(1) (2006).
2. Del. Code Ann. tit. 8, § 141(b).
3. Model Bus. Corp. Act Ann. § 8.03.
4. Ibid. § 1.40.
5. The law is the same in other states. See, e.g. *Ute Indian Tribe of the Uintah & Ouray Reservation v. Ute Distribution Corp.*, 2010 WL 956905 at *5 (D. Utah Mar. 12, 2010), aff'd, 455 F. App'x 856 (10th Cir. 2012) ("Utah statute specifies that a director must be a natural person who is at least eighteen-years-old."); *Rohe v. Reliance Network Training, Inc.*, 2000 WL 1038190 at *9 n.22 (Del. Ch. July 21, 2000) (quoting the Texas Business Corporation Act as requiring that "natural persons" serve as directors); Michael A. Budin, Prepare LLC Documents with Care: Issues to Consider to Achieve the Desired Results for Your Client, 74 *Pa. B.A. Q.* 27, 38 (2003) (stating that § "1722(a) of the Pennsylvania Business Corporation Law requires each director of a business corporation to be a natural person"); see generally Shawn Bayern, The Implications of Modern Business-Entity Law for the Regulation of Autonomous Systems, 19 *Stan. Tech. L. Rev.* 93, 98 (2015) ("This restriction is standard across American law.").
6. 75 Cal. Rptr. 2d 893 (Cal. App. 1998).
7. Ibid. at 899 n.5.
8. NYSE Listed Company Manual § 303A.01.
9. Ibid. § 303A.02(a)(i).
10. See ibid. § 303A.04–.06.
11. Ibid. § 303A.02 cmt.

12. See, e.g. 17 C.F.R. § 240.10A-3(b)(1) (2013) ("In order to be considered to be independent for purposes of this [section], a member of an audit committee of a listed issuer that is an investment company may not, other than in his or her capacity as a member of the audit committee [have a material relationship with the company].").

13. Pub. L. 111–203, § 952, 124 Stat. 1376, 1900–03 (codified as amended at 15 U.S.C. § 78j-3 [2012]).

14. MBCA § 8.03(a) cmt.

15. Ibid. § 303A.03.

16. *Bulawayo Market and Office Co Ltd.*, [1907] 2 Ch. 458, 463 (U.K.).

17. Norton Rose Fulbright, Update on Corporate Directorships (Dec. 2010), www.nortonrosefulbright.com/knowledge/publications/32739/update-on-corporate-directorships.

18. U.K. Dep't for Business, Innovation, & Skills, Corporate Directors: Scope of Exceptions to the Prohibition of Corporate Directors 4 (2014) [hereinafter Exceptions Paper].

19. U.K. Dep't for Business, Innovation, & Skills, Final Stage Impact Assessments to Part A of the Transparency and Trust Proposals (Companies Transparency) 155 (2014) [hereinafter Impact Assessments Paper]. Part of the problem may be that the latter survey included limited liability partnerships, while the former apparently did not. Ibid. at 160 n.20.

20. See ibid. at 228 (stating that "over 85% of the 67,000 companies with corporate directors file accounts as if they were small companies").

21. Exceptions Paper, at 8.

22. Ibid. at 6.

23. Impact Assessments Paper, at 152.

24. Companies Act § 156A (2015) (U.K.).

25. Exceptions Paper, at 4 (stating that "we seek views on circumstances where the use of corporate directors could continue, under exceptions to the prohibition").

26. See Theresa Grech, Legal Changes Businesses can Expect in 2017, www.SouthWestBusiness.co.uk (Jan. 25, 2017) ("It was originally thought that the ban would come into force last October, but it now looks as though it is likely to be April or June this year.").

27. Impact Assessments Paper, at 228.

28. Ibid. at 183.

29. Louis D. Brandeis, *Other People's Money, What Publicity Can Do* 92 (1932).

30. Impact Assessments Paper, at 4.

31. Michael Roach, An Analysis of the UK's New Register of Beneficial Owners (Apr. 13, 2016), www.lexology.com/library/detail.aspx?g=d9dc907f-6997-4d7a-b9c5-4afa89c5a2d3.

32. Ibid.

33. Corps. Act § 201B(1) (2001) (Aus.).

34. See Exceptions Paper, at 6 (noting that Australian law does "not allow corporate directors at all").

35. *Grimaldi v. Chameleon Mining NL and Another* (No 2), 200 FCR 296 ¶ 33 (2012).

36. Ibid. at ¶ 34.

37. Ibid. at ¶ 32.

38. Ibid. at ¶ 141.

39. Corps. Act § 9 (2001) (Aus.).

40. See, e.g. *Buzzle Operations Pty Ltd (in liq) v. Apple Computer Australia Pty Ltd*, 238 FLR 384 ¶ 231 ("It has been held more than once and assumed on many occasions that a company can be a shadow director.").

41. Ibid.

42. Ibid.

43. Business Corporations Act § 105(1)(c) (1985) (Can.).

44. Barry J. Reiter, *Directors' Duties in Canada* 77 (2006).

45. Minkang Gu, *Understanding Chinese Company Law* 140 (2006).

46. Ibid.

47. Ibid.

48. Companies Act § 151(1) (1993) (N.Z.).

49. *Commercial Management Ltd v. Registrar of Companies*, 1 New Zealand L. Rep. 744, 746 (1987).

50. Ibid. at 747.

51. Barry Conway & Aoife Kavanagh, A New Departure in Irish Company Law: The Companies Act 2014—An Overview, 16 *Bus. L. Int'l* 135, 151 (2015).

52. Ibid.

53. Singapore Companies Act § 145(2) (2009) (Sing.).

54. Rajah & Tann, Appointment of Directors: Requirements, Qualifications and Procedure 5 (June 2001), http://eoasis.rajahtann.com/eoasis/lb/pdf/ Directors_Appointment_v2.PDF.

55. Report of the Steering Committee for Review of the Companies Act 1-5 (2011), www.mof.gov.sg/cmsresource/public%20consultation/2011/Review %20of%20Companies%20Act%20and%20Foreign%20Entities%20Act/S C%20Report%20Chpt%201%20Directors.pdf.

56. Basil H. Hwang & Selina Wong, Setting Up a Company in Hong Kong, *Bus. L. Today*, June 2013, at 1, 2.

57. Ibid.

58. Seaman Kwok, *The New Hong Kong Companies Ordinance – Restriction on Corporate Directorship for HK Listed Companies*, http://hk.lexiscn .com/asiapg/uploads/metadata/1455855608.pdf. See also Abdul Majid et al., Company Directors' Perceptions of Their Responsibilities and

Duties: Hong Kong Survey, 28 *Hong Kong L. J.* 60, 64 (1998) (stating that "except in the case of an exempt private company, a director must be a natural person").

59. Review of the Hong Kong Companies Ordinance: Consultancy Report 117 (Mar. 1997).

60. Similar rationales are suggested in Ji Lian Yap, De Facto Directors and Corporate Directorships, 7 *J. Bus. L.* 579, 582 (2012).

61. Corporate or Individual Directors and Trustees?, 5 *Private Client Bus.* 274 (2005).

62. Paul L. Davies & Klaus J. Hopt, Corporate Boards in Europe-Accountability and Convergence, 61 *Am. J. Comp. L.* 301, 347 (2013).

63. See Franklin A. Gevurtz, Globalizing Up Corporate Law, 68 *SMU L. Rev.* 741, 748 (2015) (stating that "procedural barriers to enforcement actions in many countries, as for example China, reduce the potential liability inattentive directors face").

64. See Frank H. Easterbrook & Daniel R. Fischel, *The Economic Structure of Corporate Law* 14–15 (1991); Larry E. Ribstein, The Mandatory Nature of the ALI Code, 61 *Geo. Wash. L. Rev.* 984, 989–991 (1993).

65. See Easterbrook & Fischel, *Economic Structure,* at 2 (stating that an "enabling statute allows managers and investors to write their own tickets, to establish systems of governance without substantive scrutiny from a regulator.").

66. Del. Code Ann. tit. 8, § 141(a).

67. See Unif. Partnership Act § 202(a) (stating that "the association of two or more persons to carry on as co-owners a business for profit forms a partnership, whether or not the persons intend to form a partnership").

68. Ibid. § 102(14).

69. See ibid. § 401(h) ("Each partner has equal rights in the management and conduct of the partnership's business.")

70. See Larry E. Ribstein, An Applied Theory of Limited Partnership, 37 *Emory L.J.* 835, 868–871 (1988) (discussing incorporated general partners).

71. Del. Code Ann. tit. 6, § 17–101(5).

72. Ibid. § 17–101(14). See generally Robert W. Hamilton, Corporate General Partners of Limited Partnerships, 1 *J. Small & Emerging Bus. L.* 73 (1997) (noting the availability of corporate general partners).

73. See *Feeley* v. NHAOCG, LLC, 62 A.3d 649, 669 (Del. Ch. 2012) ("[T]he LLC Act and the Delaware Statutory Trusts Act ... permit entities to serve in managerial roles ... ").

74. 15 U.S.C. § 80a-2.

75. 301 F.2d 458, 460–461 (2nd Cir. 1962).

76. Ibid. at 460–461.

77. 368 U.S. 403 (1962).

78. Ibid. at 410 ("Lehman Brothers would be a 'director' of Tide Water, if as petitioner's complaint charged Lehman actually functioned as a director through Thomas, who had been deputized by Lehman to perform a director's duties not for himself but for Lehman.").

79. *Feder* v. *Martin Marietta Corp.*, 406 F.2d 260, 263 (2nd Cir. 1969) (citing Blau, 368 U.S. at 408–409).

80. Edward P. Welch et al., *Folk on the Delaware General Corporation Law* § 141.03 (6th edn. 2013).

81. Model Bus. Corp. Act Ann. § 8.03.

82. Ibid. § 8.03 cmt.

83. 11 U.S.C. § 704.

84. Ibid. § 321.

85. Kurt F. Gwynne, Employment of Turnaround Management Companies, "Disinterestedness" Issues Under the Bankruptcy Code, and Issues Under Delaware General Corporation Law, 10 *Am. Bankr. Inst. L. Rev.* 673, 686 (2002).

9

BSPs and the Emerging Federal Law of Corporations

As we've noted at several points, the vague statutory responsibilities of corporate boards of directors under state law have gradually been supplemented by far more specific duties imposed by federal law and stock exchange listing standards. In this chapter, we therefore turn to the question of whether BSPs will be able to carry out the duties required by the emergent federal corporate law.

Many of the provisions discussed in this chapter were controversial when they were first proposed and many remain controversial to this day.[1] Some have been targeted by Congressional Republicans for repeal, although as yet there has been no movement in that direction. For present purposes, however, we take the existing rules as given. The question we tackle here is not whether BSPs should have to comply with SOX and Dodd-Frank, but how they will do so.

DIRECTOR INDEPENDENCE

In promulgating SOX, Congress and the SEC left much of the heavy lifting on board reform to the stock exchanges. All three major exchanges – the NYSE, NASDAQ, and the American Stock Exchange (AMEX) – amended their corporate governance listing requirements to require that a majority of the members of the board of directors of most listed companies must be independent of management. All three also adopted new rules defining independence using very strict, bright-line rules.

The NYSE has long required that all listed companies have at least three independent directors.[2] A director was treated as independent unless, inter alia, (1) the director was employed by the corporation or its affiliates in the past three years, (2) the director had an immediate family member who, during the past three years, was employed by the corporation or its affiliates as an executive officer, (3) the director had a direct business relationship with the company, or (4) the director was a partner, controlling shareholder, or executive officer of an organization that had a business relationship with the corporation, unless the corporation's board determined in its business judgment that the relationship did not interfere with the director's exercise of independent judgment.

The NYSE's pre-SOX listing standards also required that listed companies have an audit committee composed solely of independent directors. The committee had to have at least three members, all of whom must be "financially literate." At least one committee member had to have expertise in accounting or financial management.

In the wake of the Enron debacle, however, the NYSE adopted new listing standards requiring that all listed companies have a majority of independent directors.[3] In addition, as we will see, the NYSE has mandated the use of several board committees consisting of independent directors.[i]

The key issue for BSPs under these rules is whether they will qualify as independent. NYSE Listed Company Manual § 303A.02 sets out a number of tests for determining whether a director is independent:

(i) The director is, or has been within the last three years, an employee of the listed company, or an immediate family member is, or has been within the last three years, an executive officer, 1 of the listed company.

(ii) The director has received, or has an immediate family member who has received, during any twelve-month period within the last three years, more than $120,000 in direct compensation from the listed company, other than director and committee fees and pension or other forms of deferred compensation for prior service (provided such compensation is not contingent in any way on continued service).

(iii) (A) The director is a current partner or employee of a firm that is the listed company's internal or external auditor; (B) the director has an immediate family member who is a current partner of such a firm; (C) the director has an immediate family member who is a current employee of such a firm and personally works on the listed company's audit; or (D) the director or an immediate family member was within the last three years a partner or employee of such a firm and personally worked on the listed company's audit within that time.

---

[i] The NASDAQ and AMEX standards are substantially similar. Note that all three exchanges exempt controlled companies – those in which a shareholder or group of shareholders acting together control 50 percent or more of the voting power of the company's stock – from the obligation to have a majority independent board.

(iv) The director or an immediate family member is, or has been with the last three years, employed as an executive officer of another company where any of the listed company's present executive officers at the same time serves or served on that company's compensation committee.

(v) The director is a current employee, or an immediate family member is a current executive officer, of a company that has made payments to, or received payments from, the listed company for property or services in an amount which, in any of the last three fiscal years, exceeds the greater of $1 million, or 2% of such other company's consolidated gross revenues.[4]

The NYSE cautions that "it is best that boards making 'independence' determinations broadly consider all relevant facts and circumstances. In particular, when assessing the materiality of a director's relationship with the listed company, the board should consider the issue not merely from the standpoint of the director, but also from that of persons or organizations with which the director has an affiliation."[5]

The first four tests may occasionally create difficulties for BSPs whose employees have such conflicts. It is the fifth, however, that poses the most serious difficulty. Although a BSP technically is not precluded from being deemed independent by the strict text of standard (v), the requirement that the board determine "that the director has no material relationship with the listed company" implicitly calls test (v) into question by way of analogy. Just as an employee of a company that "received payments from" the listed company has a conflicting interest, so does the company itself. To solve the problem, the NYSE should exempt fees paid for serving as a director from test (v) just as it does in test (ii).

A similar problem requiring a similar solution is presented by influential proxy voting advisor Institutional Shareholder Services, which defines an "affiliated outside director" as someone who has "any material transactional relationship with the company or its affiliates (excluding investments in the company through a private placement)."[6] ISS presumes that a material transactional relationship exists if the company makes annual payments to the director "exceeding the greater of $200,000 or 5 percent of the recipient's gross revenues, in the case of a company which follows NASDAQ listing standards; or the greater of $1,000,000 or 2 percent of the recipient's gross revenues, in the case of a company which follows NYSE/Amex listing standards."[7] In addition, the ISS treats someone as an "affiliated outside director" if they provide "professional services to the company, to an affiliate of the company or an individual officer of the company or one of its affiliates in excess of $10,000 per year."[8] "Professional services" are defined for this purpose "as advisory in nature, generally involve access to sensitive company information or to strategic decision making, and typically have a commission- or fee-based payment structure."[9] ISS recommends that the institutional investors who use its services vote against election of affiliated outside directors if, inter alia, the individual serves on the audit, compensation, or nominating committees or independent directors make up less than a majority of the board.[10] Again, it will facilitate the use of BSPs if ISS makes clear that payment of directors' fees to the BSP does not implicate these restrictions.

BSPS AND THE CEO/CHAIR DUALITY ISSUE

In the UK, public companies must either have an independent chairperson or explain in their disclosure statements why they chose not to do so. Some corporate governance commentators have long advocated a similar rule in the United States, which came to partial fruition in Dodd-Frank § 972. It instructed the SEC to adopt a new rule requiring reporting companies to disclose whether the same person or different persons hold the positions of CEO and Chairman of the Board and to explain why it made the choice it did. As adopted, the rule thus requires a company's annual proxy statement "to disclose whether and why it has chosen to combine or separate the principal executive officer and board chairman positions, and the reasons why the company believes that this board leadership structure is the most appropriate structure for the company at the time of the filing."[11]

A company would thus simply disclose that it has a board with one independent member – the BSP – and that the question of CEO/chair duality has been rendered irrelevant to the company's leadership structure. The required § 972 disclosure also is where the company likely would explain to its shareholders why it has chosen a BSP-based leadership structure.

THE AUDIT COMMITTEE

The data contained in a corporation's financial statements is the market's best tool for evaluating how well a firm's managers perform. Because management prepares the financial statements, however, how can the market trust those statements to represent fairly and accurately the company's true financial picture? Would managers really tell the truth if it meant losing their jobs?

To ensure that the financial statements are accurate and complete, the SEC requires corporations to have those statements audited by an independent firm of certified public accountants. In order to prevent management and the outside auditor from getting too cozy with one another, it has long been considered good practice for the corporation's board of directors to have an audit committee. As defined by SOX, that committee is "established by and amongst the board of directors of an issuer for the purpose of overseeing the accounting and financial reporting processes of the issuer and audits of the financial statements of the issuer."[12]

For decades, the NYSE required listed companies to have an audit committee consisting solely of independent directors. The committee had to have at least three members, all of whom were "financially literate." At least one committee member had to have expertise in accounting or financial management.

When Sarbanes-Oxley was under consideration by Congress, a consensus quickly formed in favor of imposing a tougher version of the NYSE requirements on all public corporations. Sarbanes-Oxley § 301 therefore ordered the SEC to adopt rules requiring that the stock exchanges and NASDAQ adopt listing requirements mandating the creation by listed companies of audit committees satisfying the following specifications:

- Committee Responsibilities: The audit committee is responsible for appointing, compensating, and supervising the company's outside auditor. The outside auditor "shall report directly to the audit committee." The committee also must resolve "disagreements between management and the auditor regarding financial reporting."[13]
- Independence: All members of the audit committee must be independent.[14]
- Whistle Blowers: The audit committee must establish procedures for handling complaints about the way the company conducts its accounting, internal audit controls, and outside audits. The procedure must include a mechanism for "the confidential, anonymous submission by employees . . . of concerns regarding questionable accounting or auditing matters."[15]
- Hiring Advisors: In addition to empowering the audit committee to hire and pay the outside auditor, the company also must empower the committee to hire "independent counsel and other advisors, as it determines necessary to carry out its duties," with the outside advisor's fees paid by the company.[16]

As finally amended post-SOX, NYSE Listed Company Manual § 303A.06 therefore requires that each listed company have an audit committee. Unlike the nominating and compensation committee requirements, even companies with a controlling shareholder must comply with the audit committee rules.

In § 303A.07, the NYSE sets out additional committee requirements:

- The committee must have at least three members. Note that a growing number of firms are appointing as many as five individuals to the audit committee so as to help share the high workload imposed on this committee's members.
- All committee members must be independent, both as defined in Sarbanes-Oxley § 301 and the NYSE Listed Company Manual.
- All committee members must be "financially literate" and at least one member "must have accounting or related financial management expertise."[17] It is left up to the company's board of directors to decide what that means and whether the members qualify.
- The audit committee must have a written charter specifying its duties, role, and powers.
- The committee is charged with oversight of "(1) the integrity of the listed company's financial statements, (2) the listed company's compliance with legal and regulatory requirements, (3) the independent auditor's qualifications and independence, and (4) the performance of the listed company's internal audit function and independent auditors."[18]
- The committee must prepare an annual report on the audit process to be included in the company's annual proxy statement.
- The audit committee must have the power to engage independent counsel and other advisors and to pay such advisors.
- The committee must have the power to set the compensation of the outside auditor.
- At least once a year, the committee must receive a report from the outside auditor on the adequacy of the company's internal controls.
- The committee is to review the company's annual and quarterly disclosure reports, specifically including the MD&A section, as well as the financial statements.
- The committee is to review earnings announcements and other guidance provided to analysts.
- The committee must meet periodically in executive session with both the company's internal and outside auditors.
- The committee must review any disagreements between management and the auditors.

The NASDAQ rules are less detailed but otherwise are substantially similar to the NYSE provisions.

In sum, the audit committee is SOX's central clearinghouse. The audit committee must approve any nonaudit services performed by the company's outside certified public accounting firm. The audit committee supervises the company's whistle-blower policies. The audit committee is required to ensure that the outside auditor can perform its audit unimpeded by management. The audit committee acts as a liaison between management and the outside auditor, especially with respect to any disagreements between them or any other problems that arise during the audit. The audit committee should review the CEO and CFO's certifications with the outside auditor. The audit committee must ensure that every five years the outside auditor rotates both the partner principally responsible for conducting the audit and the partner responsible for reviewing the audit.

The SEC put additional teeth into the exchange's audit committee requirements by mandating that corporate proxy statements include a report from that committee containing a variety of disclosures. The report, for example, must state whether the committee reviewed and discussed the company's audited financial statements with management and the firm's independent auditors. The report also must state whether the audit committee recommended to the board of directors that the audited financial statements be included in the company's annual report on Form 10-K.

Studies of how these requirements have impacted audit committees suggest that having a BSP carry out the audit committee's functions would result in considerable improvements in corporate governance. A study of the relation between the probability of financial misstatements by a firm and various corporate governance features found a negative correlation between financial expertise on the part of audit committee members and the probability of financial misstatements.[19] In other words, expert directors make superior monitors, which is hardly surprising. A BSP brings to the table not just expertise, but also a cohesive team of experts who are experienced at working together. A substantial body of sociological and economic literature reports that such groups generally outperform atomized individuals at tasks involving the exercise of critical evaluative judgment,[20] which is precisely what audit committees spend most of their time doing. Of course, a multi-member audit committee may eventually develop beneficial group dynamics, but they will always remain part-timers who will inevitably be at a disadvantage vis-à-vis a collegial group who work together full time.

SECTION 404 INTERNAL CONTROLS

At first glance, SOX § 404(a) looks like a simple disclosure rule. It requires that public corporations include a statement in their annual report acknowledging management's responsibility for "establishing and maintaining an adequate internal control structure and procedures for financial reporting" and "an assessment, as of the end of the most recent fiscal year of the issuer, of the effectiveness of the internal control structure and procedures of the issuer for financial reporting." In addition, just as the corporation's outside auditors have long been obliged to attest to the company's financials, Section 404(b) requires that the company's independent auditors attest to the effectiveness of the company's internal controls.[i] Yet, these seemingly simple requirements have, in Ralph Ward's words, brought more "woe and compliance spending to corporate American than all [SOX's] other provisions combined."[21] Audit committees have borne the brunt of the load.

The audit committee must review management's assessment, which obviously requires that the committee be highly familiar with the design and operation of the company's internal controls. If management or the outside auditor identified any deficiencies, the audit committee must supervise the process of remediating them. In short, as former SEC Commissioner Roel Campos observed, audit committees have been required to "take more affirmative roles in rooting out accounting and internal control issues."[22]

As currently structured, however, audit committees are poorly suited for this important role. Although all audit committee members are supposed to be financially literate and at least one is supposed to be a financial expert, the SEC's definition of financial expert is so loose as to allow most businesspeople to qualify. There is no requirement that any member of the audit committee – let alone all – be qualified accountants or auditors with the professional training necessary to sniff out deficiencies. Even when some or all of an audit committee's members are experts, moreover, they are part-timers.

There is considerable evidence that these deficiencies matter. Firms whose audit committees are staffed by expert accountants or auditors have fewer earnings restatements. The quality of reported earnings at such firms is higher

---

[i] Small public corporations with an aggregate worldwide market value of their common stock held by its nonaffiliates of less than $75 million have been exempted from the outside auditor attestation requirement, but still must comply with § 404(a). SEC, Internal Control Over Financial Reporting in Exchange Act Periodic Reports of Non-Accelerated Filers, Exchange Act Rel. No. 62,914 (Sept. 15, 2010). This is widely believed to have significantly reduced the financial burden of compliance on these corporations, but the continued requirement of a management attestation means that even for them the audit committee remains actively involved in supervising the company's internal controls.

than at firms lacking such experts. Higher audit committee expertise is also positively correlated with fewer material misstatements.[23] BSPs marketing themselves to corporations and competing to be elected by shareholders likely will address these concerns by including experienced and highly trained accountants and auditors on the team servicing the client and ensuring that those team members take the lead in carrying out the responsibilities respecting internal controls currently assigned to the audit committee.

Time matters too. Corporations whose audit committees meet more often have lower incidence of earnings manipulation than do companies whose audit committees meet less often.[24] As with other board tasks, having a dedicated BSP working full-time should result in results superior to the current system.

THE COMPENSATION COMMITTEE

Under NYSE Listed Company Manual § 303A.05, the board of directors of all listed companies must have a compensation committee, which must consist solely of independent directors. The committee must adopt a written charter setting out its purpose, responsibilities, and powers. At a minimum, the charter must authorize the compensation committee to set the metrics by which the CEO will be evaluated, to use those metrics to evaluate the CEO's job performance, and to set the CEO's pay, perquisites, and benefits. Recognizing that it is customary for companies to rely on compensation consultants in setting the CEO's pay, the committee must be given exclusive power to hire, fire, and compensate compensation consultants.

Since 2006 the committee also has had primary responsibility with respect to the required Compensation Discussion and Analysis (CD&A), which is a narrative evaluation of the CEO's pay and performance. It must lead off the compensation section of the Form 10-K and proxy statement. In addition, the SEC requires an annual "Compensation Committee Report," in which the company states whether the compensation committee has discussed the CD&A disclosures with management and whether the committee recommended that the CD&A be included in the company's annual Form 10-K and its proxy statement.

Nothing in these requirements precludes a BSP from serving as the compensation committee for the company simultaneously with serving as the board as a whole. As with other board tasks, we believe that a BSP would do a better job than compensation committees staffed by individual independent directors. The BSP's usual advantages with respect to time, expertise, and specialization obviously apply here as elsewhere. They are especially relevant in this context, however, because compensation committees "have traditionally lacked members (particularly a chair) with strong executive pay or human resources background."[25] The result has been a host of compensation committees that fail to understand the complex mix of pay, options, bonuses, perquisites, and benefits that make up CEO pay packets and therefore tend to simply rubber-stamp the recommendations of their compensation consultants.[26] In contrast, a credible BSP will have team members assigned to each client with the relevant expertise and experience to meaningfully match CEO compensation to job performance.

THE NOMINATING COMMITTEE

NYSE Listed Company Manual § 303A.04 requires that listed companies set up "a nominating/corporate governance committee composed entirely of independent directors," which must have a written charter specifying how it will go about identifying and selecting candidates for board membership. In addition, the listing standard includes "corporate governance" as part of the nominating committee's job. Although this element of the committee's responsibilities is poorly defined, the intent seems to be that the nominating committee serve as the board of directors' principal liaison to the shareholders.

This requirement is superfluous in the BSP model. To be sure, it may be desirable for the BSP to take over the nominating committee's role as a key liaison with the shareholders. With the BSP serving as the corporation's sole board member, however, there is no need for a committee to select new directors. After all, one would hardly expect the BSP to nominate someone else? Instead, we propose that the nominating committee requirement be replaced with a version of proxy access, as discussed in the next chapter.

Notes

1. See, e.g. Stephen M. Bainbridge, Dodd-Frank: Quack Federal Corporate Governance Round II, 95 *Minn. L. Rev.* 1779 (2011) (critiquing Dodd-Frank's governance provisions); Roberta Romano, The Sarbanes-Oxley Act and the Making of Quack Corporate Governance, 114 *Yale L.J.* 1521 (2005) (critiquing SOX's governance provisions).
2. NYSE, Listed Company Manual § 303.01 (2001).
3. Ibid.
4. Ibid. § 303A.02(b) (commentary omitted).
5. Ibid. § 303A.02(a) cmt.
6. ISS, 2014 U.S. Proxy Voting Summary Guidelines 15 (2014).

7. Ibid. at 16 n.viii.

8. Ibid. at 15.

9. Ibid. at 16 n.vii.

10. ISS, United States Concise Proxy Voting Guidelines: 2016 Benchmark Policy Recommendations 16 (2016).

11. SEC, Proxy Disclosure Enhancements, Release No. 9089 (Dec. 16, 2009). Exchange listing standards require appointment of an independent lead director if the company's CEO serves as the chairman of the board of directors. The lead director presumably chairs the required executive sessions of the independent board members. Because the lead director's identity and contact information must be disclosed, he also acts as a point person for shareholder relations. Best practice guidelines suggest that the lead director should have a voice in setting the board's agenda, as a check on the CEO/Chairman's control of board meetings, and be prepared to act as a rallying point for the other independent directors in times of crisis, especially those involving CEO termination or succession. In the BSP model, this requirement is superfluous.

12. The Sarbanes-Oxley Act of 2002, Pub.L. 107–204, 116 Stat. 745), § 2(a)(3) (July 30, 2002) [hereinafter SOX].

13. 15 U.S.C. § 78j–1(m)(2).

14. Ibid. § 78j–1(m)(3).

15. Ibid. § 78j–1(m)(4).

16. Ibid. § 78j–1(m)(5).

17. NYSE Listed Company Manual, supra note 2, at § 303A.07(a) cmt.

18. Ibid. § 303A.07(b).

19. Anup Agrawal & Sahiba Chadha, Corporate Governance and Accounting Scandals, 48 *J.L. & Econ.* 371, 375 (2005).

20. See generally Stephen M. Bainbridge, Why a Board? Group Decisionmaking in Corporate Governance, 55 *Vand. L. Rev.* 1 (2002) (reviewing the relevant literature).

21. Ralph Ward, *The New Boardroom Leaders: How Today's Corporate Boards Are Taking Charge* 18 (2008).

22. Roel C. Campos, Remarks of SEC Commissioner, 55 *Case W. Res. L. Rev.* 527, 537 (2005).

23. For a review of the relevant literature, see Alan Levitan, The Number of Professionally Certified Accounting Experts on Audit Committees and Confidence in Earnings: A Study of Retail Investors' Perceptions, 17 *J. Accounting, Ethics, & Pub. Pol'y* 721 (2016).

24. Raghavan J. Iyengar et al., Does Board Governance Improve the Quality of Accounting Earnings? 23 *Accounting Res. J.* 49 (2010).

25. Ward, *Boardroom Leaders*, at 24.

26. Ibid.

PART IV

BSPS AND THE FRONTIERS OF CORPORATE GOVERNANCE

In this part, we apply the BSP concept to several cutting-edge debates in policy circles in corporate governance. We consider how the BSP could be used to resolve debates about shareholder access to the corporate proxy, about proposals to increase managerial power, and about how the board may evolve into a role that involves more than just monitoring. The punchline from this part is that the BSP is a tool that could be used to better achieve whatever the policy choice is, be it to increase shareholder power, managerial power, or board power. The proposal as such is not biased one way or the other in the Corporate Wars; it is merely a tool to increase the efficiency of corporate governance.

10

BSPs and Proxy Access

Since at least 2003, shareholder access to the proxy has been one of the hottest issues in corporate governance. Proponents contend that shareholders should be able to nominate directors and have those nominations appear on the company's proxy statement so that shareholders can choose between the directors nominated by the incumbent board and those nominated by the shareholders. Opponents argue that activist shareholders may use proxy access to nominate directors whose loyalty would be to the activist rather than the company's shareholders as a whole; incumbent directors are better positioned to choose new board members than shareholders; and discordant factionalism is likely when proxy access leads to a board consisting of a mix of members nominated by the incumbent board and those nominated by shareholders. One of us has taken a position on that debate in other work,[1] but for present purposes the merits of that debate are not at issue. Instead, the question is how BSPs and proxy access would interact. In our view, moving to the BSP model would allow companies to capture the benefits of proxy access while mitigating the disadvantages.

A BRIEF OVERVIEW OF PROXY ACCESS

Under both state corporate laws and federal securities regulations, the incumbent board of directors controls the process of nominating directors. When it is time to elect directors, the outgoing board nominates a slate, typically consisting of the same members, which is included in the company's proxy statement. Although in theory a shareholder may attend the annual shareholder meeting and put forward one or more nominees, there is no mechanism for a shareholder to put a nominee on the company's proxy statement and use the company's proxy card to collect votes for the shareholder's choices. In addition, many companies have advance notice bylaws sharply limiting shareholders' ability to even make nominations from the floor. As a result, a shareholder who wishes to nominate directors must incur the considerable expense of conducting a proxy contest to elect a slate in opposition to that put forward by the incumbents.

In 2003, the SEC proposed a rule that would have permitted shareholders, upon the occurrence of certain specified events and subject to various restrictions, to have their nominees placed on the company's proxy statement and ballot.[2] A shareholder-nominated director thus could be put to a shareholder vote in a fashion similar to the way shareholder-sponsored proposals are put to a shareholder vote under Rule 14a-8. The SEC never acted on the proposal, however.

In response to the SEC's inaction, activist investors began waging a company-by-company campaign for proxy access, using Rule 14a-8 proposals to amend the bylaws to permit shareholder access to the company proxy. Over the next decade, multiple regulatory and legislative developments culminated in the SEC's adoption of a revised version of proxy access. Under the rule as adopted, companies would include in their proxy materials the nominees of shareholders who owned at least 3 percent of the company's shares and had done so continuously for at least the prior three years. A shareholder could not use the rule to conduct a de facto proxy contest, because the rule only allowed a shareholder to put forward a short slate consisting of at least one nominee or up to 25 percent of the company's board of directors, whichever was greater.[3] Shareholders had very little chance to make use of the newly created power, however, because a federal court struck down the rule on the grounds that the SEC had failed to conduct an adequate cost-benefit analysis.[4] To date, the SEC has not attempted to revive proxy access by rule.

As a result, activist shareholders have returned to their company-by-company campaign of obtaining proxy access via the bylaws. As of 2016, over a third of S&P 500 companies had adopted proxy access bylaws either voluntarily or because of a shareholder proposal. The basic features of such bylaws are now well established. They typically allow a shareholder who has owned at least 3 percent of the company's stock for at least three years to nominate a short slate of up to 20 percent of the board. Many bylaws allow shareholder groups to act together to meet the 3 percent requirement, although those bylaws often cap the maximum number of shareholders who may collaborate at twenty. The shareholder nominee's biographical information must be included in the company's proxy statement and provision made on the company's proxy card for shareholders to vote for those nominees.[5]

PROXY ACCESS AND BSPS

As presently configured, proxy access and BSPs would only work where BSP employees serve as members of the board rather than the BSP serving as the board. In such cases, shareholders satisfying the requirements of the company's proxy access bylaw could nominate persons unaffiliated with the BSP – whether they are drawn from an alternative BSP or are wholly independent of BSPs – to hold up to 20 percent of the available board seats. This result strikes us as undesirable, since it will encourage the same sort of factionalism and cliquishness that likely accompany proxy access even in the absence of BSPs.

If companies adopting the BSP model were to modify their proxy access bylaws to permit shareholders to nominate a substitute BSP, however, significant corporate governance gains might be produced. The risk of a proxy contest that would replace the incumbent BSP, and presumably the top management team as well, provides an incentive for both the BSP and company managers to maximize shareholder welfare in the hope of avoiding such a contest. The *in terrorem* effect of proxy contests therefore should reduce agency costs.

Under the present legal regime, however, incumbent boards face only a very tiny risk of a proxy fight. To be sure, anyone can run for a board seat, but bearing the cost of identifying, contacting, lobbying, and tallying the votes of shareholders is prohibitively expensive for the gain of a single board seat. Accordingly, proxy contests are usually conducted only by those seeking control of the entire board, who typically are holders of large economic stakes in the firm. Hence, the shareholder activist community embraced proxy access as a next best solution.

In contrast, the BSP model and proxy access could be combined to produce an alternative superior both to traditional proxy contests for control and the short slate contests envisioned by proxy access. Specifically, corporations could specify in their articles of incorporation or bylaws a nomination and election process designed to create competitive elections. One option would be for someone, say the outgoing pre-BSP board, to initially nominate two (or more) BSPs to run at the first annual shareholder meeting of the BSP era. Shareholders would then choose one of the nominees to serve as the board for that year. Annual turnover might be too frequent, so one can imagine companies prescribing in advance a minimum term (subject to removal by shareholder vote), such as three years. (We discuss a variant of this idea in the next chapter.)

At subsequent elections, the incumbent BSP could stand for reelection, but shareholders holding a prescribed number of shares for a specified period could nominate alternative BSPs. It might also be desirable to permit the company's top management team to nominate an alternative BSP, because they will work closely with the incumbent BSP and thus be well informed as to its effectiveness. It likely also would be desirable to cap the number of BSPs that could be nominated at any election, so as to avoid overwhelming the shareholders with choices. The BSP receiving a plurality of the votes would then serve until the next election or, if preferred, a runoff could be held between the top two finishers so as to ensure that the chosen BSP had the support of the holders of a majority of the company's voting stock. The latter would alleviate concerns that a cohesive minority might be able to foist their preferred BSP on the company even where that BSP is not ideal from the perspective of shareholders as a whole. In particular, it mitigates the risk that the BSP would favor the interests of such a minority.

Notes

1. See Stephen M. Bainbridge, *Corporate Governance after the Financial Crises* 222–233 (2012) (arguing that proxy access was unwise).
2. For a detailed description and critique of the proposal, see Stephen M. Bainbridge, A Comment on the SEC's Shareholder Access Proposal, *Engage*, April 2004, at 18.
3. Facilitating Shareholder Director Nominations, Exchange Act Rel. No. 62,764 (Aug. 25, 2010).
4. *Bus. Roundtable* v. *SEC.*, 647 F.3d 1144 (D.C. Cir. 2011).
5. Alexandra Higgins & Peter Kimball, The Finer Points of Proxy Access Bylaws Come under the Microscope, www.issgovernance.com/finer-points-proxy-access-bylaws-come-microscope.

11

The BSP as an Alternative to Quinquennial
Board Elections

In Chapter 10, we looked at how BSPs could be used to achieve the goals of advocates of proxy access. If it would be optimal to give shareholders *more* power to discipline directors through elections, the use of the BSP would make this much more efficient and effective than the current board model. Elections would be less costly, more transparent, and more likely to result in informed choices of shareholders.

In this chapter, we show how BSPs could also be used to give shareholders *less* power. There is a view that insulating managers from the pressure of shareholders would enhance corporate value by permitting managers to focus on creating long-term corporate value through investments that might not satisfy the short-term preferences of some shareholders. We do not take a view on the relative merits of this idea, or the one presented in Chapter 10. Our point here is simply to show how BSPs can make it easier to effectuate managerial power, and to make that power more accountable and efficient.

INTRODUCTION

In April 2017, Luxembourg-based JAB-Holding Company, the investment arm of the Austrian billionaire Reimann family, took Panera Bread private in a deal valued at about $7.2 billion. For Panera's founder and CEO, Ron Shaich, the transaction was not just a windfall of entrepreneurial rents. It also freed the company from the short-term whimsy of activist investors. In one interview, Shaich ridiculed activist investors and lamented their impact on companies: "These guys show up, they're renting the stock and they tell you what to do – it's not a positive way to have dialogue."[1] He went on to claim that Panera can now focus more on the long term, to invest more in innovation, and to focus on delivering value to customers, instead of trying to satisfy the selfish greed of a small subset of investors.

Shaich is not alone. A survey of over 400 senior executives found a strong preference for satisfying accounting estimates over generating economic returns.[2] Three in four CEOs would leave money on the table to smooth out earnings in an attempt to satisfy short-term investors. (This is really bad for everyone, except of course CEOs and short-term investors.) One might discount this survey result on the grounds that CEOs might be distorting their answers to protect their jobs. After all, if their responses create the impression that short-term investors are bad (when they aren't), this might lead to new rules that insulate CEOs more from them.

But commentators decrying short-termism are not all CEOs or board members. Many corporate observers share this view of the current market in which corporate control is available for sale on a daily basis. In an article in the *Harvard Business Review* entitled "Focusing Capital on the Long Term," Dominic Barton (the head of McKinsey & Company) and Mark Wiseman (the head of a large Canadian investment firm) argue that the short-term pressure of activist investors is having "far-reaching consequences, including slower GDP growth, higher unemployment, and lower return on investment for savers."[3] The claim is buttressed by some recent empirical work by two Bank of England economists, Andrew Haldane and Richard Davies. They find that "short-termism is both statistically and economically significant in capital markets," and "[i]t appears also to be rising."[4] They conclude that the impact is negative for everyone in society.[5]

The law has recognized this potential problem to some extent by giving managers wide latitude in adopting takeover defenses, including the use of staggered boards (which can delay a takeover for long enough to make it unappealing) or the use of a poison pill (which can make any takeover a suicide pact). In addition, many states, even Delaware, have anti-combination statutes and so-called stakeholder statutes that deter or provide ammunition against unwanted takeovers.

While these takeover defenses might be justified in some instances, they are an overly blunt instrument, since they protect selfish managers, as well as ones looking after shareholders. One could reasonably conclude from all this that the net effect is that the law insulates managers and directors too much, making the vast majority of elections relatively meaningless and directors less informed than they should be. Even advocates of more shareholder activism believe that the current system of elections leaves a lot to be desired.

Corporate governance is an arms race. Annual elections of directors with the possibility of an involuntary change of control beget takeover defenses, which then beget demands for more shareholder control. At each stage, complexity is added. Managers innovate and create elaborate ways to protect control; shareholder activists then try to overcome these defenses, expending resources, generating lawsuits, and engendering ill will between management and shareholders. Courts have developed a rich body of case law to decide who is right and wrong in a particular case, but there is lots of uncertainty and significant costs (both in real terms and in the opportunity costs and chilling effects on management). When takeovers do happen, they result from destructive games of brinksmanship. The end result is a very costly game in which the parties to economic production end up in warring camps – management versus shareholders – instead of collaborating together. This is all thought to be necessary because the market for corporate control is necessary (to police bad management), but might be overly biased toward short-termism if not properly checked.

Two lawyers with experience in the takeover battles of the past several decades proposed a solution intended to improve this state of affairs. Martin Lipton and Steven Rosenblum, lawyers at the New York law firm Wachtell, Lipton, Rosen & Katz, argued in a 1999 law review article for quinquennial (that is, every five years) board elections.[6] The idea is to give board members and managers the time and insulation from the pressures of short-term investors to focus on creating long-term shareholder value. While this seems to put Lipton and Rosenblum squarely in the managerial-power camp in the debate between shareholder and manager control, they claim there is another potential benefit of their proposal: It would simultaneously raise the stakes for the elections that happen every five years with the goal of making these real elections where shareholders could focus their attention. Yes, corporate elections would be rarer, but they would be more meaningful and salient too. Most importantly, the proposal would be a form of détente, in which both sides agreed to disarm and come together in a predetermined way to collaborate on the future of the corporation.

Much more could be written about the Lipton and Rosenblum proposal, and we are not necessarily convinced that their proposal, as it is, would be welfare-enhancing. But if the idea of quinquennial elections has any merit, and we think it does, BSPs could be used to compliment the approach. If we are correct that BSPs can improve board performance, then that should be true whether the board is being elected every year or every five years. In fact, there are aspects of the combination of the BSP with quinquennial elections that may make the idea one that is viable, whereas it has yet to take off with the traditional sole-proprietor board model.

Let us first look briefly at Lipton and Rosenblum's idea, and then turn to a preview of what it might look like in a world with BSPs.

THE QUINQUENNIAL ELECTION PROPOSAL

Lipton and Rosenblum propose to make corporate elections look much more like presidential elections by holding an election for the board every five years, with limited ability (akin to impeachment) to remove directors in the interim. They sum up the proposal this way: "to convert every fifth annual meeting of stockholders into a meaningful referendum on the essential questions of corporate strategy and control, and to limit severely the ability of stockholders to effect changes in control between quinquennial meetings."[7] This may seem like a device to entrench, and thereby unjustly enrich, management, but it is far from obvious that it would work to that end. Moreover, although it is deceptively simple, if adopted it would cause profound changes by vastly simplifying the legal regulation of corporate governance.

The Lipton and Rosenblum proposal has the following features:

First, the quinquennial election would be the "sole means of accomplishing nonconsensual changes of control."[8] Directors could be removed for "criminal conduct" or "willful misfeasance" (that is, be impeached), or in cases in which the corporation fails to meet almost all of its plans and 20 percent of its shareholders call for a special election.[i] Otherwise the board would be insulated from shareholder accountability during that period. This would allow them, according to the proponents, to focus on a five-year plan for the corporation. Lipton and Rosenblum would limit any shareholder to less than 10 percent of the company's shares without board consent, thus preventing any one investor from acquiring de facto control or making the result of the five-year election a fait accompli.

Second, the quinquennial system would eliminate the need for takeover defenses, whether they are imposed by virtue of the company's charter, bylaws, or practice, or imposed by statute or regulation. Accordingly, a whole litany of controversial features of corporate law would go the way of the dodo: poison pills, staggered boards, standstill provisions, the *Unocal/Revlon* line of Delaware cases, control acquisition statutes, business combination moratorium statutes, Rule 14a-8, shareholder access to the proxy, unequal voting shares, and on and on would all be moot. (What would corporate law professors have left to write about!) The vast landscape of corporate law would be cleared of an enormous amount of doctrinal detritus and argument.

---

[i] Lipton and Rosenblum give this a bit more treatment in their article, but not enough to make it workable without more. If a quinquennial approach is utilized, we suspect that the details of the impeachment process would require a great deal of contractual specification and a yet-to-be-developed case law to define its parameters. This is because it will likely be utilized far more than impeachment is in the political process.

Importantly, a significant piece of leverage for plaintiffs' lawyers in mergers and acquisitions lawsuits, allegations that the board acted in violation of its fiduciary duties in enacting takeover defenses of one sort or another, would be eliminated. The modern tendency for multiple lawsuits to arise from every business combination transaction would end. Finally, managers and shareholders would, for the five-year periods, be in ceasefire, thus freeing managers to focus on building rather than protecting the corporate bastion.

Here is how Lipton and Rosenblum describe the impact:

> Eliminating the takeover battleground should remove much of the current friction between managers and institutional stockholders, which is often centered around takeover battles and anti-takeover defenses. Institutional stockholders have mounted anti-poison pill stockholder resolution campaigns. Incumbent boards have adopted a panoply of takeover defenses. Legislatures have enacted anti-takeover legislation. Stockholders complain that directors are simply trying to entrench themselves. Managers complain that stockholders only care about takeover premiums. The whole debate engenders a degree of distrust and hostility that undermines the necessary spirit of patience and partnership essential for long-term operating success in today's business world.[9]

As noted earlier, the Lipton and Rosenblum proposal is akin to a ceasefire and a call for serious elections to be the means by which we resolve issues of corporate control.

Third, given the increased stakes of the quinquennial election, Lipton and Rosenblum would require the company, in the year of the election, to send to shareholders at the end of the fiscal year a detailed report on the performance over the five years and the plan for the next five years. They would also require the board to choose an external expert, such as an accounting firm or an investment bank, to submit an independent review on the past and future prospects of the company. Shareholders of sufficient size (more than five percent or $5 million, whichever is lower) would then have sixty days to submit rival nominees to the board (on the company's proxy materials) for consideration at the quinquennial election. The details of the proposal are negotiable technicalities that should not obscure the key point about making elections rarer and more consequential.

The quinquennial election proposal has political roots, just like the board itself. Article II of the US Constitution provides that the President of the United States of America "shall hold his Office during the Term of four Years." The founders believed that a term of four years struck the right balance between accountability and authority. By giving the president a four-year term without the possibility of removal (except in extraordinary cases), the Constitution enables the president to focus on the long-term and avoid bending to the blowing of short-term political winds. But, by limiting the term, it allowed voters to hold politicians accountable and provided some check on abuse. Moreover, regularly scheduled elections allow the president, Congress, and political rivals to plan their legislative and political strategies with certainty about timing. Instead, elections could be held every two years (as for members of the House) or six years (as for the Senate), or even every year (as for most corporate directors). Another possibility would be for elections to be held on an episodic basis, as in the parliamentary system used in the United Kingdom and elsewhere. The tradeoff is between executive and voter power.

Just like voters elect the president, shareholders elect directors. And the same tradeoff between accountability and authority is present. Today, director elections happen annually, although in practice the elections look more like those in North Korea than those in North Dakota. Directors are nominated as a group (known as a "slate") to shareholders via the company's proxy voting materials, but run as individuals. Because directors generally run unopposed, the shareholder vote is more advisory than anything else. Indeed, under traditional plurality voting rules a vote of less than 50 percent suggests only shareholder dissatisfaction, because directors with even a single vote can continue to serve.[10] Of over 17,000 individual directors who stood for election to publicly traded firms in 2012,[11] only six directors (0.04 percent) stepped down or resigned because they did not get shareholder support.[12] Forty-one directors lost their elections (by conventional understanding of the term) in 2012 and yet remained as directors.[13] The only sure way to remove a director is through a proxy contest, in which a rival pays, win or lose, the full costs of distributing ballots to shareholders and convinces them to vote for the rival. Firms pay incumbents' costs no matter what, and incumbents are effectively spending shareholders' money to maintain their jobs.[14] Given the asymmetry of costs and benefits of this strategy, proxy contests are exceedingly rare, and are seen primarily in cases in which the benefits of winning a board seat include gaining control of the entire board, and thus the economics of the entire firm.[15] There is no market for corporate governance, only a market for corporate control.

Accordingly, most shareholders are rationally apathetic. This is true even of many large, institutional shareholders. Investors have an interest in companies being well run, but good governance benefits all shareholders equally, and therefore individual shareholders may have muted incentives to make investments in it. Accordingly, most large shareholders – representing ownership of something like 90 percent of shares – rely on third-party corporate governance experts, such as proxy adviser firms like ISS and Glass Lewis who sell their expertise, making recommendations to investment funds about how to vote. But while outsourcing a fund's votes may be efficient in theory, academic critics have identified cases of biased and self-serving behavior on the part of these advisers. Blind reliance on third-party recommendations is increasingly viewed as an abdication of a fund's duty to act in its investors' best interest.

Some investors use another approach – creating in-house governance teams that make recommendations to a fund's managers. These teams prepare corporate-governance reports, issue and evaluate governance guidelines, and engage with management and the board. But there is reason to believe that these teams are not up to the task. As of October 2016, Vanguard's governance team employed 15 people to cover some 13,000 companies; BlackRock employed about 20 for its 14,000 companies; and State Street employed fewer than 10 for about 9,000 companies.

The quinquennial proposal could make this process much more manageable. For one, elections would happen only every five years, dramatically reducing the amount of voting required by shareholders. In addition, hostile takeovers would be a thing of the past, thereby eliminating high-stakes, episodic voting in which informational asymmetries and incentives may be at their worst for shareholders vis-à-vis managers and other shareholders. Finally, the stakes of quinquennial elections would heighten attention on the preparation and analysis of managerial plans and performance, reducing information asymmetries during these elections relative to today's annual elections or proxy fights. Both investors and their advisors could focus their attention on the limited number of contested, five-year elections.

THE QUINQUENNIAL ELECTION AND THE BSP

The use of BSPs could be the silver bullet that makes a world with quinquennial elections more palatable. The flexibility of our proposal is demonstrated because one could alternatively tweak the appointment and election rules to go not in the director of shareholder empowerment but rather toward what one of us refers to as director primacy.[16] To encourage an even more robust form of director primacy, while simultaneously reducing the potential for shareholder disenfranchisement or abuse, one could imagine fixed five-year board terms for BSPs with no removal during that period (except for cause) but with mandatory rotation. Of course, the term need not be five years, and one can imagine competition among firms in their corporate charters on the optimal amount of insulation needed.

In fact, we think that the use of BSPs dramatically improves the case for Lipton and Rosenblum's proposal for quinquennial elections. Their proposal relies on individual directors, acting as sole proprietors, with all of the shortcomings of this approach discussed earlier. Without additional changes, shareholders would have limited information about individual director performance, directors would be subject to only weak market forces to discipline their behavior, and directors would still face the transaction cost problems of hiring expertise, instead of associating with it in a corporate form.

Lipton and Rosenblum implicitly recognize these problems, but propose solving them by requiring the company to make a significant disclosure every five years, supplemented by an independent report by outside experts. While in theory this could be a useful corrective, in practice the success of this approach is subject to several problems. One would need to define what should be in the report, consider the incentives of those creating and evaluating it, and take account of the effectiveness of any review of it by courts or regulators. The reporting process would inevitably generate litigation that would undercut one of the key arguments in favor of the proposal in the first place. It is a command-and-control approach to the information asymmetries between shareholders and directors. As such, it leaves unsolved a host of other problems, such as the fact that directors are elected individually but perform as a group.

BSPs offer a potentially more elegant solution that could simplify the quinquennial proposal (and thus also corporate law) even further. If BSPs improve board performance in general, they should do so for boards in a quinquennial or an annual election cycle. There is nothing about quinquennial elections that would make the BSP less appealing. In fact, we think the combination of a BSP with more episodic elections could be a potentially revolutionary positive change for corporate governance.

As discussed earlier, BSPs would bring increased reputational accountability, transparency, and competency to boards. This would have at least two positive impacts on the quinquennial election system. First, the fact that BSPs would be repeat players in a market for corporate governance would reduce the possibility that the behavior of the board would deviate from shareholders' interests during the five-year period between elections. After all, if BSPs want to preserve their reputation for doing good work, they will have to deliver during their exclusive management period. While market forces also operate to some extent for sole proprietor directors, these forces would be stronger, all else being equal for BSPs. For publicly traded BSPs, their performance would be measured in their stock price and in the analyst reports evaluating their performance at individual firms. For other BSPs, we expect there to be independent evaluation of their work by analyst equivalents, since those buying BSP services will demand someone make an assessment of their work.

Second, the BSP would make the elections at the end of the five-year period better. They would create an electoral environment that reflects informed shareholder choice and that incentivizes good behavior on the part of boards. As discussed in Chapter 6, the BSP would bring several positive features to the elections. Most obviously, a BSP with a brand-based reputation would be easier for shareholders to evaluate than a group of disparate, individual directors. BSPs would likely be able to communicate their plans and performance more efficiently than a board comprising individuals. In addition, it would easier for external rivals to the board to mount a campaign to oust the current board. The BSP could use its national reputation as a means of lowering transaction and communication costs. Large BSPs could also spread the costs of mounting an election campaign across many potential elections, thus reducing the costs through diversification. The net effect would be better communication, more competition in quinquennial elections, and therefore improved incentives for board performance.

The company could, of course, enhance the possibility of a contested election, if it believed that an election about corporate governance (as opposed to corporate control) were in the interests of shareholders. This could be because of performance of a particular board or as a means of more generally creating a competitive environment for governance. Whatever the reason, the company could invite particular BSPs to run for election at the quinquennial meeting. A public or private call, akin to a RFP, could be utilized to express an interest in presenting shareholders with a choice at the quinquennial meeting.

Or, one could imagine rules, either as part of a particular corporate charter or in federal or state law, that permit shareholders with certain characteristics to nominate BSPs to run in the quinquennial election. For instance, borrowing from the proposed proxy access rules, one could imagine that shareholders holding a certain percentage of shares (say, 5 or 10 percent) for a certain period of time (say, at least one year) be permitted to use the company's proxy to run an alternative board or BSP. This was part of the original Lipton and Rosenblum proposal – they permitted shareholders holding the lesser of five percent or $5 million to nominate rival slates during the quinquennial election. This could be adopted by a firm or regulator as part of a BSP approach, although using a BSP would make any mandatory rule less necessary because BSPs will likely have stronger incentives and lower costs to mount rival campaigns in the first place.

We could go a step further and make the quinquennial election even more salient by requiring the incumbent board to step aside every five years. We consider this modification next.

QUINQUENNIAL ELECTIONS AND MANDATORY ROTATION OF THE BSP

Although we expect a quinquennial election with BSPs as a possibility to bring meaningful choice to shareholders, an additional tweak could ensure that the quinquennial election presented shareholders with a consequential election. A company or a regulator (the SEC or a state corporate code) could provide a limited period of service by any BSP to encourage competition, gain a fresh perspective, and ameliorate concerns about conflicts of interest (across companies) or concentration in the BSP market. For instance, the rules for a company or for all companies could term limit a BSP to a particular number of terms or years for a particular company.

Returning to the analogy to politics, the 22nd Amendment of the US Constitution provides an analog. Section 1 of that amendment provides:

> No person shall be elected to the office of the President more than twice, and no person who has held the office of President, or acted as President, for more than two years of a term to which some other person was elected President shall be elected to the office of President more than once.[17]

There is a tradeoff between experience and potential for corruption or stale thinking inherent in any system where one person or entity has executive power. This amendment reflects a view that two terms totaling eight years is the optimal point in this tradeoff – it gives the people the opportunity to reward a good job, while ensuring that the political system refreshes itself regularly.

One could take a similar approach with BSPs elected during quinquennial elections. It might look something like this: A company would nominate at least two BSPs to stand for election. Shareholders would elect one to serve a set, say five-year, term. During that five-year term, the BSP would have all the powers enumerated by Lipton and Rosenblum, as well as the limitations they proposed. For instance, the board could not be removed except for conduct that was illegal or amounted to gross malfeasance of duty. As such, the board would have the power to resist any hostile takeovers, since its control of the corporation for that period would be nearly absolute. Then, at the end of the five-year term, the incumbent BSP would have to rotate off and a new BSP would be elected.

Or, consistent with the approach taken by the 22nd Amendment, the BSP could be reelected to control the company for one additional five-year term, but could serve no more than two such terms. This would provide similar incentives as the electoral rules do for term-limited politicians: incentives for good work, but a check against abuse of power. Of course, the idea of term limits is not applied universally in the political context. Presidents are term limited, but members of Congress are not.

There is an analogy here to the mandatory rotation of auditors. After the accounting scandals of the late 1990s and early 2000s, the idea of mandatory rotation of auditors became a live issue. As of this writing, the Public Company Accounting Oversight Board (PCAOB) is considering mandatory rotation of auditors, such that an audit firm would serve a maximum number of years before it would have to be replaced by another firm. (Auditing firms are currently required to rotate the lead partner every five years.[18]) The tradeoffs between experience and potential misbehavior (intentionally or otherwise) are the same.

One can imagine adopting this approach for BSPs either alone or in combination with other governance arrangements. For instance, a firm could put in its charter or the legislature could require a mandatory rotation of BSPs after a set number of years. The arguments here for and against such a requirement are straightforward, and are similar to those now being debated by the PCAOB with respect to accountants.[19] Mandatory rotation has the benefit of reducing capture by managers, bringing new ideas, and reducing agency costs. On the downside, any rule will be both over-inclusive – forcing out competent boards – and under-inclusive, allowing incompetent boards to remain in place longer than they deserve. One might think that a company would have the proper incentives to optimize how long a board stayed in place, thus making any mandatory rule unnecessary. While we think there are reasons to doubt that companies' incentives are perfect, in the absence of some significant experimentation, it is far too early to propose a set time period as optimal, assuming one exists across many firms.

Another point in the same vein is worth mentioning. While Lipton and Rosenblum chose a five-year term for the board's exclusive governance period, there is nothing sacrosanct about this number. To be sure, they probably didn't pick it out of a hat. We suspect it is based on their intuition about the optimal tradeoff between accountability and authority. We suspect the founders at Philadelphia writing the US Constitution made the same sort of intuitive judgments about terms for House (2), Senate (6), and President (4). We could imagine different numbers in both the corporate and political context. But without experimentation, we cannot know for sure whether the number chosen is optimal.

Herein lies a difference between the corporate and political worlds. A statute is not needed to cover all corporations with the same rule – thousands of corporations can experiment with different BSP terms, and regulators can take note of the results of these experiences. Of course, it is also possible that the optimal board period varies across firms, making any legislative solution a bad idea. It is for this reason that we think the best approach (at least until we know more) is for the question of terms to be left to the market to sort out. Firms that choose optimal board terms will be rewarded in the market; those that don't will be ground under.

This assumes that firms will innovate. None have yet adopted the Lipton and Rosenblum approach that we know of, and this undercuts an organic market evolution story to some extent. However, this is likely because the necessary requirement that nonconsensual changes in control be banned during the five-year periods would be held unconstitutional under state law if adopted as part of a corporate charter. It is for this reason that Lipton and Rosenblum argue for a tweak to state law to permit firms to implement such a rule.[20] This would free firms to experiment.

One reason why no state has yet done this might be because without BSPs, there would be a worry that the board and the election would not have the effect Lipton and Rosenblum imagine, but would just further entrench management. Therefore, two state-law changes are necessary: the elimination of the natural person requirement and the exclusive governance possibility. We think this combination could be a potential game changer, but we could be wrong. There is no reason, however, for a state to offer this possibility to encourage governance innovation. If it turns out badly, the rules can always be repealed.

If we were legislators, we would require that firms put these governance rules in their charter either at the IPO stage or, for firms that are already public, via shareholder-approved amendment. For the latter, moreover, special voting rules might be warranted to ensure that the change is not designed as an entrenchment tool. A majority of the minority or other supermajority voting rule might make sense. More work would need to be done to develop the optimal legislative package. For instance, perhaps it would be best to require firms opting for quinquennial elections to use a BSP, to nominate two (or more) BSPs as alternatives in the first election, and so on.

SUMMARY

The chief advantage of combining our idea with that of Lipton and Rosenblum is that the virtues of BSPs help reduce the potential objections to their quinquennial election proposal. BSPs would be more accountable, more agile and able, and more transparent in terms of performance, thus reducing the risks from giving them free reign for a period of five years. If courts impose stronger fiduciary duties on BSPs, as we expect, boards are staffed with more capable individuals, board performance in terms of governance is measured by the market, and BSPs have large reputational capital, there is less reason to suspect that reducing shareholder oversight to once every five years would result in more managerial slack or self-serving behavior.

Of course, there is nothing about our proposal that requires a move toward quinquennial or any other type of election process. This then highlights that our proposal has no ideological or particular substantive corporate governance valence. The use of BSPs would not necessarily result in more shareholder power or more managerial power. What it would do, however, is make either of these options more likely, depending on the other forces at work. If shareholder access to the proxy with the goal of more competition for board seats is desired, our proposal can achieve this more directly, at lower cost, and with less downside than the current model. On the other hand, if what would maximize shareholder value is greater managerial control and a longer-term view for board decision making, our proposal could be adapted to this goal as well. In short, both corporate governance experts like Lucian Bebchuk (shareholder power) and Martin Lipton (managerial power) should see the value in our proposed board model. We are trying to reconceptualize the board, not necessarily move it in a particular direction.

Notes

1. Craig Giammona, What the CEO of Panera hates about Wall Street, *St. Louis Dispatch*, Aug. 22, 2017, available at www.stltoday.com/business/lo cal/what-the-ceo-of-panera-hates-about-wall-street/article_bcbd89f1-890b -53f9-a401-5dde8b2c345b.html.
2. John R. Graham, et al., "The Economic Implications of Corporate Financial Reporting" 40 *J. Accounting and Econ.* 3 (2005).
3. Dominic Barton and Mark Wiseman, Focusing Capital on the Long Term, Jan.–Feb. 2014, available at https://hbr.org/2014/01/focusing-capi tal-on-the-long-term.
4. Andrew G. Haldane and Richard Davies, The Short Long, presented at the 29th Société Universitaire Européene de Recherches Financières Colloquium, Brussels, May 2011, available at www.bankofengland.co.uk/ archive/Documents/historicpubs/speeches/2011/speech495.pdf.
5. There are commentators on the other side. In a prominent article in the prestigious *Journal of Finance*, Alon Brav, Wei Jiang, Frank Partnoy, and Randall Thomas examined activist hedge funds during the period 2001 to 2006. They find evidence that activist hedge funds had a significantly

positive impact on operating performance over a multi-year period, as well as increasing CEO turnover and reduced executive compensation. See Alon Brav et al., Hedge Fund Activism, Corporate Governance, and Firm Performance, 63 *J. Fin.* 1729 (2008); see also Lucian A. Bebchuk et. al., The Long-Term Effects of Hedge Fund Activism, 115 *Colum. L. Rev.* 1085 (2015) (finding "no evidence that activist interventions, including the investment-limiting and adversarial interventions that are most resisted and criticized, are followed by short-term gains in performance that come at the expense of long-term performance.").

6. Martin Lipton & Steven A. Rosenblum, A New System of Corporate Governance: The Quinquennial Election of Directors, 58 *U. Chi. L. Rev.* 187 (1991).

7. Ibid. at 225.

8. Ibid. at 240.

9. Ibid. at 243.

10. Until recently, state law merely required a plurality shareholder vote. DGCL § 216(3) formerly provided, for example, that "Directors shall be elected by a plurality of the votes of the shares present in person or represented by proxy at the meeting and entitled to vote on the election of directors." Stephen M. Bainbridge, *Mergers and Acquisitions* 153 (3rd edn. 2012). Today, however, state law permits – but does not require – firms to adopt various schemes having the effect of requiring director candidates to receive a majority of the votes cast in order to serve. See ibid. at 154–157 (discussing state law developments).

11. James B. Stewart, For Boards, Re-Election is a Slam Dunk, Mar. 30, 2013.

12. Ibid. Although sixty-one directors received less than a majority of shareholder votes, directors run unopposed and therefore even a single vote (which could be their own!) suffices to be elected as a legal matter.

13. See, James B. Stewart, When Shareholder Democracy Is Sham Democracy, *NY Times*, Apr. 12, 2013, available at www.nytimes.com/2013/04/13/business/sham-shareholder-democracy.html?_r=1&adxnnl=1&ref=jamesbstewart&adxnnlx=1366121251-7wtOwup7xCraPpGPvzw79A.

14. See, e.g. *Eisenberg v. Flying Tiger Line, Inc.*, 451 F. 2d 267 (2nd Cir. 1971) (describing reimbursement rules for proxy contests). For a general discussion of these issues, see Lucian Arye Bebchuk, A Framework for Analyzing Legal Policy towards Proxy Contests, 78 *Cal. L. Rev.* 1073, 1086 (1990) (analyzing proxy contests, including reimbursement asymmetries, using a law and economics approach, and noting how the rules strongly favor incumbents).

15. Stephen M. Bainbridge, *Corporate Governance after the Financial Crisis*, 177 (2012) (discussing rarity of proxy contests and reasons therefor).

16. Stephen M. Bainbridge, Director Primacy and Shareholder Disempowerment, 119 *Harv. L. Rev.* 1735 (2006).

17. US Constitution, Amendment XXII, section 1.
18. See SEC Release No. 33–8183, Strengthening the Commission's Requirements Regarding Auditor Independence, Jan. 28, 2003, available at www.sec.gov/rules/final/33–8183.htm.
19. See Dena Aubin, "PCAOB's Debate over Auditor Rotation Moves to Congress" (Reuters) (http://blogs.reuters.com/taxbreak/2012/03/29/pcaob s-debate-over-auditor-rotation-moves-to-congress/).
20. Lipton & Rosenblum, Corporate Governance, at 250.

12

The BSP in a Post-Monitoring Board World

Times are changing. Unfortunately, boards are not. While the size, scope, complexity, and risk of modern businesses have increased dramatically over the past five decades, there has been nearly zero innovation in corporate governance. No doubt boards are better today at some things than they were a few decades ago, but these improvements have come at a large cost. A focus on oversight and monitoring has taken attention away from strategy and risk optimization. Fetishizing independence has eroded firm-specific and industry-specific knowledge, and this has diminished the credibility of the board as an arbiter of the value of the company in the hands of managerial rivals. There is a hydraulic effect at work – given the constraints law puts on the kinds of governance possible, pushing here reduces effort or effect there. And there is increasing evidence that modern boards are just not up to the tasks in front of them.

Consider the venerable investment bank, J.P. Morgan. In 1986, J.P. Morgan reported a net income of $872 million based on about $76 billion in assets. In 2016, J.P. Morgan made a net income of nearly $25 billion from over $2.5 trillion in assets. A bank deploying $2.5 *trillion* in assets is a completely different animal than one managing less than $100 billion. The bank has grown internationally, as well. Then, it had major operations in eleven foreign countries, with assets there of about $18 billion; today, it operates in dozens of countries, and has assets of nearly $600 billion. In short, J.P. Morgan has grown about thirty times in thirty years.[i]

It hasn't just got bigger. It is also much more complex. Back then, J.P. Morgan was a plain-vanilla investment bank, while today it engages in lending, consulting, and wealth management. It also runs hedge funds, enormous

---

[i] We thank Professor Jeffrey Gordon of Columbia University Law School for inspiring this example.

fixed-income and currency trading operations, and has sophisticated deriva-tives businesses. It is safe to say that if a seventy-year-old banker, out of the business for a few decades, found his way back to the floor on a typical trading day at J.P. Morgan, they would find it utterly unrecognizable.

The enhanced regulatory environment, both domestically and internation-ally, has also added to the complexity. In just the past two decades, the business of banking, already one of the most highly regulated industries in the world, has become even more intensely regulated. Congress added significant new responsibilities for managers and boards with the reforms in SOX and Dodd-Frank. The former, a response to the accounting scandals that roiled the economy during the dot.com boom, dramatically increased board responsi-bility for financial and accounting statements. Although financial institutions were not at the center of the scandals, the size, risk, and complexity of modern banks made internal control systems, risk management practices, and account-ing oversight an especially large challenge for banking boards. The latter, a response to the financial crisis that was precipitated on Wall Street, intensified regulatory obligations in ways unheard of in the history of banking. Dodd-Frank, measuring approximately 2,400 pages, mandated countless new respon-sibilities for corporate managers and boards regarding the oversight of bank risk-taking. Just one of these, the so-called Volker Rule, covering seventy-one additional pages of regulation, has generated enormous regulatory compli-ance costs for firms and risks for boards.

Older laws, like the Foreign Corrupt Practices Act (1974) and the Bank Secrecy Act (1970), have become much more important over time as well, increasing the burden on directors. Anti–money-laundering rules promul-gated under these laws have become major oversight obligations in a world of globalized financial transactions that permit money and new currencies, like bitcoin, to be transferred instantaneously and anonymously across the globe in fractions of a second.

A sense of the regulatory scope of the modern bank is captured by the growth of compliance professionals needed to manage this burden. In an April 2015 letter to shareholders, Jamie Dimon, the CEO of J.P. Morgan Chase, announced the hiring in that year of 8,000 new compliance professionals, bringing the bank's total to nearly 25,000. The growth is staggering: The bank employed fewer than 7,000 in compliance roles at the beginning of 2012, and far fewer just a decade or two earlier.

And yet, the number of bank directors has not scaled in accordance with the greater stakes, work load, demands of expertise, and complexity. J.P. Morgan had approximately a dozen directors in the 1980s, the same number that it has today. Why has J.P. Morgan added more than 20,000 compliance professionals during the past several decades, while keeping the number of board members constant?

One reason is that the current model of the board as a collegial, team-based group of individuals may face diseconomies of scale. While the production of most things becomes cheaper and more efficient as the scale of the enterprise increases, governance in a team-based model may not. After all, it would be incredibly difficult to have a consensus-seeking, collegial board with a thousand or even a hundred members. No board that we know of contains greater than twenty individuals, and this likely reflects the limitations on achieving scale in governance under the current model. One could imagine, as we do in this book, alternative board models that would permit some efficiencies in scale to address the increase in complexity, but due to the ancient structure of boards, the problem is acute.

Another problem facing boards when addressing increasing complexity is the limited amount of time board members can spend on board-related work for a particular company. The rise of the monitoring board (replacing the strategy board) has brought with it an increased emphasis on board independence. These independence rules essentially ensure board members are part-timers who cannot devote more than a fraction of their time and effort to their board work.

The NYSE listing rules, for example, require (following federal law) that independent directors comprise a majority of the board of directors. (NASDAQ has similar rules.) Independent directors must also be a majority of key committees, such as the audit committee, compensation committee, and nominating committee. To satisfy the independence requirement, a board member must have no "material relationship" with the company, "either directly or as a partner, shareholder, or officer of an organization that has a relationship with the company."[1] The NYSE, like other exchanges, does not define the entire scope of "material relationship," but offers a few bright-line rules that would disqualify any director as independent. These include any employment relationship of the director with the company over the past three years, payment of more than $120,000 from the company during the past three years (other than for director services), and being a current employee. In short, directors are legally required to spend mere days on the business they are supposed to be managing at a high level. And, moreover, any attempt to increase the amount of board member effort would potentially compromise the important incentives to monitor the firm on behalf of shareholders and other stakeholders created by the independence requirements.

The complexity of modern governance is not the only factor that is putting pressure on the traditional board model. The changes in stock ownership over the past few decades – with massive outflows from actively managed accounts and inflows into passive index funds – are also putting pressure on boards in new ways. There is an emergent school of thought contending that shareholder activism is a response to alleged shortcomings of the monitoring model and the phenomena described earlier.[2] Proponents of this line of argument contend that boards need to evolve to a "thickly informed" director model, in which the board would develop deep knowledge about the company and its industry. This would require significant changes in what directors do and how board structure might evolve to support this broader role. In our view, the BSP model is an ideal vehicle for implementing such a post-monitoring board.

THE THICKLY INFORMED BOARD

Two years after we published the *Stanford Law Review* article in which we first proposed BSPs,[3] the Millstein Center for Global Markets and Corporate Ownership hosted an event on May 5, 2016 entitled, "A New Model for the Public Corporation Board." Professors Ronald Gilson and Jeffrey Gordon framed the discussion by proposing an alternative to the current board model, which they called the "thickly informed board." In a blog post, Gordon set out a problem with corporate governance that he believes explains the rise of activist investors:

> [T]he board of a large public company, as presently constituted, cannot credibly evaluate management's strategy or respond to activist criticisms of that strategy. The current model of corporate governance is a product of academic thinking of the 1970s, which produced the "monitoring board" staffed by "independent directors" whose main source of monitoring capacity is the stock price performance of the company over time and compared to peers. These directors are decidedly part-time; relying on information supplied by management and stock market prices, they are "thinly informed." In its time, this model of board governance was an advance and suited the needs and capacities of dispersed shareholders.[4]

But, as Gordon noted, shareholders are no longer dispersed. Institutional investors, such as index and pension funds, have reconsolidated the ownership of American companies into a small group of hands. For instance, nearly 90 percent of public companies count one of three large institutional investors – State Street Global Advisors, Vanguard, and BlackRock – as their largest investor.

Activist investors supporting a change in management or strategy at their portfolio companies frequently pitch their ideas to these large investors.

Management thereupon typically responds with a counter that the firm is doing just fine, leaving institutional investors to make a choice between obviously self-interested proposals by both sides in these corporate battles. This is where the board of directors should come in and play a vital inter-mediating role. After all, it can safely be said that the two primary jobs for a board are to hire and fire the CEO and to make informed and independent valuations of the business during a potential change in control. But here is where, according to Gordon, the current board model falls woefully short:

> The thinly informed independent director has no answer to the activist's counterplan and thus is not a credible adjudicator for the institutional investor. That is, given the present board model, the institutional investor cannot say, "we know management is biased, but the directors, who have deep knowledge of the firm and the industry, have looked closely at the activist's counterplan and have rejected it, and *therefore so should we*."[5]

The critics who decry all activists as greedy short termers are misguided, Gordon believes, because much of the activist money is tied up in long-term (seven to ten year) hedge funds. But certainly, there are some activist investors who are focused on a quick buck at the expense of the long-term value of a particular company. Unfortunately, as Gordon notes, there is no credible institutional mechanism for sorting between these two activist types. Management is likely to oppose both, and activists don't reveal their type and can't credibly commit to being a good guy.

In the recent battle for control of Arconic, discussed in an earlier chapter, Elliott Management and the management of Arconic (the successor to Alcoa's downstream business) were locked in a battle for the future of the business. Elliott proposed a rival slate of directors to that proposed by Arconic in an attempt to chart a new course for the company, which it argues is under-performing. Both sides waged costly campaigns to convince shareholders to vote for their board candidates. Elliott, for its part, issued a 336-page PowerPoint presentation making its case to shareholders, as well as numerous press releases, videos of directors and their plans, and other communications. It spent many hundreds of thousands of dollars making its case. Arconic management countered with its own sixty-page deck and a more limited set of public communications about its directors and their plans for the company.

The recipients of this information were, by and large, institutional investors and their advisors at proxy advisor firms, like ISS or Glass Lewis. This situation is far from ideal for several reasons. First, the proxy advisor firms are well known to be interested more in advancing their own special interests than in being fair arbiters of corporate governance advice. Second, institutional investors, like Fidelity, Vanguard, and Blackrock, are rationally apathetic about the recommendations made by proxy advisors and their own votes. Most funds are heavily indexed, meaning their votes for one firm do not materially change the value of their portfolios. While everyone is interested in good governance, the stakes are relatively low for index funds in any election. Is it any wonder that they aren't sophisticated shoppers for voting advice or spending hours digesting hundreds of pages of PowerPoint slides? Third, the law regulating shareholder voting is flawed. Most obviously, it requires institutional investors to vote, even when they have weak incentives to choose wisely. A better rule would be to permit funds to vote only when it matters to them and when they have a reasonable basis for their votes, or believe the proxy advisors' opinions are well founded. Liability might even be appropriate against funds if they blindly rely on the unsupported recommendations of proxy advisors.

In any event, the situation is hardly tenable. A relatively weak and uninformed board simply cannot play the role of intermediary in this battle. A phenomenal board might be able to overcome these structural failures, but the Arconic board, like many others, suffered from institutional weaknesses. For one, the Arconic board was plagued with severe conflicts of interest. The lead independent director, Pat Russo, also served as chair of the Hewlett-Packard (HP) board, of which the CEO of Arconic, Klaus Kleinfeld, is also a director. Russo was charged with overseeing Kleinfeld's compensation at Arconic, while Kleinfeld oversaw Russo's compensation at HP. Such conflicts of interest, which are all too common among modern, interconnected boards, disable the board even further.

In the spirit of our work, Professor Gordon therefore proposes a new role for the board:

> [C]redibly evaluating and then verifying that management's strategy is best for the company (or making changes if it is not). Boards need directors who will have that credibility, which is won through deep knowledge about the company and its industry and an appropriate time commitment. Venture capital and private equity firms attract funds for long term investing because they provide a different style of corporate governance that includes directors who are engaged and knowledgeable. Such "thickly informed" directors provide "high powered" monitoring of managerial performance. They enable investors to trust that the firm is pursuing a planning horizon that is suited to its genuine opportunities, "right termism." Public corporations will be better run if their boards are staffed by directors with such capacities.[6]

But Gordon does not offer a specific, detailed plan for operationalizing his proposal for staffing current boards with better directors who can distinguish between "management's claim of market myopia and activist's claim of managerial hyperopia."[7] The reader will not be surprised to learn, of course, that we believe the BSP offers a solution to this problem.

In a presentation at the Millstein conference, Professor Fabrizio Ferri offered some evidence from the literature about what works and what does not work for board members today with the hope of informing the question about how to make directors better. His diagnosis of the problem, citing the board of Lehman Brothers at the time of its collapse, is familiar at this point. The *Wall Street Journal* noted at the time that the Lehman board, which "carried the health of the world's financial system," was a lackluster group: "Nine of them are retired. Four of them are over 75 years old. One is a theater producer, another a former Navy admiral. Only two have direct experience in the financial-services industry."[8] As we've noted throughout this book, this state of affairs is all too common.

In his presentation, Ferri considered a variety of potential director attributes to more thickly inform the board, but does not propose a mechanism (other than jawboning) to make the changes he hints might be valuable. First, he considered industry expertise. Surveys of board members and executives suggest that industry expertise is the most sought-after director qualification, but during the first half of the Aughts, only 25 percent of independent directors in the S&P 500 had relevant industry experience.[9] Ferri also cited a handful of studies supporting the intuition behind these survey results. One empirical study shows a positive impact of industry experience on firm value, greater pay-for-performance sensitivity, and better innovation.[10] Another finds higher accounting reporting quality when audit committee members have relevant industry experience.[11] The same holds true, according to another study, when board members on the compensation committee have industry experience.[12]

Ferri also looked at other attributes, such as diversity of various kinds, skill sets, experience as CEOs, country of origin, and a variety of others. None seemed to have a significant impact on firm value according to the existing literature. One somewhat surprising result is a finding that "professional directors" – directors whose sole employment is as a director – are associated with worse corporate performance. According to a recent paper – "Does the Market Value Professional Directors?" – these directors, which account for about 40 percent of independent directors, lead to lower valuation, worse pay-for-performance sensitivity, and worse results from acquisitions.[13] The market also reacts negatively to the announcement of a professional director. Although not "professional directors" in the sense proposed by corporate law reformers, the evidence nevertheless suggests caution when it comes to believing the solution to boards is as simple as greater independence and fewer outside commitments.

We are persuaded by Professor Gordon's and Professor Ferri's diagnosis of the central problem with corporate boards today. There are two fundamental changes to the market that are stressing the current monitoring role played by boards and the longstanding model of board composition: first, the increasing complexity and risk of corporate activities, and second, the changes in stock ownership that have intensified activist investing and put boards in the difficult position of intermediating two rivals with competing claims, but not having the information or tools to effectively evaluate those claims.

But, we have yet to see a specific, concrete proposal for how to improve boards. As we've noted throughout this book, reform proposals abound from all quarters on how to improve boards. None of them, however, address the force of the Gordon critique or the problems with boards that we have outlined at length in this book. How can we create a "thickly informed" board that can intermediate the claims of rivalrous groups with competing claims on the best way to promote long-term corporate value? It is very unlikely that the way to do this, in the face of ever-increasing pressure on boards, is to simply rely on the market to choose better board members, especially when the law does so much to limit the kinds of board services and the ways that they are provided.

We think that providing board or governance services through a BSP offers the most likely way of creating a "thickly informed" board that can both monitor the increasingly complex functions and activities of corporate America, and can credibly serve the role of reliable intermediary between passive and active shareholders vying for control over the direction of corporate activity. We also think that BSPs can do so without the negative market reaction currently associated with professional directors, because we believe the market will recognize the advantages a firm brings to the task relative to an individual.

THE BSP AS THICKLY INFORMED BOARD

The corporate board is increasingly ill suited to dealing with the realities of modern business. Large American corporations are operating on a global scale of unprecedented size and interconnectedness, dealing with the most aggressive regulatory environment in history, and interacting with investors – a mix of small, aggressive activist investors and large, passive institutional investors – that are proving difficult to manage effectively. The board is the central node in this story, as in all corporate stories, by virtue of their legal status as the managerial authority of corporations. The confluence of complexity, risk, regulation, and investment management is stressing the corporate board model that has prevailed for the past century. In this world, there is an increased importance for boards to provide strategic advice and monitoring functions, and thus a greater emphasis on skills, expertise, and experience of board members. Of course, as noted earlier, the design of the current board model creates a natural tension between pushing in the direction of more professional directors with greater investment in a particular firm and the independence and other requirements of boards under current law.

The BSP is a particularly apt mechanism for creating a thickly informed board. In the previous chapters, we have described the benefits that we believe would flow from a corporation hiring a BSP to provide board services. These include the ability of corporate BSPs to devote more time to corporate governance, to improve information flows inside and outside of the firm, to provide fiat access to expertise in a wide variety of areas, to intensify incentives for those providing governance incentives, to be more accountable to share-holders and the government, and so on.

Let's return to the example of J.P. Morgan. The current board of J.P. Morgan brings a variety of knowledge and experience to the work of managing the business in its complex milieu. But these directors cannot possibility devote the time necessary or deploy the expertise necessary to address the problems that J.P. Morgan has faced and will face. Prior to the early 2000s, it is likely that no board member of J.P. Morgan had ever heard of "credit deriva-tives"; by 2007, the firm's investments in these instruments nearly led to its downfall. After the financial crisis struck, J.P. Morgan was quickly in need of expertise on the board about public relations, government relations, bank-ruptcy, and a host of other topics. The board could, of course, buy these services and expertise in the market – hiring various consultants or advisors – but it would require spending money, their own or the firm's, and entering into a formal relationship. That relationship would be one of uncertainty, since it would be at arm's length, and would be subject to various inefficien-cies by virtue of this fact.

If J.P. Morgan hired a BSP to provide board services, things might have looked differently. As credit derivatives came online in the early Aughts, the BSP could draw on in-house experts or build the in-house expertise as part of its service role. Consultancies, such as McKinsey & Company and Bain, routinely build knowledge behind the scenes that they can use to inform their front-line consultants in their interactions with their clients. The BSP would have economies of scale in the production and distribution of this knowledge, since it would likely serve multiple companies in the economy, unlike a typical board member. Then, as the crisis unfolded, the BSP could draw on other resources to address the problems that J.P. Morgan faced on a daily basis. Teams of experts could be deployed to address issues of market risk, government risk, investor relations, back office management, and so forth. These teams might work with the CEO or instead merely provide briefings to the individual or team from the BSP that served as the de facto board. Whatever the case, the major upside of the BSP is the ability to marshal greater resources and expertise, with stronger incentives, over a given problem and time frame.

We expect board services provided by BSPs would also be more adaptive to changing market conditions both across time and across firms. What worked in the 1970s or 1980s might not work today, for the reasons described earlier. By enshrining mechanisms of corporate governance in law – such as the natural person requirement of Delaware law or the independence rules of federal law and stock exchanges – the ability to adapt to local conditions is dramatically reduced. If firms were free to choose governance approaches, they would choose a monitoring board when it was optimal, and they would choose a strategy board or other type of board when that was optimal. Of course, law can change too, but it is far more sticky and resistant to change, because of the political coalitions that must be built and the status quo bias of legislators and interest groups.

Not only is one model – such as the monitoring model – potentially out of date at a particular time, but it may be suboptimal for particular firms during a time when it is the optimal approach for firms on average. Current governance practices effectively forbid such localized experimentation, instead foisting a one-size-fits-all approach on American corporations. It seems obvious that what would be optimal for J.P. Morgan would not necessarily be so for J.C. Penny's or any firm in between.

THE PRIVATE EQUITY ANALOG

In calling for academics to rethink the current board model several years after we published our original paper presenting the BSP concept, Professor Gordon described the thickly informed board as analogous to a private equity firm. In our original paper, we drew the same analogy, comparing the BSP to private equity governance. It is worth exploring this analogy a little further as a means of understanding the BSP approach and its potential benefits.

One of the chief virtues of the private equity industry is that it consolidates the ownership interests of the firm, and thus helps undo the harms that flow from the separation of ownership and control. For companies underperforming by virtue of poor management and governance, private equity offers a means of solving this problem. If board members are insufficiently skilled or attentive, or if managers hold sway over them by virtue of conflicts of interest, ousting the board, replacing the managers, and eliminating the problems of dispersed, rationally apathetic shareholders may work a fix. Managers of private-equity-owned firms have a tremendous economic stake in the success of these firms, and therefore, it is thought, better incentives to take care and make good decisions.

Although not every private equity deal is successful, the industry as a whole has performed remarkably well over the past few decades. In an assessment of this success, McKinsey & Company concluded that the gains were not from price arbitrage, financial engineering, or choosing industries that were likely to have improved prospects, but rather from better management.[14] The McKinsey study called this "governance arbitrage." The key element of which, the study concluded, was primarily the way that the boards operated in a "more engaged form of corporate governance."[15] In other words, a more thickly informed board.

When a private equity fund takes over a business, it does not populate the board with the CEO's cronies, celebrity chefs, and kids of politicians. Private equity funds stock the boards of their portfolio companies with the proprietors of the business or their representatives, as well as industry experts and governance ninjas. These directors have a strong sense of personal ownership that is enhanced by the typical carry arrangements of the fund model. These board members are actively involved in decision making at a high level, bringing their experience to bear on fundamental questions facing the business. This type of model appears to be quite effective at improving outcomes for a set of underperforming businesses.

A downside or shortcoming of the private equity model, however, is that the improved governance only obtains when the entire firm is taken over, and the public shareholders are displaced. This makes private equity expensive and risky. If there are frictions in the market for capital, it may prevent even beneficial takeovers from happening. Moreover, there will be some governance improvements that cannot be justified by the costs of capital, weighted to the risk and opportunity cost. For instance, if a $50 billion firm could be made into a $51 billion firm through an improvement in governance, but if the financing costs (the weighted cost of capital to do a takeover) cost more than $1 billion, then the improvement will not be made. This is the case even if the actual costs of improving the firm's governance are trivial.

A market for corporate governance arising from the use of BSPs could be a half step in this direction. As discussed in Chapter 7, we imagine BSPs taking a larger stake in the client company than current board members but without having to take over the entire company. BSPs could bear more risk than individual directors, and would likely have an interest in greater economic ownership than the rather low levels of current board ownership.

SUMMARY

The bottom line is that BSPs could provide the type of expert corporate governance routinely provided by private equity firms, except for a larger number of companies than the economics of investment strategy currently can accommodate. We suspect that the number of companies for which the thickly informed board could improve outcomes is far greater than the domain over which private equity is a viable investment strategy at this point. The BSP model of governance is about trying to achieve some of the improved governance benefits of the private equity model without the need for investors to stake an economic bet on the entire firm. If there develops a robust market for governance, BSP firms would be a threat to any existing board. The potential for a takeover of the board function, separate from the takeover of the firm, would be a real possibility, and with it the possibility that management could be improved by the intervention of a third party offering a better governance mousetrap. This model could, of course, be coupled with the board taking a greater stake in the economics of the firm than it currently has, a possibility that we discuss further later. The use of higher-powered board incentives would thus create a sliding scale of governance, with the full private equity model on one end and the current approach on the other. The BSP model would fall somewhere in between, depending on the incentives of the board in any particular case.

At the end of the day, of course, we do not know whether thickly informed boards will work for all firms, some firms, or no firms. Perhaps the state of the governance world today is perfect. We doubt it for the reasons discussed previously. But one does not need to think that we are correct to favor experimenting with the BSP model. There is no contesting the fact that companies today are far more complex and risky than when the current board model was invented forty years ago, and that the demands of the new landscape of shareholders adds to the importance of the board's role. This strongly suggests to us, as it does to other corporate law scholars, that changes may be necessary to the model that has served well for the past few decades but may be in need of updating. After all, the history of boards demonstrates that there is no static, first-best board model over time.

The existence and success of the "governance arbitrage" of private equity is evidence of the value of the thickly informed model of board members that underlies our argument for the BSP. It may be the case that the current approach to private equity investment is optimal when it comes to governance – that is, there are no additional benefits from expanding the number of companies that can be subject to improved governance by changing the board in the ways that the private equity funds do. But we suspect that lowering the price of making these changes, which is effectively what permitting BSPs and creating a market for corporate governance separate from the market for corporate control would do, will open up opportunities currently foreclosed by the costs of the private equity approach. It is also possible that the governance changes private equity funds deploy are inexorably linked with the economics of the private equity model. Although we imagine BSPs taking much larger economic stakes in firms than the current board model permits, we admit that private equity may be a better governance mousetrap. The argument for BSPs, however, is likely to remain, since it would operate in a world between the extremes of public ownership and private equity ownership. We find it highly unlikely that these two worlds are the only possible solutions to optimal corporate governance, especially given the increasingly difficult tasks facing the boards of American public companies.

Notes

1. NYSE Listed Company Manual § 303A.02.
2. See, e.g. Jeffrey N. Gordon, Shareholder Activism, the Short-Termist Red-Herring, and the Need for Corporate Governance Reform, The CLS Blue Sky Blog (Mar. 28, 2016), http://clsbluesky.law.columbia.edu/2016/03/28/shareholder-activism-the-short-termist-red-herring-and-the-need-for-corporate-governance-reform.
3. Stephen M. Bainbridge & M. Todd Henderson, Boards-R-Us: Reconceptualizing Corporate Boards, 66 *Stan. L. Rev.* 1051 (2014).
4. Gordon, Shareholder Activism, at 2.
5. Ibid. (emphasis in original).
6. Ibid.
7. www.law.columbia.edu/sites/default/files/microsites/millstein-center/gilson-gordon_slides.pdf.
8. Where Was Lehman's Board?, *Wall Street Journal*, Sept. 15, 2008.
9. Cong Wang, Industry Expertise of Independent Directors and Board Monitoring, 50 *J. Financial & Quantitative Analysis* 929 (2017).
10. Olubunmi Faleye et al., Industry Experience on Corporate Boards, Rev. of Fin. & Accounting (forthcoming).

11. Jeffrey R. Cohen, et al., The Effect of Audit Committee Industry Expertise on Monitoring the Financial Reporting Process, 80 *The Accounting Rev.* 243 (2014).
12. See Wang, Industry Expertise.
13. Aida Sijamic Wahid and Kyle T. Welch, Does the Market Value Professional Directors? (Dec. 3, 2016), available at SSRN: https://ssrn.co m/abstract=2930117.
14. www.mckinsey.com/business-functions/strategy-and-corporate-finance/o ur-insights/what-public-companies-can-learn-from-private-equity.
15. Joachim Heel and Conor Kehoe, "Why Some Private Equity Firms Do Better Than Others," McKINSEY QUART. (Feb. 2005), available at: www .mckinsey.com/business-functions/strategy-and-corporate-finance/our-ins ights/why-some-private-equity-firms-do-better-than-others.

PART V

CONCLUDING THOUGHTS

In this final part, we address what we anticipate are the most powerful objections or counterarguments to our proposal to permit BSPs to operate. We have tried to make the best case against our idea. It is only by overcoming the best arguments against it that the BSP idea has any chance to live beyond these pages.

13

Anticipating Objections

Although we think our proposal is a straightforward application of the enabling nature of American corporate law and has deep intuitive appeal centered on the increasingly common use of firms to provide various services, we understand that legal change is often difficult. We do not expect our proposal to be adopted overnight, if at all. In this chapter, we try to understand why that might be. Our goal is to anticipate and respond to what some of the objections to the proposal are likely to be. At the end of the day, we are not persuaded that the net impact of these criticisms and costs is greater than the benefits of the BSP model that we've described at length in this book. But you be the judge.

OVERCOMING THE STATUS QUO BIAS

The biggest objection to our proposal is likely to be that we've had corporate boards of individual persons for hundreds of years, and changing anything with this history will be very difficult. This is especially so because there are thousands and thousands of powerful people and entities with a vested interest in protecting the status quo. Although many objections will be couched in substantive terms, we suspect that most will be based on aversion to change. We are not suggesting that the individuals making these arguments are disingenuous, but rather that the economic and social forces at work are usually a more powerful descriptor of resistance than arguments for the merits. For this reason, we look first at the status quo bias.

Most of us prefer the status quo most of the time. The phenomenon is sufficiently well documented that psychologists and behavioral economists have a name for it: the status quo bias. A wealth of empirical evidence from human subject research confirms that people will stick with the status quo even if given the opportunity to make a change that would improve their welfare.

Examples are all around us. We know, for example, that most employees who invest in 401(k) retirement saving plans subsequently make no changes in how their assets are allocated in that plan even if doing so would make their investments safer or pay a higher rate of return.[1] Car owners tend to stick with either no-fault or fault-based insurance depending on the default law of the jurisdiction, even if a switch would save them money.[2]

Even supposedly sophisticated people, like lawyers and businesspeople, exhibit the status quo bias. When the law creates a default rule – that is, a rule that governs unless the parties agree to the contrary – lawyers tend not to advise their clients to contract out of the rule even when doing so would be beneficial to their clients.[3] Businesses are reluctant to change their strategy even when they would benefit by doing so.[4]

The status quo is the status quo for a reason. What seems to us to be irrational, unfair, inefficient, wrongheaded, or just plain stupid may actually be vital and important for reasons beyond our comprehension. And, changing it, even out of a purely benign motive, may cause more harm than good.

Accordingly, it shouldn't surprise us that even successful business firms tend to be risk averse when it comes to corporate governance innovations, even when such innovations would enhance shareholder wealth.[5] Critics of our proposal thus may argue that even if legislators changed the law so as to allow BSPs to serve as directors, companies might stock with old-fashioned boards, even if a BSP would be superior.

Such critics might point to the fact that in jurisdictions in which corporate entities have been permitted to serve as boards or in board-like roles, BSPs did not arise naturally. In our view, however, the robust nature of US capital markets and the prominent governance role played today by investors and other stakeholders (such as proxy advisory services, law firms, and consultants) distinguishes the United States from most, if not all, of the jurisdictions in which corporate directorships are allowed.

After all, the status quo bias only means that the status quo tends to be sticky. We must first understand deeply and completely before we should change and before the status quo will give way. Put another way, the status quo bias acts like friction keeping an object in place. Put enough oomph into pushing the object, however, and that friction will be overcome and the object will move. Similarly, put enough money on the table, and the status quo bias will give way.

We think there is significant potential for vertical integration of the existing board services industry to generate creation of BSPs. Because we already have a plethora of consulting firms (not to mention law and accounting firms, which easily could spin off consulting ventures) serving as advisors to existing sole-proprietor board members, the costs of integrating various board service providers into a BSP will be lower than would be the case if new firms had to be created to start the industry from scratch. The current corporate governance space is replete with activist shareholders, institutional investors, and good governance advocates, moreover, all of which may have an incentive to encourage experimentation with the BSP model if they can be convinced that doing so would result in significant corporate governance improvements.

One mechanism for achieving some movement in the direction of a robust market for BSPs is the possibility that a court could hold managers of a particular firm liable for failing to consider, if not hire, a BSP. If we are correct that hiring a BSP could bring substantial governance improvements, then for an underperforming company with an entrenched board, the failure to open the board up to competition from a BSP or a move to shut out a BSP from competing for control of the board could be viewed as a violation of managers' and board members' fiduciary duties.

We both respect the status quo as a signal of value. But history is also littered with longstanding practices that persisted despite their value. That slavery, feudalism, communism, and countless other practices lasted for long periods of time tells us very little about their value. Sometimes new ideas come along. We all carried and dragged our suitcases around airports for decades until someone had the idea of putting wheels on them. More relevant to this case, however, are the people who may lose out or may think they will lose out if BSPs are adopted. Current board members may worry about losing profitable work, doubting that they will be hired by BSPs. Managers may resist the additional discipline and transparency that BSPs would bring to governance. Incumbent service providers, like compensation consultants and others offering advice to boards, may resist giving up some of their profits in what we suspect will be a more efficient market for them. But some bold ones may be inspired, if the law would get out of the way, to bring the efficiencies of scale and vertical integration to the board room.

REDUCED ACCOUNTABILITY

A common objection that we have heard is that BSPs will be less accountable than boards composed of individual human directors. A naïve view is that corporations are somehow able to skirt liability by their nature, by virtue of limited liability (as if it were liability limited at the entity level), or because of political power and so on. We reject these more or less out of hand. There is nothing special about corporations in this regard. In fact, we subscribe to the contractarian school that views corporations as mere labels that stand in for the various human actors and contracts that cooperate to do a particular activity. As for limited liability, it would indeed prevent the shareholders of BSPs from being held *personally* liable for the debts of the BSP, but they would have their investments in the BSP on the hook – the BSP entity could be held liable for its wrongdoing. Society is generally comfortable with corporations engaging in far riskier and more dangerous work than providing board services, and we see no reason why if limited liability is not a problem there, it would be here. This objection then might boil down to an attack on limited liability itself. For a strong defense of limited liability, we reference our book on the subject.[6]

Not only do we think that the concept of entities performing board services is not a problem, as we argued earlier, we believe it is a benefit of the BSP model. It is a feature, not a bug. Entities providing board services should be *more* accountable. Even a thinly capitalized BSP will have deeper pockets than any individual. Moreover, BSPs will be more transparent almost by definition, since there is almost no transparency about directors and boards today. Reputations will also be greater. As noted above, we expect enhanced legal scrutiny of BSPs than of individual directors. It is important to compare the expected liability of BSPs with the reality of modern board practice. In the past several decades, the number of instances of personal liability for individual directors can likely be counted on one hand, two at most. Instead, directors pay damages, such as there are, from insurance policies paid for by the firms they serve. We would expect BSPs to largely self-insure, and thus offer potential plaintiffs at least as good a base against which accountability can be grounded, and likely far better.

LOSS OF PERSONAL SERVICE

Another objection grounded in tradition is that the longstanding practice of individual directors may suggest a deep wisdom about personal service that would be lost in the move to the BSP model. The objection would go something like this: Not only have boards since the days of the Dutch East India Company been composed of individual sole proprietorships, but also board members may simply be another category of leader that we think of as necessarily being individuals. For instance, the Constitution requires the president to be an individual person, and it would seem strange to suggest that we hire Presidents-R-Us to be President, even though many of the arguments advanced in this book could apply to that situation as well. The same could be said about a variety of leaders, from mayors to law school deans.

One response is that our proposal is about corporate directors, not political leaders, and the cost-benefit calculation may be quite different in those cases. For instance, firms have to compete in various markets, and markets provide discipline for bad governance choices in ways that political leaders do not feel as intensely. We pick a president every four years, whereas the governance of Microsoft is priced every second. Another response is that boards are different than the president or a law school dean because of the nature of the role they play. While it might make sense to hire a firm to be a dean or president, there is something personal about leadership in these cases that is not as true in the board context. Individuals feel invested in the personal connection with political leaders for reasons deep in the human psyche, but it is difficult to imagine that any corporate stakeholder – be it an employee, customer, or investor – feels this way about a particular board member or the board as a whole. It is possible that some CEOs serve this function, and that this may make the use of a firm to provide CEO services more problematic, but it is hard to see this value for the board. As noted previously, the board provides a variety of functions, none of which concerns the kind of personal leadership that we commonly associate with individual leaders.

A final response is to point out that the use of boards is largely a product of historical path dependency, and that the reasons for their initial use no longer seem as strong as they once did. As noted in Chapter 1, Franklin Gevurtz traced the origin of corporate boards back to medieval guilds and towns, concluding that corporate board antecedents were "a reflection of political practices and ideas widespread in Western Europe in the late Middle Ages."[7] Gevurtz's detailed historical account concludes that the reason corporate boards developed was in order to give "political legitimacy" to corporate activity. While his article concludes with a sop to modern defenders of boards and greater shareholder participation in corporate affairs, there is nothing about our idea that would upset the idea of "consent through elected representatives" continuing as part of the corporate tradition. In fact, our proposal is likely to increase the political legitimacy of corporate boards by opening up possibilities for more transparent and active participation of shareholders in deciding who will represent their interests in supervising corporate management.

But, as we've noted in other sections, perhaps we are missing something deep. If that is true, then no firms will adopt BSPs, even if they are permitted and run against an incumbent board. Or, maybe firms will adopt them, and then find that something is missing – perhaps the value of personal service – and then go back to the traditional model. We are open to that possibility.

We expect, however, that this argument is a convenient one for incumbent board members vested in the status quo. Moreover, we suspect that whatever benefits there are from personal service of individual directors can be replicated (and even enhanced) within the BSP model. If firms value personal service, BSPs will want to deliver it to them. This could be done through employment, staffing, and incentive decisions within the BSP. If having ten individuals akin to the current board members feel personal ownership of a particular firm maximizes governance, then BSPs will structure their service in this way. They will appoint a board, like the current board, to make decisions just as it does today, except with the resources, reputation, and assets of the BSP standing behind it. Or, perhaps a smaller group or a larger one than is manageable today would work better. Whatever the size or scope, the job descriptions, work flow, compensation, and performance evaluation can be structured by the BSP to maximize the value of personal service, without giving up the benefits of entities performing particular functions.

LOSS OF ADVANTAGES OF GROUP DECISION MAKING

As just noted, boards of directors have been around for a very long time. While giving due deference to the principle that an appeal to tradition is not probative, persistence of an institution in the heat of economic competition forces one to consider the possibility that there is something unique about multi-member boards that has considerable survival value.[i]

Put another way, the best argument for the board as monitor has to do with the nature of the board as a group of individuals, and how this may resolve a tricky problem of delegated authority. To see this, and why BSPs do not eliminate the economic advantages of group decision making, we have to look at various types of hierarchies and how they generate accountability.

The Advantages of Multi-Member Boards

As we've already noted at various points, one of us has argued elsewhere that the board of directors' utility arises out of the very fact that it places a collective body rather than a single individual at the head of the corporate hierarchy.[8] On one hand, the old joke that a camel is a horse designed by a committee captures the valid empirical observation that individuals are often superior to groups when it comes to matters requiring creativity. On the other hand, there

---

[i]   Interestingly, at one time, many states required that the board have at least three members, although most have eliminated that requirement. MBCA § 8.03(a) cmt.

is considerable evidence that groups are superior at evaluative tasks requiring the exercise of critical evaluative judgment.

The Advantages of Group Decision Making

Decision-making requires the use of scarce resources for four purposes: (1) observation, or the gathering of information; (2) memory, or the storage of information; (3) computation, or the manipulation of information; and (4) communication, or the transmission of information.[9] Groups are superior to individuals at some of these tasks, most notably memory and computation.[i] As to the former, groups develop a sort of collective memory that consists not only of the sum of individual memories but also an awareness of who knows what. Consequently, institutional memory is superior when the organization is structured as a set of teams rather than as a mere aggregate of individuals. There is some laboratory evidence, moreover, that the collective memory of groups leads to higher quality output.[10] Group members, for example, seem to specialize in memorizing specific aspects of complex repetitive tasks.

As for computation, an actor can economize limited cognitive resources in two ways. First, by adopting institutional governance structures designed to promote more efficient decision making. Second, by invoking shortcuts; that is, heuristic problem-solving decision-making processes. Group decision making is an example of the former, because it provides a mechanism for aggregating the inputs of multiple individuals with differing knowledge, interests, and skills. Numerous studies suggest that groups benefit from both by pooling of information and from providing opportunities for one member to correct another's errors.[11] In the corporate context, the board of directors thus emerged as an institutional governance mechanism to constrain the deleterious effect of bounded rationality on the organizational decision-making process.

Groups and Agency Costs

Individuals are subject to the temptations to shirk or self-deal. As we saw in Chapter 2, corporations – and other large organizations, for that matter – use

---

[i] By providing access to multiple sources of information, multi-member boards may make it less costly to gather information. But it seems unlikely that directors qua directors do much to facilitate the observation process. Any such savings, moreover, likely are offset by increased communication costs. By decentralizing both access to information and decision-making power, group decision-making requires additional resources and imposes additional delays on the decision-making process.

hierarchal monitoring to deter and punish shirking. Suppose the shareholders created a vertical hierarchy by hiring a single individual, for example, call her Agent X, to monitor the CEO. If Agent X is supposed to serve the shareholders' interests by monitoring the CEO, this begs the question of who will monitor Agent X?

The problem with hierarchal monitoring was one well known to the Romans, who famously asked *Quis custodiet ipsos custodes?* Dr. Seuss amusingly explained the problem in his 1973 book *Did I Ever Tell You How Lucky You Are?*

> Oh, the jobs people work at!
> Out west, near Hawtch-Hawtch,
> there's a Hawtch-Hawtcher Bee-Watcher.
> His job is to watch . . .
> Is to keep both his eyes on the lazy town bee.
> A bee that is watched will work harder, you see.
> Well . . . he watched and he watched.
> But, in spite of his watch,
> that bee didn't work any harder. Not mawtch.
> So then somebody said,
> "Our old bee-watching man
> just isn't bee-watching as hard as he can.
> He ought to be watched by another Hawtch-Hawtcher.
> The thing that we need is a Bee-Watcher-Watcher."
> WELL . . .
> The Bee-Watcher-Watcher watched the Bee-Watcher.
> He didn't watch well. So another Hawtch-Hawtcher
> had to come in as a Watch-Watcher-Watcher.
> And today all the Hawtchers who live in Hawtch-Hawtch
> are watching on Watch-Watcher-Watchering-Watch,
> Watch-Watching the Watcher who's watching that bee.
> You're not a Hawtch-Hawtcher. You're lucky, you see.

In other words, hierarchical monitoring requires a never-ending series of monitors monitoring lower level monitors.

In a justly famous article, *Production, Information Costs, and Economic Organization*,[12] economists Armen Alchian and Harold Demsetz solved this problem by proposing to consolidate the role of the final monitor with that of the residual claimant. They contended that if one team member was given both the right to the firm's residual income and final monitoring authority, he would be properly incentivized to monitor the other because his reward will vary exactly with his success as a monitor.

As the saying goes, however, facts are ugly things. Alchian and Demsetz's elegant theory fails to help us understand the corporation because it doesn't take into account the separation of ownership and control. The shareholders are legally entitled to the residual claim on the corporation's assets, but they lack the power to exercise the kind of control necessary for meaningful monitoring of the corporation's agents.

Corporate law solved this problem by capping the corporate hierarchy not with an individual but with a group. A hierarchy whose governance structures provide only vertical monitoring cannot resolve the problem of who watches the watchers. But putting a group of equals at the apex of the hierarchy offers a solution to the problem because the group engages both in vertically oriented monitoring of its subordinates (that is, the CEO) and in horizontal monitoring of one another. In the latter capacity, the internal dynamics of group governance constrain self-dealing and shirking by individual team members and, perhaps, even by the group as a whole.[13] Board members may use social pressures to constrain lazy or corrupt directors in ways that would be more difficult if the board members were responsible only to people above them in a hierarchy.

Think about the relationship between a team and a coach compared with that among team members. A coach monitors a team in a vertical hierarchy, while teammates monitor each other in a horizontal hierarchy. While both means of creating incentives can be useful and more or less effective depending on the circumstances, it is easy to see how there are motivations and pressures that can be used by teammates that might be impossible for coaches to deploy. Trying hard so as not to disappoint the person in battle with you can be more powerful than trying to please a superior. This is especially the case when one suspects that the superior is not subject to effective oversight.

If this is correct, the board as a group of individuals might be a crucial component of corporate governance in restraining agency costs, and thus our proposal to consolidate the board into a single legal entity would reduce or eliminate this benefit. Accountability might be reduced. But we doubt it.

While the BSP model may seem to give up the advantages of a multi-member board by placing a single decision-maker at the top of the corporate hierarchy, that facile assumption errs by reifying the BSP. In fact, of course, the BSP will have a team of individuals working for each client, just as law firms, accountants, and other service providers do. That team will have much the same sort of dynamics as a multi-member board and thus will share the advantages of groups over atomized individuals.

In other words, if there are important constraints on shirking or stealing inherent in a team of equals at the top of the corporate hierarchy, a BSP could design its internal structure to mimic the current board model. For instance, if Boards-R-Us is hired to provide corporate governance for Apple, it could assign a specific team of individuals to be the board of Apple. The board, which might look a lot like the current board of Apple, could meet and make decisions much as it does today, with the key difference being that the vote of the team would be the decision of Boards-R-Us, which would then make that decision for Apple.

In fact, if equal team members were valuable, BSPs would have incentives to create internal work systems to deploy employees in this way. BSPs that did not would deliver worse corporate governance services, as evidenced by the greater slack and other cheating by corporate managers under their watch. Their clients would underperform in the market. Importantly, the shortcoming of the BSP would not only be evidenced by the underperformance of their clients, but also by market assessments of the BSPs themselves. As noted in Chapter 6, having board services provided by entities would produce a market for information about the BSPs, which would judge them based on how effective they are at providing board services. This is the market for corporate governance that we mentioned earlier.

If the BSP were publicly traded, the stock price of the BSP would provide information about how well the BSP were doing at providing governance services. A board that did not create an important team dynamic (if one were valuable) would trade at a discount to BSPs that did. If the BSP were not publicly traded, there would still be market signals of the value of its services. Most obviously, the prices the BSP were able to charge and its reputation would say something about how well it was doing to monitor management. More indirectly, but perhaps more powerfully, the stock price change of a publicly traded client on the announcement that a particular BSP were taking over providing governance services would be an indication of the value of that BSP.

We cannot predict the optimal structure for BSPs to use. In fact, we doubt there is a one-size-fits-all approach to governance. One of the key virtues of our proposal is premised on the idea that what works for Firm A may not work for Firm B or Firm C. A team-based approach may optimize the results for Firm A, while Firm B, for whatever reason, might be better governed by a single individual (for example, the partner of the BSP assigned to lead Firm B, with input from underlings at the BSP), while Firm C's performance might be optimized by a hybrid approach. Dialing in the right mix of equal team members, powerful individuals, expert advisors, and so on is something that is likely to be learned by experience for individual firms. A "board" of one, two, three, or ten might be optimal. Current law prohibits this exploration.

Maybe a board of tens or even hundreds of individuals at a BSP voting in a market, akin to a prediction market, would be the best approach. Imagine that the BSP set up a market in which contracts referencing the monitoring of management could be bought and sold within the BSP. For example, the BSP could float two contracts internally: Contract A would ask traders to evaluate a monitoring mechanism (like an internal controls system), call it Mechanism X; Contract B would ask traders to evaluate Mechanism Y. Contract A would be worth $1 if the client adopted Mechanism X and the company did not have to, say, restate its earnings over, say, the next five years; it would be worth $0 if the client did. Contract B would ask the same question about Mechanism Y.

If these contracts were offered for sale in a market, and then traded back and forth, the BSP could get some information about the collective views of its employees (whoever was trading in the market) about the relative effectiveness of Mechanism X versus Mechanism Y. For example, if Mechanism X were trading at $0.60 and Mechanism Y were trading at $0.40, this would reflect a prediction that X was thought by the employees of the BSP to be a better mechanism. In the extreme, the BSP could simply make the market assessment its determination.

We do not mean to suggest this is an approach that should be followed or that this simple contract would be effective. There is a robust literature on prediction markets, their design, and their current use by corporate America. We do not know how such markets might be useful in corporate governance, but we suspect that they could be useful in this area, just as they have proved to be useful in strategy and planning and other areas of corporate decision-making. We merely point out that this kind of tool is currently unavailable or underutilized in corporate governance, in part because of legal restrictions that purport to tell all companies what their optimal governance model is.

Resolving the Double Agency Problem

Some critics of our proposal may argue that we are simply doubling the agency problem. In the client firm, there is a problem that the directors may not adequately monitor the corporation's employees. If the client appoints a BSP to serve as its board, and the BSP appoints an employee (or many) to accomplish that work, you arguably have two agency problems where in the traditional mode we only had one. But this objection applies equally to any situation where a firm is providing a service. That is, it applies equally to any entity (such as a law firm or consultancy or accountancy) where there is a separation of ownership and control. A system of legal rules, best practices, contracts, and compensation structures has evolved to address the double-agency problem in those settings, resulting in a net decrease in costs. We see no reason to think that the BSP would be different.

Managing the Firm

One of us has elsewhere argued that corporate law favored multi-member boards because groups are better than individuals are at the sort of critical evaluative judgment that characterizes most board decisions. While it might seem that a BSP could undermine this by consolidating the multi-member board into a single decision-making point, this is not necessarily the case. If the client opted to have multiple representatives of the BSP serve as its board (or on a mixed board), the board itself would continue to function as a group decision-maker. If the client opted for the pure BSP model, the team within the BSP servicing that client would continue to use group decision-making as part of its process. In short, in both cases multiple individuals will be analyzing and voting, either directly or indirectly, on a particular course of conduct. We see no reason why this group decision-making process need take place among sole proprietors serving as board members instead of among employees of a BSP.

As noted in our discussion of monitoring, there are innumerable options open to BSPs about how to structure their board service function. The BSP might appoint a single individual to make decisions as the "board" of the client, with that person supported by a team of advisors and experts and support staff. Or, the BSP might create a board of individuals who would make decisions just as the current board does, with the gains of the BSP model coming from the enhanced reputation, access to fiat services, and increased transparency. Or, maybe there are hybrid models that entrepreneurs will figure out through trial and error.

In fact, we suspect that different internal decision-making approaches might be used by the BSP for different functions currently played by boards. For the monitoring function, perhaps having a single partner at the BSP responsible for oversight might be the most efficient approach, since it would intensify effort and accountability in one individual. Or, perhaps a many-minds approach with delegated authority for different oversight functions – one for accounting, another for compensation, another for compliance – would make more sense. Regardless of the approach taken for monitoring, perhaps a different approach makes sense when it comes to the board playing its managerial role. (Certainly, using multiple board members seems like the sensible approach to play the board's service role, discussed next.) After all, decisions about strategy and project choice are fundamentally different than those about whether managers are doing their best and putting the interests of the firm above their own. Collective input and critical evaluation by many individuals makes much more sense when it comes to a decision about getting into a particular business line or whether to open a plant in China, Mexico, or the United States.

The key point, however, is merely that hybrid approaches are foreclosed or made much more expensive by the legal rules that currently demand a one-size-fits-all approach to governance. These rules may also explain why boards today have a difficult time balancing the various roles they have to play. If a board has to pick only one form through which it can operate, then, given the circumstances of the time, it may have to elevate one role, say, the monitoring role, over all others, and thus choose a form that delivers it the best at the expense of the other roles. The BSP approach, on the other hand, could allow tailoring that would permit governance to serve the multiple roles more efficiently, all at the same time in the amount demanded by the market.[i]

In addition, we expect that BSPs would make better decisions than current boards, all else being equal. They would have better information, access to specialists with fewer conflicted interests, more person hours available for exercising judgment, better incentives, and so on. The BSP thus combines the advantages of group decision making with a group composition likely to be better informed and motivated.

According to Anthony Fitzsimmons, chairman of Reputability, a governance consultancy, "A fundamental manifestation of the problem with boards is information. A board has information, but doesn't know if it's accurate or has important gaps. If you don't have the right information how

---

[i] An alternative hybrid approach was suggested by Adrian Wooldridge:

> [Bainbridge and Henderson's BSP model] might deny companies the insights of genuine outsiders – people with a record of producing industry-changing ideas. The very professionalism which will make BSPs better monitors of corporate performance might make them too conservative when advising on strategy. There could be conflicts of interest if, say, rival firms used the same BSP. But all professional-service firms (such as management consultants) have such problems – and ways of dealing with them. The idea might also deprive big shareholders of a chance to nominate board members. These problems could be overcome by creating a hybrid system in which the BSP filled a majority of board positions and a minority were reserved for others. Corporate boards have always been one of the weakest parts of the capitalist system – collections of cuckolds, in Ralph Nader's phrase.

Schumpeter, Replacing the Board: The Case for Outsourcing Company Boards, *The Economist*, Aug. 16, 2014. We think the pure BSP model is superior to Wooldridge's proposed hybrid model, but we could be wrong about that. Accordingly, we would support legal change that allowed pure BSPs but also permits companies to experiment with hybrid versions.

can you be in control?" We believe that the BSP would be an easy way to enhance the information and processing ability of boards when it comes to helping corporate managers improve strategy and performance of their companies.

A final point is worth mentioning. As noted earlier, state corporate law has moved away from a requirement that boards consist of multiple members in some contexts, and this suggests that the group decision-making benefits may not alone justify the statutory bar on BSPs.

Providing Services

As noted previously, board members provide various services to their clients, including access to capital, information about industries, experience as CEOs, and so forth. For instance, research by Randall Kroszner and Philip Strahan finds that about one third of large, nonfinancial US companies had a banker on their board at the turn of the twenty-first century. They argue that bankers help improve information flows to lenders and the market and can be a signal of credibility in capital markets, thereby lowering the cost of capital. (In fact, they argue the only reason more US companies do not have bankers on their board is because lenders with board representation may find themselves subordinated [that is, going to the end of the line] if the borrower encounters financial distress).

The same role can be played by other professionals, whether they are consultants, other CEOs, accountants, engineers or technology professionals, political figures, or academics. Professional networks can bring information, signals of credibility, access to capital or other important assets, and so forth.

One might think that going to the BSP model might disrupt this possible role for boards. But this alone cannot justify a bar on the use of BSPs. While it is possible that particular BSPs will not be able to provide as diverse a set of networks as can a multi-member board of unrelated individuals, for some firms, the importance of, say, access to a network of investors, may be sufficient to outweigh the benefits of hiring a BSP. For that firm, for that particular time in its lifecycle, there is nothing in our proposal that requires the use of a BSP.

Moreover, we see no obvious reason why a BSP may not be able to provide these services. For one, modern consulting firms and investment banks provide important networks of information and access for companies without relying on individual contracts as in the board model. Large BSPs comprising hundreds or thousands of professionals, including many individuals currently serving as board members, could likely do the same thing. If current or former CEOs are valuable members of companies' decision-making processes, their services will be demanded by BSPs, which could hire them on a permanent or ad hoc basis. Finally, where this is not feasible, a BSP could serve as a matchmaker between clients, just as investment banks often do.

Summary

Indeed, for all the reasons developed in earlier chapters, we expect BSPs to outperform multi-member boards. As we have seen, BSPs will have better access to information. BSPs will be able to draw on the expertise of dedicated in-house specialists, who will have fewer conflicted interests than the outside consultants that serve current boards. BSPs will spend more person-hours exercising judgment and will have superior incentives to do so effectively. In effect, the BSP will have all the group-based advantages of current multi-member boards plus a group composition that makes it likely to be better informed and motivated.

BSPS WILL BE CAPTURED BY MANAGEMENT

Another objection we've heard is that BSPs might be even more beholden to the top management team – and thus even less effective monitors – than the current individual directors. One of the anonymous reviewers of our proposal for this book raised a related point, which is that: "Large controlling shareholders, dual class stock firms and private equity firms already have the power to select the directors they employ. BSP's would just add an additional layer of cost onto their board structures and presumably provide little additional benefit."

It is important when evaluating this objection to avoid the Nirvana fallacy – we need to compare BSPs along this dimension with current board practice, not an alternative of perfection. As we discussed earlier, the baseline level of control of board members by management is thought to be quite high. One need not sign on to the entire research agenda of law professors like Lucian Bebchuk of Harvard Law School – author of a book and series of articles outlining the ways in which managers influence and control (even dominate) their boards – to believe that there is a great deal of current control by CEOs over who is on the board, what information they receive, how they are compensated, and whether they will be invited back.

The opportunities for BSPs to mount proxy contests at much lower costs, to be more transparent, and to be more effective all push in the direction of boards being more accountable to shareholders. An independent BSP model could be implemented in a way that would make it far less likely to simply rubber-stamp the wishes of a CEO or controlling shareholder than is the case with current boards. For example, shareholders could be given the power to nominate BSPs in all cases, or perhaps just where there is a controlling share-holder, and to require that the selection of the BSP be approved by the holders of a majority of the minority shares.

In any event, state law is fairly robust in offering legal protections for minority shareholders, and there is no reason why this would be different for BSPs. The Delaware courts have emphasized the need for formal corporate governance mechanisms to police the conflict of interest inherent in transactions involving large block holders. The courts have also emphasized the duty of the board of directors, in appropriate cases, to take action to protect the interests of minority shareholders.[14] As we have argued, we expect minority shareholders to have *greater* protection from BSPs, both in terms of the quality of board services and in the enhanced legal scrutiny that we would expect from courts. If this is correct, then this would lower the cost of capital for firms (by reducing the discount minority shareholders are willing to pay for shares based on the risk of expropriation), and in turn lead to greater economic growth and opportunity.

BSP INCENTIVES INADEQUATELY ALIGNED TO SHAREHOLDER INTERESTS

Given the importance of aligning the interests of board members and share-holders, another objection we've heard is that even if BSPs are truly independent of management, BSP interests nevertheless will be inadequately aligned with those of shareholders. For example, as profit-maximizing entities, which may themselves be publicly held, BSPs may have incentives to cut costs by minimizing the number and qualifications of staff.[15]

While this is true as a descriptive matter – businesses are not famous for trying to maximize the number of staff – the argument fails for several reasons. First, again the proper baseline is not a hypothetical board with an endless staff and an infinite amount of resources, but the current board of individuals. As noted earlier, boards currently have to contract and pay for all outside advice and expertise they may need. Even if the corporation pays, as they may be obliged to under various federal laws and stock exchange listing requirements, they would be doing so only with the blessing (either implicitly or explicitly) of the CEO, who will realize that the money is being used in part to monitor her, and who, in any event, is also running a profit-making business.

Second, this argument proves too much in that it would apply with equal force to any service provider, whether they are supplying legal, accounting, consulting, or other services. Everything a company buys from another company – from coffee to computers to consulting services – is purchased from a for-profit entity. We see no reason why board services would be particularly susceptible to this concern relative to other services, such as legal services. In fact, this argument sounds like a criticism of for-profit corporations in general, not BSPs.

ISN'T THIS JUST ONE MORE COSTLY INTERMEDIARY?

One final objection that we've heard frequently is that using a BSP will just introduce another costly intermediary into a modern corporate governance framework that is already overloaded with costly intermediaries, each skimming a little from the beneficial owners? Ordinary investors may react by thinking "great – another faceless corporation is running my faceless corporation." We agree that successful BSPs may need to develop a human face, but we don't think the BSP is just another costly corporate governance intermediary.[i] In fact, we are merely suggesting improvements to the intermediary (the board) mandated by law.

The Delaware courts have emphasized the need for formal corporate governance mechanisms to manage the firm, to monitor executives, and to police the conflict of interest inherent in transactions involving large block holders. The board is that mechanism. The courts have also emphasized the duty of the board of directors, in appropriate cases, to take action to protect the interests of minority shareholders.[16]

We have argued herein that an independent BSP model could be implemented in a way that would make it far less likely to simply rubber stamp the wishes of management or of a controlling shareholder than is the case with current boards. For example, shareholders could be given the power to

[i] We are grateful to the anonymous referee who directed our attention to a newspaper article, from the *Atlanta Journal-Constitution*, Corporate, Individual Ownership Debate Continues, *Atlanta Journal-Constitution* (Feb. 16, 2003). The reporter writes:

> Most teams in baseball, basketball and hockey remain owned by individuals or by investment groups with one person as the controlling shareholder or managing partner. . . .Fans like ownership to have a face. (Which isn't to say some cities wouldn't like to change the face of an owner or two.) "Fans like individual owners because . . . they want to throw their beer on them when the teams are losing and throw confetti on them in a championship parade," said David Carter, who heads Los Angeles-based Sports Business Group and teaches sports marketing at Southern Cal. "It's easier to relate to individuals. Like them or not, the Yankees are much easier to rally behind or against with a guy like [George] Steinbrenner than if they were still owned by CBS."

nominate BSPs where there is a controlling shareholder and to require that the selection of the BSP be approved by the holders of a majority of the minority shares. As a result, we would be much more willing to invest in a company like Facebook or Google – where dual class capital structures allow their founders to wield effective control while owning tiny shares of the firm's equity – if a BSP were present to act as a check on the controlling shareholder's whims.

More generally, as it is presently structured, the board is opaque to shareholders. We doubt the shareholders of Boeing, Facebook, or Verizon can name a single board member of their firms. There is already a nameless faceless thing running their corporation, and the typical shareholder would likely be indifferent between the current board and a BSP on this dimension. In fact, we suspect that shareholders would identify more with a branded BSP than with a current board. To be sure, we think this is likely only when nationally branded BSPs arise and reach maturity. Even if we are wrong, and shareholders will miss the days of sole-proprietor boards along this dimension, the efficiency gains from BSPs would need to be weighed against these costs of moving to the BSP model. We believe the cost-benefit calculation will come out in favor of BSPs, but, as we've said repeatedly, we are merely proposing that shareholders be given the chance to make this determination themselves.

CONFLICTS OF INTEREST

Another objection we hear with some frequency is concerns about conflicts of interest and concentration in the BSP industry. The typical criticism goes like this: The BSP model will create conflicts of interest when a single BSP serves as the board of two firms in the same industry, or even in different industries, so long as the decisions of one firm influence the fortunes of competitors of the other firm. The argument then typically slides down the slippery slope to concerns about a single BSP monopolizing the market or achieving a dominant position in the market for board services. In the sophisticated version of this argument, the concern is not just increased prices for services, but also a reduction in the multiple viewpoints about governance and strategy inherent in the current model of dispersed individuals providing governance services.

These are serious problems with the use of BSPs. But, we think the problems have solutions that can reduce the concerns to a manageable level.

First, it is important to note that there are already issues regarding conflicts of interest in the current board model. Individuals commonly serve on multiple boards, and these director interlocks could create conflicts of interest. These are managed, we assume, by the individual directors and firms without too much hassle. We do not see common board members of ExxonMobil and BP or Bank of America and Wells Fargo.

There are also reasons why an individual board member serving on boards (or as an executive and board member) of rivals or firms in related industries provides value to shareholders. Expertise and information sharing can be valuable in a prosocial way. But, of course, there are differences in the BSP case that make this potentially worrisome. The BSP will have control, not just be a single voice, and this will intensify the conflict of interest.

Second, conflicts like these are common in any service industry. Firms selling legal services, accounting services, consulting services, and so on face and manage these same conflicts of interest. These firms therefore deploy sophisticated conflict-management systems that prevent putting the firm in an untenable position ethically or legally. We would expect BSPs to use similar approaches to manage these conflicts. Moreover, we would support the development of ethical standards – the ones for lawyers would probably be a good starting point – for managing BSP conflicts. While these might reduce some instances of information sharing that currently happen with certain interlocks, we doubt the value lost would outweigh the gains from moving to a BSP.

Third, if it turns out that the ethical standards or self-interest of the companies using BSPs and the BSPs themselves are insufficient to manage the conflicts of interest, state or federal legislation and the rules of stock exchanges are available to set new standards. For instance, as mentioned previously, for many years it was believed that the gains from permitting accounting firms to sell advisory services and auditing services to the same firm outweighed the conflict of interest. After a series of accounting scandals, most famously involving Arthur Andersen and its client Enron, Congress mandated in SOX that these services be provided by separate firms. The accounting profession then modified its ethical standards accordingly. There could be an analogy to BSPs. If BSP services turn out to present conflict problems that are not adequately addressed by the professional standards in the business, then legislation could require a BSP to put limits on the number of firms it can serve in an industry or related industries.

Fourth, if the problem were to be unchecked by practice, ethical rules, or legislation (a very unlikely possibility), antitrust laws are available to prevent excessive concentration in the BSP industry. It is a strange argument, after all, to prevent an industry from arising in the first place based on the prediction that someday, under some circumstances, some firms might achieve market power through illegal means or to excessive levels.

* * *

We do not mean to dismiss out of hand the legitimate worries and concerns about moving to the BSP model. There are always problems and risks when innovation happens. The question is whether the risks are of an unmanageable level and whether there are available tools to address the problems that may arise. We are confident that a well-regulated market for BSPs providing governance services would present no greater risks for shareholders or society than the current model, and, for the reasons discussed in this chapter, offer benefits that far outweigh the downside from these risks

Notes

1. Richard H. Thaler & Cass R. Sunstein, *Nudge: Improving Decisions About Health, Wealth, and Happiness* 34 (2008).
2. David Cohen & Jack L. Knetsch, Judicial Choice and Disparities between Measures of Economic Values, 30 *Osgoode Hall L.J.* 737, 747 (1992).
3. Russell Korobkin, The Status Quo Bias and Contract Default Rules, 83 *Cornell L. Rev.* 608 (1998).
4. Jeffrey J. Rachlinski, The Psychology of Global Climate Change, 2000 *U. Ill. L. Rev.* 299, 307–308 (2000).
5. See Robert B. Thompson, Teaching Business Associations: Norms, Economics and Cognitive Learning, 34 *Ga. L. Rev.* 997, 1003 (2000) (explaining that "the status quo bias in the context of human attachment to default rules ... can have similar effects in the law of business associations.")
6. Stephen M. Bainbridge & M. Todd Henderson, *Limited Liability: A Legal and Economic Analysis* (2016).
7. See Chapter 1.
8. Stephen M. Bainbridge, Why a Board? Group Decisionmaking in Corporate Governance, 55 *Vand. L. Rev.* 1 (2002).
9. Roy Radner, Bounded Rationality, Indeterminacy, and the Theory of the Firm, 106 *Econ. J.* 1360, 1363 (1996).
10. Susan G. Cohen & Diane E. Bailey, What Makes Teams Work: Group Effectiveness Research from the Shop Floor to the Executive Suite, 23 *J. Mgmt.* 239, 259 (1997).
11. See Gayle W. Hill, Group versus Individual Performance: Are N + 1 Heads Better than One? 91 *Psych. Bull.* 517, 533 (1982).
12. Armen Alchian & Harold Demsetz, Production, Information Costs, and Economic Organization, 62 *Am.Econ.Rev.* 777 (1972).
13. Bainbridge, Why a Board?, at 36 ("Within a production team, for example, mutual monitoring and peer pressure provide a coercive backstop for a set of interpersonal relationships founded on trust and other noncontractual social norms.")
14. See, e.g. *McMullin v. Beran*, 765 A.2d 910, 920 (Del. 2000) ("Effective representation of the financial interests of the minority shareholders imposed upon the Chemical Board an affirmative responsibility to

protect those minority shareholders' interests."); *Mendel* v. *Carroll*, 651 A.2d 297, 306 (Del. Ch. 1994) ("I continue to hold open the possibility that a situation might arise in which a board could, consistently with its fiduciary duties, issue a dilutive option in order to protect the corporation or its minority shareholders from exploitation by a controlling shareholder who was in the process or threatening to violate his fiduciary duties to the corporation ... ").

15. The Activist Investor blog complains in a post entitled Do BSPs Solve the AP of the BoD? (Sept. 9, 2014), http://www.theactivistinvestor.com/The_A ctivist_Investor/Blog/Entries/2014/9/9_Do_BSPs_Address_the_Agency_Pr oblem_of_the_Board_of_Directors.html, that:

> Individual directors want to keep their job. A BSP will likely want to promote its firm identity, preserve its contract with the company, and earn profits for the BSP. Neither set of interests align well with increasing company value.
>
> Relative to individual directors, a firm would likely have an even stronger motive to create a separate identity. Firms now create and promote brands, unlike individuals.

In our view, however, this overlooks the incentives the BSP would have to develop an identity as a faithful servant of shareholder interests.

> The blogger then complains that:

> [A] BSP will have a much stronger profit motive than individual directors. Incentives to hit profit goals will lead them to minimize the number and qualifications of staff. The quality of BoD oversight over executives will suffer accordingly.

This strikes us as a really odd – Occupy Wall Street-style—view of the profit motive. Others might think that the BSP would be incentivized to provide high levels of service.

> Finally, the blogger complains that:

> A company would need more extensive controls over a BSP than it would an individual.

Compared to what? to what? We have seen that current boards do a lousy job of evaluating themselves. In addition, the current multi-member board is hard for outsiders to evaluate using metrics like firm performance because it is difficult to single out the contributions or harms of one member. See Armen Alchian & Harold Demsetz, Production, Information Costs, and Economic Organization, 62 *Am.Econ.Rev.* 777 (1972) (discussing the difficulties inherent in monitoring multimember production teams). On contrast, a single BSP could be judged by such performance metrics. So BSPs should be easier to monitor.

16. See note 14 and accompanying text supra.

14

Conclusion

The secret to the success of American corporate law has not been genius but ignorance. Lawmakers have been humble, using a bare minimum of mandatory rules, and this has enabled answers to be revealed through experimentation that never would have occurred to the wisest, ablest, or purest regulator. Instead of offering answers to questions about how best to govern businesses, the American approach has been to, within a broadly prescribed range, let tens of thousands of entrepreneurs and countless millions of investors innovate, experiment, succeed, and fail, and thus reveal truths about what works in corporate governance. The answer has varied over time and across firms and industries. The story we tell in this book is one of change, adaptation, and innovation. Boards have been with us for nearly a thousand years, despite the fact that business today looks nothing like it did to English wool merchants operating in Belgium in the thirteenth century. The only explanation for this is that law has permitted boards to adapt to the needs of the time.

But several trends are threatening to change this. The combination of state-law requirements and federal rules regarding board functions and composition have locked the board into a monitoring role that is increasingly ill-suited to the demands of modern business. The so-called monitoring model of corporate boards is untenable for our large publicly traded firms when combined with the age-old requirement that board services be provided by an unaffiliated group of weakly incentivized, part-time, sole proprietors. Whether boards continue to provide mostly monitoring services or something else, it is time for the board to evolve into a more efficient and effective form. Unfortunately, law, specifically the requirements of natural person service and independence on board committees, stands in the way of innovation.

In this book, we've proposed repealing these rules to permit firms and boards to evolve to better meet the demands of the day. We think our innovation – the board service provider or BSP – is a logical mechanism for improving board services. All other services in our economy are permitted to be provided through firms, and we see no reason why board services or corporate governance services should be different. If lawyers, accountants, consultants, and other service providers are permitted to affiliate with each other, board members should be as well.

Firms are the mechanism for the vast majority of economic activity for straightforward reasons. Associating with other individuals – cooperating – permits sharing of risk, access to information and expertise on demand (instead of through a market transaction), greater reputational bonding, more transparency, and the ability to use higher-powered incentives. All of these benefits and more apply with equal force to the provision of board or governance services as they do to legal services or anything else in the economy.

We have set out the basics of what the entity that we call the market for corporate governance may look like. We already have a market for corporate control that has as a corollary, or even main driver, improvements in governance, but unfortunately the linkage between governance and control means that there may be some instances in which it would be possible to improve governance but the costs of a takeover of the entire firm make it unattractive. By separating these two distinct markets, we open up the possibility for improved governance to be brought to more firms and sectors of the economy.

The board today is a vestige of the old-boys-network of a bygone era. While reforms have dragged the board into our modern world, the model of running global businesses with a handpicked group of individuals with almost no transparency or accountability is no longer tenable. Proposals abound to tweak at the margins of the board today, trying to compel it to be more accountable to shareholders, to be more transparent, and to be better. Theory and experience tell us that this is likely to make incremental improvements, but unlikely to make the kind of fundamental changes that are required or permit boards the flexibility to adapt to changes down the road that neither we nor anyone else can predict. Instead, it is time to subject the board to the market forces that we entrust to optimize these things in all other areas of the economy. It is time to outsource the board.

Index